Go-Go Live

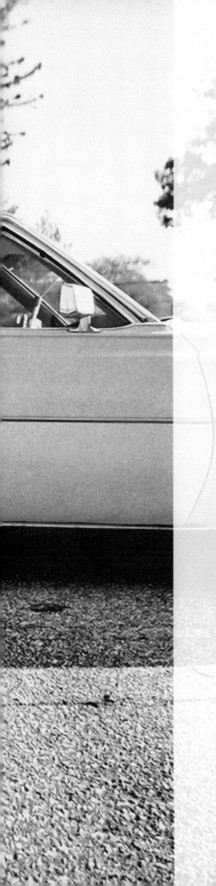

Go-Go Live

The Musical Life and Death

of a Chocolate City

Natalie Hopkinson

Duke University Press

Durham ★ London ★ 2012

© 2012 Duke University Press. All rights reserved. Printed in the United States of America on acid-free paper ♾. Designed by Jennifer Hill. Typeset in Arno Pro by Tseng Information Systems, Inc. Library of Congress Cataloging-in-Publication Data appear on the last printed page of this book.

For Serena and Terrence Hopkinson,
and in loving memory of Beverley Hyacinth McGann

Contents

Preface

Them black days are gone. You hear me? Chocolate City
and all that foolishness.—BEVERLEY McGANN, 2010

"There's a lot of chocolate cities around," George
Clinton of the funk band Parliament announced in
a recording of 1975. "We've got Newark, we've got
Gary. Somebody told me we got L.A. And we're
working on Atlanta. . . . But you're the capital, C.C.!"
He was talking, of course, about Washington, D.C.,
the U.S. capital city that earned the moniker soon
after electing its first mayor, a black man named
Walter Washington. The cover art of the Parliament
album *Chocolate City* was an illustration of the Lincoln Memorial, the National Monument, and the
Capitol dome all dipped in chocolate, proof that
blacks did not "need the bullet when you got the
ballot."

"We didn't get our forty acres and a mule," Clinton sang. "But we did get you, C.C.!"

Indeed, as far as Chocolate Cities go, there is no
more extreme case than Washington, D.C., in the
second half of the twentieth century. Beyond the
federal capital, Washington, lies a very black city,

D.C.: Black families milling around on the streets, waiting at bus stops, driving cars. Black schools taught by black teachers and run by black principals reporting to black superintendents. Black restaurants, black recreation centers. Black universities. Black hospitals run by black doctors and staff. Black suburbs. Black judges ordering black police officers to deliver black suspects to black jail wardens. For much of the past half century, it was entirely possible to live and work in the District of Columbia and not interact with a white person for months.

To wit: My dear friend Lynette recently drove into the Chocolate City with her three-year-old daughter, who woke up and peered out of the window at the corner of North Capitol Street and Florida Avenue. The corner was bustling with black people trash-talking each other on park benches, standing at the bus stop, lining up outside a carryout. Breathless, the girl asked, "Are we in *Africa*, Mommy?"

It was not the motherland, but D.C. ranked among the few major cities in the United States where black people could not be accurately called "minorities," with the whiff of inferiority that the label carries with it. When you happen to be born black in a world designed for white people, to live in a Chocolate City is to taste an unquantifiable richness. It gives a unique angle of vision, an alternate lens to see world power. In a Chocolate City, black is normal. As a rule, black people strut around town with their chests puffed out—reeking of what my sister Nicole Rose calls "black privilege." Some might call it arrogance.

So how did this curious scene happen more than a century after the end of legal slavery, in a country in which black people make up just 12 percent of the population? Much of world history has consisted of a series of racial migrations fueled by colonialism and capitalism—a global game of racial musical chairs. All along, the color of one's skin has served as a convenient shorthand for who has the money and the power and who does not. In the fifteenth century, a white adventurer "discovered" a place where brown people already lived, and he took it. The white settlers in what would become the United States of America needed someone to work the land, so boatloads of free black labor were shipped in from Africa. By the mid-nineteenth century, a new kind of industrial economy took hold, making this free black labor, always morally troublesome, an obstacle to economic progress as well. The Civil War ended slavery, but not the basic color caste system. As industry soared and cities thrived, the descendants of slaves made a steady migration from the fields of the

South to cities in the North in search of work. By the end of the Second World War, whites, in the meantime, already made a steady migration to the suburbs. Add in the gains of the civil rights movement in producing a class of black leaders and you have got Chocolate Cities from Cleveland to Atlanta.

But as the twentieth century drew to a close, yet another round of musical chairs began. U.S. suburbs sprawled, wreaking havoc on the environment, lengthening commutes, and reducing the quality of life outside the cities proper. An information-based economy now took hold. Concentrated public housing located in city centers disproportionately filled with black residents across the United States was dismantled. This coincided with a general march back to cities, increasing the population, reviving tax bases, and sparking new development. This also has led to the displacement of black communities and a slow death of the Chocolate City.

I saw it firsthand in 2000, when my husband and I house-hunted for our first home. We saw a curious scene at open house after open house in black D.C. neighborhoods: black renters being evicted and hordes of eager young white buyers hovering, waiting to pounce. For the first time in generations, billions of dollars in development had poured into D.C. Tens of thousands of luxury apartments and condo units went up. Abandoned Victorian houses in the center of the city were being snapped up and renovated. For me, the moment that punctured the veil of black invincibility came one evening, when I saw a pack of white people on rollerblades moseying down my block in the city's Logan Circle neighborhood, long after the sun had set. The words of my former political science professor at Howard University echoed in my ears: "When you see white people in a neighborhood after dark, that means they are about to take it over." "White flight" was what happened in our parents' generation. We were witnessing a "white return."

In urban centers throughout the country, this kind of racial paranoia was not new, as the desperate plea in 2006 by the New Orleans mayor Ray Nagin evinced. After Hurricane Katrina had ravaged his city, the Associated Press quoted him vowing, "It's time for us to rebuild a New Orleans, the one that should be a chocolate New Orleans.... This city will be a majority African American city. It's the way God wants it to be. You can't have New Orleans no other way; it wouldn't be New Orleans."

For as long as U.S. inner cities have been declining, allowing black people to make political and economic inroads there, we have been wondering when white people with money and power would decide to snatch it back. In 2001, as a young reporter at the *Washington Post*, I wrote an op-ed, "I Won't Let D.C. Lose Its Flavor," as a warning, a dare and a challenge to my middle-class black peers—plentiful in the D.C. area—with the means to do an about-face from the 'burbs. In buying our home not far from the "Africa" corner, my husband and I managed to snatch our piece of the Chocolate, I gloated immodestly in the *Post* essay; our peers needed to do the same before prices got completely out of control. But my message was not mature, nor was it nuanced or subtle. "We damn sure won't let white people buy up all the property in DC," I wrote.

Fast-forward ten years. The release of the U.S. census figures in July 2011 made it official: "This city, the country's first to have an African-American majority and one of its earliest experiments in black self-government, is passing a milestone," the *New York Times* soberly announced. "Washington's black population slipped below 50 percent this year, possibly in February, about 51 years after it gained a majority." Similarly, in 2010, New Orleans elected its first white mayor in a generation.

It is easy to romanticize Chocolate Cities because of their unique contributions to U.S. culture. There is so much to love about them. Located at the geographic center of the urban experience in the United States, they provide a much-needed counterdiscourse, an alternate view on everything from politics to art. George Clinton and P-Funk popularized the moniker used by the city where they found their greatest and most loyal fans, fans who, under the brilliant direction of Chuck Brown, would create a whole genre of popular music called "go-go"—the beating heart of the Chocolate City. As the poet Thomas Sayers Ellis once explained to me, go-go music is the most "radical opposition to English syntax" that exists. In the chapters of this book, I sometimes use *go-go* as a verb. At other times it becomes a noun, at others still an adjective. Throughout go-go serves as a metaphor for the black urban experience in the second half of the twentieth century.

You will find no arguments against this particular art form here. But you will find arguments about the inherently separate but unequal milieu that produced it. When boiled down to their essence, as I attempt to do in this book, Chocolate Cities are also just an expression of America's original sin, the birth defect that began with slavery and lived on through segregation. Persistent assumptions around race uphold the same color caste system that preceded the country's founding. Segregation is a circumstance, which however relatively privileged, dumps a single group of people with a disproportionate share of historical baggage and social and economic burdens, while limiting access to opportunities for greater peace and prosperity. Adding insult to this injury is the persistent but wholly false narrative that black people have destroyed urban centers and that therefore for progress to continue, black people must now be pushed out of the way.

Change is inevitable. As the poet E. Ethelbert Miller famously quipped to the *Washington Post* in 2011, "Well, chocolate melts." The rise of the multicultural, "Neapolitan" city has the potential to change the way Americans think about cities, the way we think about communities, the way we think about race, the way we think about the United States. It is a new chapter for this country, an opportunity, really. The cynic would expect for the country to slide back into a familiar pattern with the same old winners and losers. But as long as we understand and appreciate the larger historical and socioeconomic factors that led to the rise and fall of the Chocolate City, we have the potential to forge ahead toward a tolerant, inclusive, multicultural society.

In D.C. the music tells the story. In the African oral tradition, drums hold the history, tell the story, and give warning of what is to come. Just as the Chocolate City was taking its last gasps of air in 2008, news spread that Barack Obama had been elected president of the United States. Conga drums appeared on U Street. Hundreds of people of every color gathered to celebrate just as the drums appeared in streets of Nairobi.

So it goes in this book. Washington, D.C.'s go-go music and culture — the personalities, the artists, the fans, the entrepreneurs, the ministers, the fashion designers, the politicians — tell the story of race and the U.S. city in the second half of the twentieth century.

Acknowledgments

Thanks to everyone who has shared this journey with me, starting with my husband, Rudy McGann, and our kids, Maven and Maverick.

Thank you to every single person connected with Howard University, past, present, and future, for supporting an alternate view of the world right at the seat of world power—it is needed now more than ever. Thanks to the whole go-go community for giving me so much to think about for the past ten years: Especially Richard O'Connor—this would not be possible without your help. Thanks to everyone connected to the go-go community: Chuck Brown, Go-Go Nico Hobson, Kato Hammond, Thomas Sayers Ellis, Rev. Tony Lee, Bobbie Westmoreland, Delece Smith-Barrow, Kadidia Thiero, INI Band, Fatal Attraction, Backyard Band, Chi Ali, Suttle Thoughts, Eric "Tree" Hinnant, Big G, Coop, Jay Pooh, Largo Brad, Ronald "Mo" Moten, Ken and Sam Moore, Bruce Brown, RIP Marvin "Slush" Taylor, Andre "Whiteboy" Johnson, and Nina Mercer.

Thanks also to Allison R. Brown, Denise Hopkinson Ortiz, and Autumn Saxton-Ross for ignoring the bourgie haters and hanging with me at the go-go! Thanks to Glynn Jackson and Joel Dias-Porter. Ta-Nehisi Coates, thank you for your friendship and for publishing the first oral history of go-go. Thank you Natalie Y. Moore, E. Ethelbert Miller, Chris Jenkins, Mark Anthony Neal, and William Jelani Cobb for writer's triage.

Thank you to Scripps Howard Foundation for funding my doctoral research, and to all my former University of Maryland friends and colleagues: Chris Callahan, Tom Kunkel, William E. Smith. Thanks to my dissertation committee: Linda Steiner, Alice Bonner, John E. Newhagen, Jonathan Dueck, Carolina Robertson, and Nancy Struna. Thank you to my colleagues at the *Washington Post*: Lynn Medford, Kevin Merida, Deb Heard, Milton Coleman, Marcia Davis, Gene Robinson, and Nicole Arthur. Special shout to Don Graham for permission to use *Post* photography. Thanks to my colleagues at the *Root*: Lynette Clemetson, Terence Samuel, Saaret Yoseph, Erin Evans, and Henry Louis Gates Jr. Thanks to my colleagues at the Interactivity Foundation for supporting my arts and society project—wonderful synergy. And a special thanks to my parents, the original dreamers and wanderers, Serena and Terrence Hopkinson, and to Bunny McGann. And a final thank-you to my great late mother-in-law, Beverley Hyacinth McGann. There aren't enough words to say how grateful I am to you for holding me down from the beginning of this journey and giving me insights right until the very end. Please rest well— you've earned it.

1 ★ A Black Body Politic

"So . . . are you a go-go fan?"

I was just trying to make small talk with the woman sitting next me. LaTanya Anderson and I were among the thousands of mourners gathered at the Washington, D.C., Convention Center in June 2010, where the body of the legendary go-go trumpeter Anthony "Little Benny" Harley was lying in state in a baby blue casket topped by red roses. Well, the District of Columbia is not legally a state; so it was the Chocolate City equivalent of a state funeral. The mayor, city council, and the District's representative in Congress sat on a stage above the body of the forty-six-year-old trumpeter, who had died unexpectedly in his sleep. The night before, he had played a gig with his mentor, the "Godfather of Go-Go," Chuck Brown. Little Benny would not be recognized outside the Beltway, but inside the city limits, he was the kind of superstar who would bring out six thousand people to pay their respects in the middle of a workday.

Dead or alive, these were the kind of coattails you might want to ride if you were a politician facing a tough primary.

"Am I a *fan*?" repeated LaTanya, who was a forty-something government analyst, looking at me as if I had just landed from outer space. "That's a strange thing to ask. I'm a *fan* of Erykah Badu. I'm a *fan* of Ronald Isley. To me a fan is something removed, not part of your culture, part of your blood. Something you grew up with, watched develop. That's like asking someone from New Orleans if they like jazz. It *is* them. It's the culture. It's the food."

It is as the ethnomusicologist Kip Lornell and the cultural activist Charles Stephenson Jr. explained in their groundbreaking ethnography,[1] *The Beat: Go-Go's Fusion of Funk and Hip-Hop*: "Go-go is more than just music. It's a complex expression of cultural values masquerading in the guise of party music in our nation's capital."[2]

Indeed, three generations of Washington-area residents had been grooving to go-go, ever since the guitarist Brown had created the sound in the mid-1970s, borrowing the Caribbean flavor he had picked up playing for a Washington Top 40 band called Los Latinos. Go-go has been compared to everything from funk to hip-hop and reggae, but it is best described as popular music—party music—that can take many forms. When you hear it, you know it's go-go by the beat: slow-boiling congas, bass drums, timbales, cowbells, and rototoms layered with synthesizers and a horn section. You also know it's go-go because the audience is part of the band. Together the musicians onstage and the people below it create the music live—always live—through a dialogue of sounds, movements, and chants.

Go-go comes with distinctive dance moves, slang, hand-signs, and clothing—all customized and unique to life in the area surrounding the U.S. capital city. A so-called lead talker presides over the show as emcee, calling out fans and rhyming free-style. There is also usually a rapper and an R&B vocalist singing original compositions and covering pop artists from Ashlee Simpson to Ludacris. Much like jazz artists, the D.C. musicians completely transform popular standards in the live environment, funking them up with the heavily percussive go-go swing.

At Little Benny's funeral, Brown collapsed at the dais, breaking into tears mid-note during an emotional rendition of "A Closer Walk to Thee." Until his unexpected death in May 2010, the diminutive Little Benny was both a bandleader and trumpeter (sometimes blazing two trumpets simultaneously). He and some buddies at his Southeast Washington elementary school had started the seminal go-go band Rare Essence. At the time of his death, go-go had still not much broken out of the D.C. area; there were only some crossover hits from Brown, EU, Trouble Funk, Wale, DJ Kool, and others. There was also a national film release, *Good to Go*, by Chris Blackwell's Island Visual Arts (a spinoff of Island Records) in the late 1980s, followed by a memorable go-go scene in Spike Lee's musical *School Daze* of 1987, which spawned EU's Billboard hit "Da Butt."

Go-go did not stay outside D.C. for very long. But there was plenty of work for go-go musicians in the Chocolate City. Hundreds of musicians played go-go in the D.C. region seven nights a week anywhere the genre's musicians and audience gathered—backyards, street corners, high school proms, firehouses, community centers, parks, government buildings, restaurants, skating rinks, corner stores, nightclubs, and college campuses. The most popular go-go bands, such as TCB, still played four gigs a week, drawing anywhere from two hundred to one thousand fans per night, with clubs turning people away at the door on a good night. The foundation of go-go was a large, extended network of local and almost exclusively black-owned businesses. Mom and pop storefronts sold local clothing lines of urban wear, live recordings, and concert tickets. Graphic design firms created and printed advertisements. The city's most popular FM stations (WKYS 93.9 FM and WPGC 95.5 FM) had nightly go-go hours devoted to the music. Then there were security companies and club and restaurant owners. By the early 2000s, as gentrification steamrolled the city core, much of the go-go industry had been shoved deeper and deeper into exurban Maryland.

The majority of go-go enthusiasts were black. But blacks do not make up a monolith, especially in the Chocolate City. Not *all* black Washingtonians liked, or even supported, go-go. As Lornell and Stephenson noted, go-go "wears the mantel of low-class or blue-collar music."[3] It would be rare to find go-go music on, say, the campus of historically black Howard University. Club owners of various races and ethnicities openly banned the music, keeping deejays from playing the rump-shaking music and turning away bands that carried the telltale conga drum sets.[4] D.C. politicians often railed against the music as a magnet for violence and illicit activity. A few politicians in Maryland and the District pursued aggressive campaigns to yank the liquor licenses of venues hosting go-go music.[5] In early 2010, the District of Columbia police force boasted at a news conference about an initiative called the "Go-Go Report," designed to keep tabs on what band was playing where and when. Officers credited this surveillance of conga players with the falling murder rate and with changing D.C.'s reputation as the "Murder Capital."[6]

In the late 1990s and early 2000s, hip-hop artists were subject to some of the same police scrutiny after a spate of well-publicized killings, including the deaths of the rappers Biggie Smalls and Tupac Shakur. After years of denying rumors of a "hip-hop task force," New York and Miami police admitted to the *Village Voice* in 2004 that they had units keeping tabs on hip-hop artists.[7] This revelation sent everyone from the rap mogul Russell Simmons to the former NAACP leader Ben Chavis Muhammad and Georgetown University law professors howling. "Hip-Hop behind Bars" blared a *Source* magazine cover. In the Chocolate City, however, there were few political consequences for disparaging go-go, as class often trumped race — except, of course, during an election year.

Yet at the time the city made arrangements to pay for Little Benny's funeral, black working- and middle-class D.C. voters were united around one sentiment: the mayor, Adrian Fenty, had become a problem. Polls showed Fenty to be in deep political trouble, losing support to his rival, the sixty-seven-year-old city council chairman named Vincent Gray. True, Fenty, a hard-charging thirty-nine-year-old triathlete, kept the trains running. Under his watch, the renaissance of the city raced ahead, with new doggy parks, renovated schools and recreation centers, and sparkling new libraries. But Fenty seemed to relish any opportunity to defy establishment elders as he made an aggressive show of remaking D.C. into what he called a "world-class city."[8] In a city that often communicated via subtext, many wondered if by "world-class" the mayor meant the opposite of "Chocolate."

As the city gentrified, it grew more diverse, but it remained far from a postracial melting pot. In fact, the influx of wealth into the city made the economic disparities between white and black residents in the city even more dramatic. Much like the rest of the country, D.C. was in the midst of heated class warfare about how public resources should be spent. Whites in the District had a median household income of $92,000, while blacks earned a median income of $34,000. (Latino and Asian D.C. residents also out-earned blacks, with a median household income of $44,000 and 84,000, respectively.[9])

When Fenty was sworn in as mayor in 2007, D.C. had a higher concentration of people living in extreme poverty—10.8 percent—than any of the fifty states, including even Mississippi and Louisiana, the latter still reeling from the effects of Hurricane Katrina.[10] Four years later, as Fenty campaigned for reelection, the increase in poverty among the city's black children was even more breathtaking: it had shot up to 43 percent, from 36 percent in 2008 and 31 percent in 2007, according to an analysis of U.S. census data.[11] By comparison, the white median income had grown, and the number of white children living in poverty was 3 percent at the time of Little Benny's funeral.

The bottom line was that D.C. remained a Chocolate City, and black residents still outnumbered white residents by a margin of one hundred thousand. Black residents were more likely to look to the city to provide a social safety net, while white residents looked to the city to provide the perks, brick sidewalks, bike lanes, and doggy parks now available thanks in part to the extra taxes they had brought into the city.

D.C.'s large and politically active black middle class could have provided a swing vote for Fenty, especially since the mayor was one of them, a D.C. native; member of a black fraternity, Kappa Alpha Psi; and a graduate of Howard University. As his London-raised wife Michelle Fenty said in an interview, "He doesn't just care; he grew up with these people."[12] But Fenty had antagonized many black middle-class voters, too, with his aggressive overhaul of city agencies, whose jobs and contracts had helped to produce the black middle class in the first place. Fenty appointed few black faces to the upper levels of his administration. This would not seem odd if the city were not home to the most educated, accomplished concentration of black talent in the country, many of whom knew their way around D.C.'s odd, quasi-colonial government structure.[13] Then there were the mass firings of veteran black public school teachers, replaced en masse by young, often white, Teach for America temporary workers recruited by his schools chancellor, a young education entrepreneur named Michelle Rhee.[14]

Few things infuriated black voters of all income levels more than Fenty's scorched-earth, erase-everything attitude toward their schools.[15] Parents in the District had spent a generation learning how to navigate the resource-starved public school system, which had, for at least a century, been a plaything of Congress. Like the rest of the city services that took a hit during the lean years when the city experienced a shrinking tax base and deteriorating infrastructure, the schools were far from ideal. But instead of leaving the city for greener suburban pastures, generations of Washingtonians had stayed loyal and learned to make do. Now, thanks to a booming local economy and skyrocketing real-estate values, the city finally had the resources to do more. Public school parents—three-fourths of them black—resented the disparate impact of school "reform" that eradicated neighborhood schools in some black communities. While traditional public schools in majority-white neighborhoods were largely left alone, black neighborhood schools were allowed to wither on the vine before being closed. (In the rash of 2008 closures that followed Fenty's election, the city's green, leafy, and majority black Ward 5 community, for instance, was left without a single freestanding neighborhood middle school.[16]) They also resented the implication of Rhee's portrait in *Time* magazine, on whose cover she appeared wearing a grim expression and wielding a broom. Did "reform" mean that black people were the dirt being swept away?[17] They did not believe there were no qualified black professionals available to run schools. They also balked at Fenty's and Rhee's statements—often to national corporate audiences they courted for donations—that the system was such a morally decrepit wasteland that parents and teachers should have no input in their reform.[18]

Fenty, who had a white mother and a black father, had attended D.C. public schools during the "Murder Capital" 1980s. He also attended Oberlin, and then the Howard University School of Law. So he could not pretend to be naïve about the racial undertones governing change in D.C. The city was replacing public housing projects located on prime real estate with so-called mixed-income housing. The scarcity of affordable housing disproportionately hit the poorest—and blackest—corners of the city. Construction and other blue-collar jobs once held by blacks were now going to Latino immigrants. The black middle class was feeling the squeeze too. Far from reflecting a postracial meritocracy, the city's elite institutions in academia, in the think tank, the nonprofit organization, on Capitol Hill, and in the media were generally whiter than a Sarah Palin rally, even in 2010. Now their grip on the Chocolate City institutions that provided them professional and economic refuge was slipping away.

There were a few notable black exceptions to Fenty's colorblind hiring policies. A few of Fenty's fraternity brothers got multimillion-dollar no-bid parks contracts at greatly inflated rates, which raised the ire of government watchdogs and the city council.[19] And Ronald "Mo" Moten, an ex-con turned go-go promoter and antiviolence activist, got $10 million in no-bid city contracts for working with "at-risk" youth.[20] Yet for the most part the young mayor charged ahead with a racially blind overhaul of what many were calling the "new D.C." As Fenty "classed" up the joint, the subtext was clear: black meant decline, white meant progress. Census projections showed that black voters would soon be a minority of the city's population. But Fenty, along with almost the entire establishment news media,[21] governed the city as if black people were dead weight—or worse, already gone.

When the voices of angry black citizens from across the city became too loud to ignore as his reelection campaign was well under way, Fenty turned to the go-go community for help—in particular to one associate, Moten. With Mo at his side, Fenty hosted go-go concerts, code-switched, spoke Ebonics from park stages, and did old-school go-go dances at rallies. He put out a video, "Go-Go 4 Fenty: We Got the Facts, Not Fiction," featuring endorsements from popular go-go artists including Chi Ali of Suttle Thoughts, Big G of Backyard Band, and Sugarbear of EU.

And, of course, Moten—and Fenty—were front and center at Little Benny's funeral. Among the audience in the Convention Center, filled with customized "RIP Little Benny" T-shirts and embroidered work uniforms, there were plenty of sighs, whispers, and eye rolls at the spectacle of Fenty and the rest of the city's political brass shamelessly standing above the trumpeter's dead body, giving what amounted to stump speeches. As the mayor took his turn at the dais, a string of boos rang out from among the mourners, many of whom had already moved to Maryland. Reverend Deron Cloud, who had delivered a eulogy backed by a go-go band, jumped to the microphone to chastise the crowd for spurning the mayor as though he had just sung off-key at the Apollo. "This is the house of the Lord," he snapped. "We are not here for that, family."

Well, not exactly. This was not the house of the Lord. And they were not "family." The Convention Center was the $800 million house of District taxpayers. Even so, as Little Benny was laid to rest that June, it was Fenty who quickly arranged for the public to pick up the tab.

A Black Public Sphere

Little Benny's funeral was just one example of how go-go embodied a certain racialized part of the public in the nation's capital. The centrality of music to Washington's local political scene is a throwback to the African oral tradition that puts music at the center of all things. But go-go also hearkens back to the Western notion of the public as described by the German philosopher Jürgen Habermas. In his seminal book *The Structural Transformation of the Public Sphere,* Habermas traced the origins of the modern idea of a public to feudal Europe. Because commoners rarely had the opportunity to enjoy music outside of church or noble society, the first music concerts constituted an early form of publicity: "For the first time an audience gathered to listen to music as such—a public of music lovers to which anyone who was propertied and educated was admitted . . . within a public everyone was entitled to judge," Habermas writes.[22]

While music played a small early role, to Habermas, the eighteenth-century culture of the European coffee house was the ultimate expression of the public sphere. These cafés were the physical locus of critical debate about the people's business. In the first decade of eighteenth-century London alone, Habermas notes the operation of three thousand coffee houses, each with its core group of regulars who debated individual and collective issues face to face.[23]

Over time, technology allowed these discussions to move to the realm of mass communication—newspapers and magazines, radio and television. Independent journalism replaced the coffee house and salon scene as the primary vehicle to challenge and criticize the government. But Habermas believed something vital was lost when discussions stopped happening face to face. Their public purpose became muddled as the mass media became increasingly commercialized. Advertising-supported journalism focused less on informing the public and on criticizing leaders and more on promoting consumer culture and consensus. "Along with its communal basis, the public sphere lost its place," and no longer presented a transparent, comprehensive view, Habermas writes.[24]

Many critics have rightly pointed out that Habermas's idea of "comprehensive" excluded many people. Women, people of color, the poor, anyone not a landholding white man. And of course, Habermas's definition of the public sphere does not exactly explain the kind of public found in a Chocolate City. In the mid-1990s, a group of black scholars called the Black Public Sphere Collective explored this glaring oversight:

> The black public sphere—as a critical social imaginary—does not centrally rely on the world of magazines and coffee shops, salons and high-

brow tracts. It draws energy from the vernacular practices of street talk and new musics, radio shows and church voices, entrepreneurship and circulation. Its task is not the provision of security for the freedom of conversation among intellectuals, as was the case with the bourgeois public spheres of earlier centuries. Rather it marks a wider sphere of critical practice and visionary politics, in which intellectuals can join with the energies of the street, the school, the church, and the city to constitute a challenge to the exclusionary violence of much public space in the United States.[25]

In his book *What the Music Said*, the culture critic Mark Anthony Neal noted that after the dismantling of chattel slavery, a black "public" emerged in the form of several institutions: the black church, the black press (newspapers and magazines), and black music. These institutions constituted the primary sites of public expression and vehicles to critique the black experience. Neal noted that black music venues, such as the so-called chitlin' circuit of black nightclubs, juke joints, and after-hours clubs, helped create common aesthetic values throughout the black diaspora.[26]

Bars, dance halls, blues clubs, barbershops, beauty salons, and street corners offered a window into what Robin D. G. Kelley called "the private worlds of black working people where thoughts, dreams, and actions that were otherwise choked back in public could find expression."[27] Even as American blacks scattered and migrated after the Second World War, these segregated black institutions helped knit together a black public, according to Neal. During the civil rights movement, music became its own form of cultural and leadership capital in and outside the black church, as Houston A. Baker has explained.[28] The music became the soundtrack for the freedom struggle.

In the post–civil rights era, the black community became even more dispersed as desegregation opened up suburban neighborhoods and regions previously unavailable to them. In the era of black middle-class flight from formerly segregated urban communities, black music continued to function as the glue that held the black body politic together. Still, a sizeable number of black Americans remained in the urban core, both in residential neighborhoods, in public housing, and in the mayor's office of places like Detroit, Cleveland, Newark, and Washington, D.C. These are the communities George Clinton called Chocolate Cities, and they became hotbeds of cultural innovation. This social, political, and economic transformation of postindustrial urban centers in the 1970s allowed for the emergence of new kinds of public spheres. White and black middle-class flight and the abandonment of the city left a power vacuum in the United States. This allowed for the rise of underground economies that snatched their own cultural and economic power. In the Bronx in the mid-1970s, that was hip-hop. In Washington, D.C., during the same time, it came in the form of go-go.

In their first decade of life go-go and hip-hop cultures developed along roughly parallel tracks as communicative mediums knitting their respective local urban communities together. Chuck D (né Carlton Ridenhour) of the hip-hop group Public Enemy described the early days of rap as a "Black CNN." He claimed the rapper or emcee would paint a visual picture with his words to describe the life of the community for those outside it, so that "people all over could get informed about black life in those areas without checking the [mainstream] news. Every time we checked for ourselves on the news they were locking us up anyway, so the interpretation coming from Rap was a lot clearer."[29]

Hip-hop began as a community-based art form that included deejaying, emceeing or rapping, breakdancing, and graffiti. But its geographic location in New York and then Los Angeles proved critical to deciding its future trajectory. The economy of New York, the U.S. financial capital, and that of Los Angeles, the entertainment capital, made it possible for private companies to co-opt and globalize hip-hop. Cable television promoted the music; multinational corporations signed and promoted artists. Hip-hop eventually became a dominant expression of youth culture worldwide.

In its divergent path go-go can be viewed as a kind of cultural and economic counterdiscourse to hip-hop. In chapter 4 I discuss how live go-go performances remain faithful to a centuries-old cross-Atlantic dialogue between West Africa and the black diaspora. Economically, the go-go public sphere is black-owned and heavily guarded,[30] a possibility that only exists because of the cultural geography of Washington, D.C. The metropolitan area is a recession-proof government town that boasts the largest, best-educated, and most prosperous black economic base in the country. I discuss the historic and political roots of the concentration of black wealth in the U.S. capital in chapter 2.

In the 1980s, when go-go was at the height of its popularity, Washington, D.C., was also home to a specific underground economy: one of the nation's most lucrative crack cocaine markets. With the economic support of what Patillo-McCoy called either "decent" or "street" elements of the black community, the go-go industry managed to survive as a cultural and economic island in the nation's capital.[31]

Long after mainstream hip-hop ceased to serve this function, live go-go performances are still a "Black CNN." Go-go has guarded this network by stubbornly resisting the standardization of youth culture via hip-hop. There are of course hip-hop fans and artists in the District, but in Washington go-go has remained the dominant manifestation of black youth culture, with locally rooted fashion styles, slang, and dance.

Go-go has accomplished this position by relentless innovation, constantly adapting its business, aesthetic, and production models. Rare Essence, the band founded by Little Benny and his elementary school friends, offers a perfect example. Although most of the founding members had moved on, Rare Essence remained a marquee brand in go-go known for its constantly changing lineup. "Rare Essence is not a band," Kevin "Kato" Hammond, the editor of *Take Me Out to the Go-Go*, a web magazine he founded in 1996, told me in 2006. "It's a company that employs musicians."

Through constant evolution, go-go remained an authentic *place* to communicate and share the reality of life in Washington, D.C. It has also grown into an industry that has capitalized on the links among consumption, identity, and economic power. "We got two things in this town, urban wear and go-go," Steve Briscoe, a local black clothing line owner, told me. "This is our culture, our identity."[32] In 2004, he organized with dozens of other District-based black colleagues in the garment industry to fend off piracy from a Korean competitor. Preserving and protecting this market allowed the same dollar to circle endlessly through a single community. This in itself is a statement that is deeply political in a way that Booker T. Washington would appreciate—if not Habermas.

Washington's "two cities" are a cliché commonly invoked by both the media and residents to describe the geographic and psychological divisions between mostly black D.C. residents and Washington, D.C., the seat of world power. Indeed, the body politic on view at Little Benny's funeral looked much different than the national public conversation taking place blocks away in Congress and the White House. However, as I will argue in this book, federal Washington and the Chocolate City share the same geography, the same history, the same values, and often quite literally the same space. They are two sides of the same coin rapidly fusing into something brand new while the Chocolate City fades away.

Election

The boos among the mourners at Little Benny's funeral died down as Fenty took the microphone. He announced a plan to rename a street off the historically black U Street corridor "Lil' Benny Way." No one in the room could have missed the symbolism of this proclamation. U Street had once been the city's segregated black entertainment district, a city within a city, or "Black Broadway." By the time Little Benny died, it had become a racial melting pot. Hipster publications had declared the neighborhood the cutting edge of urban cool. On any given day you might find tour buses, which before 2000 would have never crossed the city's racial boundary of Fourteenth Street. Shortly after his 2008 election, Barack Obama became the first president to patronize the iconic U Street greasy spoon, Ben's Chili Bowl. When the French president Nicolas Sarkozy visited the White House in 2010, he did the same.

"Lil' Benny Way" would be located steps from The Spirit of Freedom, a ten-feet-tall sculpture of uniformed black soldiers that died in the Civil War. The go-go trumpeter's name could be seen alongside a memorial listing the names of each of the 209,145 U.S. Colored Troops. His musical contributions would be commemorated right there, next to his ancestors who fought to prevent the country from cannibalizing itself over the issue of slavery.

His announcement earned Mayor Fenty a hearty round of applause. But sitting next to me, LaTanya Anderson just rolled her eyes. She knew the (sort of) state funeral and the permanent memorial to her childhood friend would not have happened if not for the political currents swirling in the melting Chocolate City. Most white voters praised Fenty's work "cleaning things up." Black voters were equally passionately against Fenty, finding him the perfect vessel to carry their resentment and bitterness about rising racial inequalities in the city. White minority public opinion was just as plainly racialized as black majority opinion. At a time when gentrification and governance decisions created clear winners and losers, few national and local observers of the 2010 mayoral election problematized the benefits and privileges that drove white perceptions of the city's leadership. Little Benny's funeral was yet another example of how go-go provided a forum, a physical space, to provide an alternate interpretation. By September 2010, the city may have been getting whiter, but black voters remained the majority in this overwhelmingly Democratic city, representing 63 percent of likely Democratic primary voters.[33] If they spoke with one voice, black voters could easily take Fenty out—a final exercise of black privilege.[34] Sitting next to me, LaTanya just shrugged: "Election year, sweetie."

2 ★ Club U

The Frank D. Reeves Municipal Center is an imposing eight-story building made of green glass and brown stone, located at the corner of Fourteenth and U Streets. The center was named in honor of a black, Canadian-born Howard University law professor who advised President John F. Kennedy and helped end legal segregation in public schools. By day, more than a thousand Washington, D.C., government workers toiled in the Reeves Center at agencies such as the Emergency Management Administration, the Department of Transportation, and the D.C. Lottery. Other city bureaucrats pushed pencils nine to five for the Management and Employee Services Administration, Customer Service and Records Management, Recruiting and Personnel Actions, and the Office of Special Review.

But on some nights, in the wee hours, after the ties and the St. John knits had gone home, the ground floor of the building transformed into a place called Club U. At weekly concerts hundreds of revelers popped bottles as the dance floor exploded with the sounds of the city's hottest go-go bands. Well into the early-morning hours deejays from Washington's top FM radio stations broadcast "live from Club U."

This weekly transformation had been happening for more than a decade, but it ended one fateful pre–Valentine's Day night in 2005.[1] On that boozy night, Rare Essence commanded sweaty bodies on the dance floor. When a patron saw his girlfriend dancing with another man, he knocked her out—and did the same to one of the woman's friends who tried to intervene. Seasoned Club U bouncers ejected the boyfriend from the club, but when outside he spotted the ambulance carrying his girlfriend and her friend to the hospital, he took out a pistol and took aim from the sidewalk. He missed.

In an unrelated incident back inside Club U, Terrance Brown scuffled with another patron on the dance floor. No one noticed a wound as club bouncers carried him outside. The bouncers had just propped him up against the wall outside the building when their walkie-talkies chirped that another fight had broken out. They raced back inside. When police arrived, Brown told them that he had been stabbed with an unidentified object, but he refused to elaborate. He was taken by ambulance to Howard University Hospital. Brown was pronounced dead the next day.

The Brown tragedy ignited months of a racially charged debate over whether to continue to allow the venue to operate. But they were really fighting over the future of the Chocolate City. During more than forty hours of testimony before the city's alcohol licensing board, a parade of witnesses gave passionate arguments on both sides. On one end were police who linked go-go music to crime and politicians representing the mass of young, increasingly white professionals now populating the U Street neighborhood. Many newcomers residing in newly built luxury apartments and refurbished row houses and condos on U Street expressed shock and dismay when they learned that District of Columbia officials had in effect been throwing the equivalent of a rent party in a public building.[2] They and police argued that the D.C. government should not be in the nightclub business, especially in one where things had gotten so out of control that someone had lost his life.

On the other end, Club U supporters pointed out an unbroken chain of black musical tradition on that corner since the 1920s, when segregated U Street rivaled Harlem as the black cultural capital. In a rare display of black solidarity across class lines, dozens of black grass-roots activ-

ists, civil rights, business, and education leaders came to the defense of
Club U. To them, Club U constituted a black sanctuary, a refuge for a rare,
authentic black Washington under attack. They viewed the effort to shut
down Club U as a ploy to expunge black people from their "home."

"U Street has always been a quick-change artist," the *Washington Post*
noted.[3] "Old Jim Crow shaped its earliest existence, creating rigid rules
of engagement, but also, perversely, carving out a niche where black folks
could be. African Americans didn't have a place to go, so they made their
own. And they owned it. U Street was it." Not anymore.

The Darker Nation

It might seem odd to imagine that a single building could house two very
different realities depending on the time of day. Strange also to imagine
a U.S. city where the government participated in the nightclub business.
Stranger still that that said nightclub would operate less than two miles
from the White House. But the story of Club U shows how tightly music
is woven into the tapestry of the black public domain, where boundaries between private and public are often obliterated. And all this is only
strange until we recall the peculiar set of historical circumstances that
produced the Chocolate City.

In 1791, Maryland and Virginia, both slave states, donated swampland
to create the diamond-shaped District of Columbia, which would serve
as the capital of the United States of America. Because it was established
as the seat of national power, the municipal structure does not resemble
that of any other place in the country. The District of Columbia is not a
state, has limited representation in the U.S. House of Representatives,
and none in the Senate. A congressional committee of members elected
from throughout the United States rules Washington.

This unique structure means that the city reflects the mood of the
whole country. It has also generally served to amplify the black voice and
voices favorable to black people. That slavery was legal in the early history of the District angered many Northern abolitionist members of Congress who lived in the city part-time. According to Constance Green's
fascinating *Secret City*, abolitionist congressmen sent so many bills on the
topic of slavery in the District of Columbia that in 1836 the feds called an
eight-year moratorium against introducing the topic.[4] This began a pattern of federal elected officials using the District of Columbia as a "politi-

cal football"—a testing ground for political innovations that might not pass in congressional home districts. D.C. citizens served as lab rats for public policies on education, public health, safety, and housing that might later be applied to the country at large.

Thus, from the beginning, the District has been a national Petri dish for urban affairs, and especially issues of race. In 1862, Congress passed a law that required public schools in the District to admit blacks. It also emancipated the thirty-one hundred slaves owned by District citizens, paying the slaveholders $300 per slave. Legislators passed this law nine months before Abraham Lincoln signed the Emancipation Proclamation, which legally freed slaves in the rest of the Union but provided no such windfall in the District.

The pattern continued after the Civil War and Reconstruction. In 1866, Congress overrode Andrew Johnson's veto and extended the right to vote to African American men living in the District. Blacks in the rest of the country would not enjoy these same freedoms until nine years later, when the federal Civil Rights Act was passed in 1875.

Local white municipal leaders objected to these racial policies, fearing they would transform the city into a haven for blacks.[5] They were right. Like many Southern slave states, Washington always boasted a high black population—roughly a third was black. By 1865, forty thousand "human contraband," or former slaves, had flocked to the District. The end of the Civil War coincided with a wave of urbanization. In 1867, Congress approved the only federally chartered university for the education of freed slaves in Washington, D.C., Howard University. The university's graduates took advantage of the federal government's hiring policies that gave opportunities that educated black people lacked in the private sector. Many educated blacks that came for federal civil service and military jobs stayed. Compared to the rest of the country, black Washingtonians were educated and prosperous. The city was regularly regarded as a "colored man's paradise."[6]

Washington, D.C., boasted the largest urban black population in the United States until Harlem overtook it in 1920. The capital city was the incubator for what would later become known as the Harlem Renaissance: key figures such as Alain Locke and Sterling Brown taught at Howard University, and Zora Neale Hurston graduated from there. Langston Hughes wrote evocatively of the time he spent in Washington after college, but he found Washingtonians "arrogant." In an essay of 1927 he wrote: "Negro society in Washington, they assured me was the finest in the country, the richest, the most cultured, the most worthy. . . . She is a graduate of this . . . or he is a graduate of that . . . frequently followed introductions. So I met many men and women who had been to college and seemed not to have recovered from it."[7]

By 1957, blacks had become the majority of the District's residents, exceeding numbers in any major city in the United States. The jazz great and U Street denizen Duke Ellington often said that his black nationalism stemmed from his upbringing in segregated Washington. Growing up there gave Ellington a "sense of being part of a historic procession."[8] He named his first band in New York City "The Washingtonians." In his autobiography Ellington remembered his education at an all-black high school in Washington, D.C.:

> She taught us that proper speech and good manners were our first obligations, because as representatives of the Negro race we were to command respect for our people. This being an all-colored school, Negro history was crammed into the curriculum, so that we would know our people all the way back. They had pride there, the greatest race pride, and at that time there was some sort of movement to desegregate the schools in Washington, D.C. Who do you think were the first to object? Nobody but the proud Negroes of Washington, who felt that the kind of white kids we would be thrown in with were not good enough.[9]

In 1967, Lyndon B. Johnson appointed the first black urban mayor, Walter Washington. Washington was one of three black men chosen to become mayors of major U.S. cities that year. Richard Hatcher of Gary, Indiana, and Carl Stokes of Cleveland both emerged victorious from elections for their posts, while Washington was appointed.

But for all the perks of living in the nascent Chocolate City, Congress still pulled the strings. Washingtonians had no voice in the congressional body that ruled them. Thanks to the city's federal status, residents of the District lived under some of the least democratic conditions in the United States with neither voting representation in Congress nor ultimate authority over municipal government. And efforts to give the District a voice in Congress were complicated by the city's darkening complexion.

In the late 1970s, there was reason to hope that would change. Both the House and the Senate passed the Civil Rights Act in 1978, which would allow the citizens of the District to elect two senators and either one or two House members. When the seven-year clock on approving the amendment timed out, less than half the necessary thirty-eight state legislatures had given their approval. Senator Ted Kennedy, a Democrat from Massachusetts, publicly speculated about the real reason behind the states' rejection. There was, he said, a "fear that senators elected from the District of Columbia may be too liberal, too urban, too black or too Democratic."[10]

At the time George Clinton was singing his ode to the Chocolate City in the 1970s, District voters made Walter Washington the city's first elected mayor. As was the case in many Chocolate Cities, the victory was rich in symbolism but hollow in outcome for many black residents. Like almost all postindustrial cities in the 1970s, the city suffered from middle-class (white and black) flight to the suburbs, which drained the municipality's tax base. That meant fewer resources to match rising demands for social services in areas such as education, housing, public safety, and health. While other urban areas could tap into state coffers propped up by wealthier suburban jurisdictions, D.C. had only the whims of Congress.

As the District's socioeconomic fortunes deteriorated, the psychological barriers erected around "white spaces" associated with federal Washington and the "black spaces" comprising most residential areas continued to move in opposite directions. Whites ran Congress and the White House; blacks ran the mayor's office, the police and fire departments, and schools, and they constituted the overwhelming majority of the city workforce.

The paradox of desegregation is that middle-class flight only left the urban core poorer, blacker, and more isolated. In Washington it essentially produced two different places in the nation's capital: white federal Washington and black local D.C. Until the beginning of the twenty-first century, this double-consciousness could be felt most vividly in a neighborhood called U Street.

The Life of U Street

For decades, U Street constituted the cultural epicenter of black Washington, the place where love and hate, mourning and celebration, life and death mingled freely. When black money had no value at theaters and restaurants downtown, the corner of Fourteenth and U Streets in particular was the command center for black social and economic power in the city. In the 1930s, the New Negro Alliance gathered at that corner to agitate for the end of such discrimination.

Segregation automatically implies inferiority. But the relative abundance of U Street obscured this reality. Located in the shadow of Howard University, by the 1930s the corridor had become the center of a black "city within a city," where more than three hundred black businesses — theaters, nightclubs, jazz clubs, billiard halls, and restaurants — catered to the black population.[11] They called it "Black Broadway." U Street was the meeting place, the place to go show off your Easter Sunday finest, to have tea, to celebrate after boxer Joe Louis knocked out his white challenger. To listen to jazz, go to a bar. Seeing black people in their finest on U Street, one could almost believe that separate could be equal. Almost.

With the end of legal segregation in the 1950s and 1960s, blacks of means left for the suburbs and other less dense parts of the city. Retail and residential spaces were abandoned. Many of those left behind were black and of limited means. The once-proud U Street strip experienced a brain drain. But even as it fell prey to the decline experienced in major urban centers throughout the United States, the corner of Fourteenth and U Streets remained a special nerve center for many Washingtonians. "That's where the people gathered and whether it was positive or negative," said U Street "mayor" John "Butch" Snipes. "I'm a Washingtonian and I grew up in Washington, been on U Street all my life. Had a chance to go anywhere in the world that I wanted to go, but I chose U Street because that is part of my home. And I've been down there to fight so that we could have progress."[12]

So it was on Thursday, 4 April 1968. Martin Luther King Jr. was planning a Poor People's March on Washington that was to begin that weekend. Many out-of-town activists and others who planned to participate had gathered at the corner of Fourteenth and U Streets. So the crowds were already there when news spread that King had been assassinated in Memphis.

The riots began at that corner of the District and spread fires across black neighborhoods throughout the city. One thousand of them were set and nine hundred businesses went up in flames.[13] The once proud Black Broadway was burned to a crisp. Speaking to the public, Mayor Washington put words to the events: "There is a voice coming from this city's ghetto neighborhoods. That voice says: 'We would like to be relevant to what happens in our communities. We would like to have entrepreneurship. We would like to be part of the American Dream.'"[14]

The riots of 1968 accelerated the brain drain afflicting U Street and other black economic hubs such as H Street. Those left behind were largely desperate and poor. Police felt overwhelmed. Criminal forces supplanted the role of government in imposing order. And after the riots another fault line, one upheld by real-estate agents and conventional wisdom for decades, hardened into cement: whites never ever were to live east of Fourteenth Street.

By the early 1980s the corner of Fourteenth and U Streets had become a dangerous and often deadly eyesore. Prostitution, open-air drug markets, X-rated bookstores, and peep shows formed a notorious red-light district. The District government needed to rein things in. It began by opening the U Street stop on the Metro, the city's award-winning public subway system. It also started plans to build a new municipal center to house city agencies. Many of the city's workers had moved to the Maryland suburbs and to less dense areas of the cities. But during the day, they (and their paychecks) would be there. The workers had to eat. And just maybe the upwardly mobile workers might stick around after hours.

In 1986 Mayor Barry cut the ribbon on the Frank D. Reeves Municipal Center at the scarred intersection. It would still take some time for the development to catch on. The hundreds of government officials who worked along the strip faced abysmal choices for retail and food. In 1992, Warren Williams Sr., the owner of a liquor store, heard that the city was looking for entrepreneurs to open a restaurant to feed the government workers. Paul D. Gwynn, Williams's partner and the president of Coach and IV, the company that owns Club U, testified at the alcohol board hearing about their initial trepidation concerning the venture.

> Half of U Street was closed down. There was no lighting in that area. And [Club U owner Warren] Williams came to me one day and said, excuse the expression, "Just what do you see there?" I said. "Man, beauty is in the eye of the beholder." Because what you see now don't necessarily have to be. . . . Metro here is developing and there is a government building here, let's take our shot at the business.

They opened a restaurant on the building's first floor, catering largely to government workers. That clientele ebbed and flowed as various government offices moved in and out. Williams decided to expand and begin hosting happy hours. Then the Williamses began to bring in live music. A promoter approached Warren Williams Jr., the owner's son, with an idea to promote live go-go shows. Club U was born. It proved to be the biggest draw to the building, one that would sustain the business financially.

But Club U would provide no haven from violence, as speakers at the 2005 alcohol board hearings would testify:

> ALCOHOLIC BEVERAGE CONTROL BOARD MEMBER ISAAC: So Mr. Snipes, sir, are you saying that historically Fourteenth and U has been actually an intersection at which the violent activity has occurred?
>
> SNIPES: You can't solve it, but I'm just in my mind, and this is the mindset of the average person that you see in Washington, D.C., that understands Washington, D.C. Maybe they don't approve of what goes on.

The Death of Club U

In 2005, a parade of witnesses appeared before the city's Alcoholic Beverage Control Board to decide the future of Club U. Emergency personnel, patrons, and workers at the building told a story of chaos the night of Terrance Brown's death. The D.C. councilman Jim Graham, one of the few white speakers, testified about many problems that the club had faced throughout the years. He had convened a press conference hours after Brown's stabbing, calling for the club's closure. Graham read a letter from the city's police chief requesting the city to revoke its liquor license. He also left the hearing early to attend Brown's funeral.

Officer Larry D. McCoy, the Third District's commander of the Metropolitan Police Department, cited a string of crimes that had occurred outside the club before the hearing room audience. In November 2003, a group of drunken Club U patrons had been ejected from the club and then began to fight. A man shot two of his friends, then sped his car out of the parking lot nearby. A police officer chased the driver before he crashed into the corner of Fourteenth and U Streets. The assailant got out of the car and shot the officer in the finger. Earlier in the month, another victim had been stabbed outside the club, dying several days later. McCoy showed the panel a statistical map of crime around Club U, indicating a high incidence of crime taking place within one thousand feet of the establishment on days when the club operated. When asked if he believed the club should be closed, McCoy responded: "Yes, ma'am, I do. I think it should be closed. Some nights, depending on the crowd. You bring in a good crowd in there, there are no problems. You have, you know, this go-go draw. I mean, I'll just tell you whenever I was over in the Seventh District, any place—if you have a black tie event, you don't have any problems, but you bring go-go in, you're going to have problems."

Taking the stand shortly after, another police officer, Paul Johnson, agreed. He described arriving on the scene at Club U the night of Brown's deadly stabbing. He said Brown had told officers that he had been stabbed with an unidentified object but that he was otherwise uncooperative with police. In his testimony Johnson presented his own theory about the source of problems at the site, echoing McCoy's:

ALCOHOLIC BEVERAGE CONTROL BOARD MEMBER THOMPSON: In your professional opinion, what do you think of this club? Do you think it is a danger to the public?

PAUL JOHNSON: I wouldn't say it's the club. I would say in my professional opinion, it's the—whenever we have the go-go music, there's violence that comes with it, I guess. And I guess I can associate it with the music because several of the clubs have go-go. And every time there is a go-go going on at the club, there is a higher tendency to have violence . . . I mean serious violence, not just, you know, fighting.

THOMPSON: Meaning someone is going to get hurt?

JOHNSON: Yeah, yeah.

In her testimony, another police officer, Inspector Diane Groomes, noted that in the previous two years, three homicides had occurred near the club. In 2003 there were 383 calls to summon police to the Reeves Center, and in 2004, 483 calls. She also told the board about crime statistics that linked violent crime to the operation of Club U. She said the kind of people the club attracted helped create the violent conditions there. She was even more specific in identifying the "problem" demographic.

DIANE GROOMES: On Saturdays, it's Rare Essence night, which is a go-go band, and that brings a lot of our young youth from the city.

ALCOHOLIC BEVERAGE CONTROL BOARD MEMBER ASTRA: And younger means more problematic?

GROOMES: A lot—I mean, I guess due to immaturity and alcohol mix. It doesn't mix well.

A stream of witnesses took the stand during several months of hearings to offer different perspectives on the club. Some pointed out that the high crime rates preceded the club and would likely continue whether a "magnet" such as Club U existed or not. They claimed violence was a social ill in the United States that transcended any form of music or the management of a particular space. Club U's lawyer, David Wilmot, told the board that his clients were being unfairly scapegoated: "We need to be concerned about [the murder of Terrance Brown], and that's well beyond what Club U can do. That's well beyond what [the owners] can do. That's well beyond what they can do alone. . . . There's a cause and effect. . . . What is causing this cancer within our community?"

Numerous witnesses, some inspired by an e-mail and an FM radio campaign called "Save the Go-Go," lined up to testify on the club's behalf. Few of the witnesses chosen to take the stand were actual go-go fans. Many of Club U's defenders were members of the city's black grass-roots political, business, and education establishments. They told the board what Club U represented to local neighborhoods, where they were seen as responsible and sensitive community members.

Shelore Ann Cary Williams, who lived near the club on Fourteenth Street and who formerly served as the principal of a private black Catholic school located two blocks away from Club U, testified about her warm working relationship with the owners. She noted that they paid to clean the whole street "spotless" after their parties, and that they hired a school security guard to escort patrons to their cars. Williams was also the chair of the Development Corporation for Columbia Heights, which issued a resolution in support of Club U keeping its license soon after Brown's murder, providing a forceful statement of the owners' right to operate in that environment. Williams told the board:

> [Club U owners] are model operators in the sense that they don't just give for political vote. They give to senior citizens. They give to the homeless. They give to the sick and shut-in. They give to children. They give to families each and every time you ask. . . . I honestly believe that a name may carry you, may carry your image. And Coach and IV is a great name, and a lot of people respect that name and so forth.

Lawrence Guyot, another advisory neighborhood commissioner, lawyer, and civil rights activist, spoke on the role of the owners' contributions to the community. Guyot described how they sponsored elementary school mother-daughter teas and provided food for civic association meetings in nearby LeDroit Park: "It was a place that the community could feel that they were welcome. For example, on many occasions, persons in the community have asked the management to hold wakes, which are very important to many of us in the minority communities, where we don't have places for wakes after funerals. And I've never once heard of them refusing to help people with wakes."

Another witness, Sinclair Matthew Skinner,[15] who owned a dry cleaning shop nearby and was a past advisory neighborhood commissioner, spoke on behalf of the Black U Street Association, for which he served as executive director. The mere existence of such a race-specific group spoke to the U Street community's defensive position at a time when the neighborhood remained overwhelmingly black. The group gathered more than five hundred signatures in support of the club, in particular, and of go-go music in general, and demanded that the police do a better job protecting citizens. Skinner testified that the focus on a particular music genre was a red herring for the fundamental problem that the death of Brown exposed: community policing. He said, "We wanted to make sure that all of the attention given, that we had a murderer still on the loose. We have a lot of the politicians bring up go-go music. Should that stay or go? Clubs, should they stay and go? . . . Somehow all of the media was on clubs and not on which way did he go and what did he have on, which to me seems more appropriate."

The Birth of the New U

Cultural landscapes are always changing, and so it is, too, with U Street. By 2005, the view at Fourteenth and U Streets depended on how long you had been looking at it. The economic development of U Street initially set in motion by black actors caught on at a speed that took many by surprise. By that year, the neighborhood found itself in the throes of a housing and retail boom. Rapid gentrification challenged the identity of Washington as a Chocolate City. According to the U.S. Census Bureau, in 2005, when the alcohol board hearings took place, for the first time in decades blacks no longer constituted the majority of homeowners in the District of Columbia. In 2000, 54 percent of D.C. homeowners were black, 41 percent white. But the decline of six thousand black homeowners during that five-year period and a surge of seven thousand additional white homeowners brought the two groups to parity in 2005.[16]

And in the early part of the 2000s, an even more impressive symbolic space was erected at the intersection of Thirteenth and U Streets: the year 2004 saw the completion of the Ellington Plaza Apartments. It was a $46 million, eight-story, and 186-unit building of luxury apartments, one that dominated most of the block and overshadowed everything else on the U Street corridor. The building's inhabitants were overwhelmingly upper middle class and predominantly white.

The Ellington complex towered over the new landscape on U Street, now billed by real-estate agents as "New to U." The complex drew in new retail and entertainment outlets that catered to a more upscale clientele. There were high-end furniture stores and a booming theater district further down Fourteenth Street. Perhaps most symbolic, Sun on U, the corridor's first tanning salon, opened on the Ellington's ground level. The strip was filled with live poetry places, ethnic restaurants, and clothing boutiques. The Reeves Center, which had since 1986 been the dominant force on the strip, now found itself in the shadows, both literally and psychologically. The center provided a bridge between the old U and the new U. It was time for that bridge to be burned.

Many old-timers wondered if black money was still good on U Street. Wilmot suggested his clients were owed a debt for being pioneers in contributing to the vitality of the strip.

> We are on the verge of a renaissance within this community. That building, the Reeves Center, was the centerpiece of that renaissance. Marion Barry and his administration fought to locate that building there to do what? To quiet the ravages of the riots of 1968. . . . Without that building there wouldn't be the economic development and the revival that's there now, and central to that was the location of businesses such as Club U.

Snipes agreed: "On the one side you have a lot of foreign people coming in, condominiums shooting up all over the place; two hundred, five hundred whatever thousand. Then you have another group of people who have been up there all their lives who don't really have a lot." One of Club U's co-owners, Gwynn, asserted that despite the change in the racial makeup, he felt that their business—and go-go—still had a place on U Street: "Well it's been a drastic change up there. The complexion of the area has changed tremendously, increase in taxes of houses, new condos, new homes, new restaurants, new nightclubs. It's a various matter of things changing up there to make this area supposedly a 'better' area. And I think we fit in that new place what's going on up there."

Williams suggested that in shutting down Club U, the city signaled a policy of evicting "problem" elements without addressing the roots of social problems. When asked what she thought was being done about violence, Williams responded, "The only thing I know that has taken place is the government appears to be moving loads of folks to somewhere else and putting high-rise buildings there at a high cost. But I don't see anything else happening." Guyot accused local alcohol beverage regulators, the local media, and officials of conspiring to purge all black elements from U Street.

LAWRENCE GUYOT: In my opinion, I've dealt with every little application on U Street or on Ninth Street, and the pattern is very, very clear. What we're really talking about here is one racial motif for blacks, another for whites. In the Wonderland [a white club], there was a stabbing. No one has heard about it. *The Post* never mentioned it. I would suspect maybe it hasn't been investigated or not. But if [Club U owner Warren Williams] were white, we wouldn't be here today.

ALCOHOLIC BEVERAGE CONTROL BOARD: You said at some point at any ANC [Advisory Neighborhood Commission] meeting that there is a constant attack upon black-owned liquor licenses in D.C.

GUYOT: Oh, yes. And it's led by [white D.C. councilman] Jim Graham and we're talking about no more than twenty people. The records of ABC [the Alcoholic Beverage Control Board] will show that. . . . So I think this, as far as I'm concerned, is a golden opportunity to really move race relations in Washington, D.C., way ahead. Let's restore this license and move on.

The Club U owner Williams had few words for the board. He told them he had lived or worked in the neighborhood for sixty years. He estimated that in his years of running Club U, at least one hundred thousand people had passed through his doors, making the Brown tragedy an aberration. He also pointed out that violence was a problem for society at large to deal with. If violence did not happen at or around his club, it would likely happen somewhere else. He worried aloud that the social problems disproportionately affecting black people were met with policies that ejected rather than rehabilitated. "If we can't behave and keep a club open at that rate, where do we go in Washington, D.C., if you close this club? Where else could I go? It's not the club I fear."

Missing a Beat

When Washington's Alcoholic Beverage Control Board voted to remove the license for Club U, it sent a clear message that a new day had come to Washington. Club U stood as a symbol of black power and of black impotence at the same time. Both proponents and opponents of the club viewed it as a container. The government saw it as a container for pathology, violence, and destruction. It was a site for the mythical boogeyman of so-called black-on-black violence and comprised menaces to society, youth gone wild, and a dysfunctional municipal government. Its defenders also viewed Club U as a container: for black cultural tradition, for economic self-empowerment, and for society's flaws. Go-go and the building that housed it had been erected by and for black people under the worst possible conditions, when many of those of means, black and white, had abandoned the urban center. The chaos and dysfunction that reigned there directly resulted from a series of historical and socioeconomic forces, forces larger than any individual actors or race.

Thriving below the mainstream radar but in plain sight, go-go had brought vitality back to the riot-scarred corridor. Through dance and song, black actors maintained a sacred public ritual space that helped exorcize the demons of the past, demons that cannot be separated from a troubled history of cities and race in the United States. Go-go's success as a quick-change artist set the stage for U Street and for many other parts of Washington to be transformed to a non-race-specific space to which people could return. Now that it had effectively paved the way for a new kind of life on the strips, Club U and its young, almost exclusively black, and sometimes rowdy working-class crowd were viewed as a blot on a brightening landscape, staining the aesthetic. Club U worked—too well for its own good.

Notably the months of hearings saw few words from the Rare Essence regulars, the go-go community, the "immature youth" themselves. An online poll on the popular message board of *Take Me Out to the Go-Go* in June 2005 tried to gauge popular opinion about Club U's future among the go-go community. The poll asked whether Club U should get their license back. Fifty-two percent answered yes. Forty-seven percent had the following response, helpfully illustrated by a photo of the actor Gary Coleman shrugging beneath captions reading: "Who Fuckin Cares?"

The go-go community took about two seconds to lick its wounds.

After thirty years, they'd come to know the drill: Hire. Fire. Repeat. It was a drill familiar to patrons of blues clubs, rent parties, early jazz community in New York, and juke joints down South and virtually every other previous manifestation of the musical black public sphere. As long as black folks own property, as long as someone can get their hands on some cymbals, a cow bell or two, a conga drum, and a microphone, folks will be getting right back up to find out where the next party is. And someone — probably black — is going to be getting paid.[17]

3 ★ What's Happening

Go-go's not like other music. It *is* what's happening. —GO-GO NICO HOBSON

A conga drum roll announces the entrance of Big G—aka Genghis, aka Anwan Glover, aka The Ghetto Prince—to the stage at the Stamp Student Union at the University of Maryland in College Park.

BOM bom BOM! Badabadabadabada BOM bom!

The six-foot-six leader of Backyard Band (BYB) glides onstage in a white T-shirt he wears over a black long-sleeved shirt, his deep chocolate brown face framed by neat cornrows with beaded tips. A gold chain with a large diamond-encrusted cross pendant hangs at his long neck. He squints at the spotlight that obscures his view of the hundreds of young fans before him. A large diamond flashes at his left earlobe.

"I wanna say what's up to Rongita," G says in a deep, guttural rasp, as the last strains of the keyboard chorus for Raphael Saadiq's "Still Ray" fade out. "I wanna thank everybody for coming out, man. For the sounds of the BYB. This how we do it."

Maryland U,
we'd like to welcome y'all to the Backyard building.
Know wha'm talkin' 'bout?
Yeah.
I'm trying to get into the groove, man.
Everybody welcome theyself.
To a beautiful party tonight.
'Till they tell us we gotta sliiiide out . . .
We gon' take over this building, this whole school.
I want everybody to be ready for it.

This was just the opening for the latest episode in the Big G show. Well before this performance for Black History Month in 2006, the crowd had been tuning into the then thirty-three-year-old bandleader and lead talker's program live. They heard his freestyle testimonies about the gangster lifestyle he had once lived. They cheered his speeches urging peace for warring crews. They watched him headline rallies for D.C. voting rights. They triumphed with him after he emerged from each stint in jail. They witnessed a disgruntled fan shoot him several times in the chest and groin while he performed onstage. They cheered him when he dragged himself onstage the next day at a rally for the first anniversary of the Million Man March, bleeding and on crutches. They followed him when he took HIV tests at city-sponsored events, and lined up to the same. They had heard his gravelly voice broadcast on the radio to prove he was not dead.

In late 2002, when I did a lengthy magazine-style profile for the *Washington Post*, I had been shadowing him for several weeks before I realized he was actually living in a halfway house preparing to be sentenced for weapons charges.[1] A judge had granted him work release, which allowed him to perform his usual four gigs per week and even allowed him to travel to Atlanta for a concert. When I pulled his criminal files at a courthouse in D.C., I found letters from then city council member Adrian Fenty, the city's youth outreach departments, and even from an assistant warden at the jail, all pleading with the judge to give him a break. His had been a story of falling and redemption — part Fela Kuti, part Tupac Shakur, part Bob Marley.

So what's happening at the University of Maryland? The back pocket of Big G's jeans holds a rolled-up script for the upcoming season of HBO's groundbreaking cops-and-crime series *The Wire*, where he is set to play the role of Slim Charles, a top lieutenant in a Baltimore drug organization.

A videographer documenting G's life buzzes around him on the stage. A motley crew of musicians and hangers-on fill the rest of the scene: A young man wearing a black wave cap and a Howard University T-shirt shifts between congas and a percussion set. Beside him are two keyboard players and two vocalists. Two members of another popular go-go group, UCB, prepare to sit in to play their local radio hit "Sexy Lady." A boy toddler sits onstage, singing into a turned-off microphone. Also onstage: young women in loud eighties fuchsia and out-to-there natural hairstyles, cherry-dyed bobs, and auburn Afro puffs and young men wearing black and gray T-shirts, sweats, and cool-pose grimaces; this group will swell as the performance wears on.

> Say what?
> How it feel?
> Where they at?

In the front row below the stage, fans thrust T-shirts in the air bearing the names of their neighborhoods and crews, as well as RIP T-shirts with the names of dead friends and hand-signs, all of them vying for inclusion in G's freestyle shout-outs or improvisations. Jay-Pooh, G's cousin, returns to the stage after cruising the dance floor taking attendance, collecting the names in the audience he's tapped into his cell phone. He shouts the names in Big G's ear, and G then feeds them into the microphone.

G snaps four fingers open and closed, then raises his hands in the air, signaling the band to launch into its classic hit, "Keep It Gangsta." The crowd answers with an explosion of movement and chants. The saxophone wails as "motorbooties" rev into fifth gear.

> G: Twenty-fifth?
> CROWD AND BAND: Rock the boat!
> G: Seat Pleasant?
> CROWD AND BAND: Rock the boat!
> G: LeDroit?
> CROWD AND BAND: Rock the boat!

The band plays several conga-inflected covers of popular songs from the rappers Nas ("Oochie Wally"), Big Boi ("Kryptonite—I'm On It"), and Kanye West ("Gold Digger"). During a Beat Your Feet dance contest onstage, a girl from Landover jumps on to the stage to try to show up a girl from Seat Pleasant.

Then time is up. But it wouldn't be a BYB show without some words of inspiration and a eulogy from the guru of go-go. "Be a leader. Don't be a follower. Love y'all so much. Keep it real. Rest in peace, Marcus 2-6-4."

★   ★   ★   ★   ★   ★   ★   ★   ★

Africa disagrees.

with subject-verb agreement.

THOMAS SAYERS ELLIS, "Marcus Garvey Vitamins"

Western audiences are used to a certain kind of story. Stories are narratives distilled into neat words with clear-cut beginnings, middles, and ends. They are taught to privilege the role of the composer over that of the performer who provides live interpretations. Those who come to go-go trying to follow those kind of linear story lines have been sorely disappointed. "The downfall of go-go's writing is a lack of new material coupled with too many songs that lack a narrative drive — that tell a compelling (or even interesting) story, or at least develop a coherent story line," Lornell and Stephenson write.[2] The hip-hop historian Jeff Chang quotes the go-go producer Reo Edwards, frustrated with the limitations of go-go's format:

> I was talking to a go-go songwriter one time. I said, "Man, you need a verse here." The guy said the roto-tom was telling the story. "Can't put no verse there, the roto-tom telling the story." Okay. Alright. You know what the roto-tom is saying. Maybe the people in the audience know what the roto-tom saying. But the people in Baltimore don't know what the hell that dang roto-tom is saying!" He shakes his head. "Go-go's got the same problem today as it did back then. You don't have no good storylines."[3]

Oh, but they're wrong! Go-go does have story lines; they are impressionistic tales — poetry as opposed to prose. Go-go is "the most radical opposition to English syntax there is," the poet Thomas Sayers Ellis told me. Chuck Brown's first two (pre-go-go) hits in the early 1970s were instructive. His first local success single, a funk song called "We the People," fretted about enduring segregation. ("When are we the people gonna sit together?" the chorus asked.) Brown told me the inspiration behind his next big local hit in 1972 with characteristic modesty: "Kids were riding bicycles. I wrote a song called 'Blow Your Whistle.' A little corny . . . mostly simple. It gave people something to sing along to. I'm not a songwriter. I write hooks that people can sing along to." The same thing for his next hit, "I Need Some Money," which used the by then signature go-go sound. The inspiration? Brown was broke.

Brown's songs reported *what's happening*. Segregation was still around. Kids were on the streets of Washington, blowing whistles that summer. He was broke. Simple. True. This is the blueprint for any live go-go performance. Call and response and audience interaction add countless other stories to the telling. These stories fly by so quickly, and through so many different mediums (from bodies to fashion to song) that they are easy to miss. It is not exactly easy reading. In 2010 I talked to a group of teenagers at a go-go club at the Knowledge Is Power Program (KIPP) Academy, a charter school in Southeast Washington, about my frustrations describing go-go. "How do you put what happens in a go-go into words?" I asked. Immediately, they shot back: "You can't." No kidding! But here goes.

Let's start with the so-called lead talker, whose hip-hop counterpart is an emcee or a rapper, the person who "raps" to the audience. In go-go, the lead talker thus "talks" to the audience. Much like news anchors, lead talkers are professional witnesses, using the microphone as their journal. Native Washingtonians spend their lives immersed in both the historic details and cultural scripts that allow them to follow the story lines. Arriving at the go-go without knowing the script is like arriving at a movie five minutes before it is over, or reading the last ten pages of a novel.

When Brown gets onto the stage, he brings his whole life history with him. His husky rasp tells of his first pull at a cigarette at age seven. His calloused hands tell of the cotton he picked traveling from farm to farm in North Carolina and Virginia, living in sharecropper shanty houses. His down-home presence manifests the humility of someone who lived in servants' quarters when his mother worked as a domestic. His is just one story among millions of black people who embarked on the Great Migration and found themselves in northern cities.[4] As he sits onstage, you won't hear him describe these struggles — you can read them on his face. As he told me in an interview in 2010:

> I shined shoes places you had to go in the back door. In 1957 was the first time I got the nerve to go into the waffle shop to order a sandwich. I walked past there and I saw a colored person. You couldn't call them black back then — that would be a fight! I said "Wow." I walked past there *again*. I saw two colored guys in there. I said "Wow." So I went into there and ordered me some waffles, sat at the table. We were

the only three colored guys in there. They were looking at us. That was the first time. You had to go down at the end of the counter and make your order. You could not sit there. Everybody knew that. They were just breaking it in. Black folks were getting ready to do that thing, integrate that thing.

Brown has scars from fights over D.C.'s shoe-shining turf about who could collect the ten-cents-a-pair prize; scars that commemorate the breakthrough he experienced when the Foggy Bottom neighborhood boss, a kid named Petey Greene,[5] gave him the OK to work his territory. Each pluck of the guitar tells of the eight years Brown spent serving time at Lorton penitentiary, learning how to play it. Each burned-out Washington building he performed in reflected his weariness about the "depressing" time after the assassination of Martin Luther King Jr. on 4 April 1968, the day he was briefly detained by police while trying to tell looting kids to go home. Forty years later, those shoe-shining memories crashed up against another triumph: walking into the gig, seeing his name on a D.C. street sign in front of the newly renovated Howard Theatre, "Chuck Brown Way."

Backyard Band's Big G tells the story of another generation of Washingtonians. His life's narrative—some of it depicted in the mainstream news media, most of it not—symbolizes the most pressing challenges to those who came of age in the late 1980s and early 1990s as the city's soaring murder rate earned it the moniker of "Murder Capital." His arrests and political activism have made him an iconic figure whose resilience is embedded in the history of Backyard Band, the larger go-go community, and in D.C. itself. Each time Big G went to jail during his adolescence it increased the anticipation and value of BYB live shows on his release. At the time of the BYB show at the University of Maryland, part of the story he told expressed the wish that his acting career would take off following the success of his role on the critically acclaimed HBO series *The Wire*.

These are two high-profile examples, but dozens of bands that play on any street in the Washington area perform a similar living archive of history, every day. At the University of Maryland show in 2006, a little-known go-go and reggae fusion band called INI Band also made an appearance. Most of the members were or had parents from the Caribbean. And the band's name derived from the Rastafarian phrase "I and I," which emphasizes the oneness of people under Jah. A majority of INI's members studied at the university, but some had been recruited from the surrounding area in Prince George's County. They discovered their bass player, for instance, when they saw him carrying an instrument on the Metro and invited him to practice. I caught up with Dice, the band's nineteen-year-old lead talker, while he was on break from his job working at the College Park campus cafeteria in 2006. Dice told me that he gives a live broadcast of what is happening in his world when he goes onstage. "I like to freestyle, like a news reporter, coming straight out of my soul," he said; "anything that you go through in your daily life."

Lead talkers do not monopolize the center stage like a voice-of-God news anchor announcing, "This is the world." During a live show, their voice is just one of many vying for recognition during the dialogue between the dance floor and the band. There are also several other people on the microphone, from vocalists to rappers or hype men; the lead talker usually simply directs traffic. The crowd experiences the lead talker's life while he experiences theirs. There are just as many stories and backstories as there are individuals at any given go-go, and the crowd aggressively vies for its time in the spotlight. Some stories have been going on for decades.

As Lornell and Stephenson indicated, go-go musicians provide a forum—a physical place—for people to speak about their everyday experiences. And just as grainy black-and-white images associated with the Second World War are seen as more credible than slick Hollywood-style productions, go-go is appreciated for its "rough" aesthetic, serendipity, lack of studio scripting and polish, and its block-by-block, neighborhood-by-neighborhood focus. Dice told me that go-go's gritty aesthetic reflects the left-behind people and communities to which it gives a voice: "It's more music of the struggle. It's more the gutter sound. In most of the neighborhoods, everybody's poor. Everybody's struggling. Go-go doesn't go mainstream. It's for the people of the D.C. area. We are not all dressed up. People look at us from the outside: 'Y'all dirty, y'all this. Y'all gangsta.' It's the whole struggle of being poor and being black in America."

Here Come the Drums

Ellis has described go-go as "a grammar"; drums are the subject, with the cowbells and timbales serving as adjectives and adverbs. At a go-go, you might find anything from cowbells to percussion sets and inverted plastic buckets. But the congas are the most critical to the go-go sound: no congas, no go-go. An earlier go-go sound was lighter and more melodious, closer to funk and reggae.

But in the "bounce beat" genre of go-go perfected by bands such as TCB (also known as the Bounce Beat Kings) musicians lean heavily on rototoms, or drums that have no shell and whose pitch can be manipulated. Rototoms reflect the attitude of a younger generation of go-go fans that are heavily influenced by hip-hop and/or street culture. In the earlier days of go-go, the rototoms came to use mostly at the climax of a performance, at the height of dance energy. Today's heavy use of rototoms reflects a new generation's heavily mediated reality of sensory overload. As Dice put it: "Now it's *bang-bang*, the rototom."

When I visited the KIPP school to speak to the go-go club that had just formed in 2010, I asked what the parents thought about their music. "They think their go-go is better than our go-go," one kid told me. Indeed, many old-school go-go heads do not consider bounce beat go-go at all. But the aesthetic shift also tells of "what's happening"; the parents' reality simply differed. Violence and poverty were still problems in many parts of the Washington region, but this generation of kids had no anchor in the traditional D.C. public school system. Since the 1980s, D.C. had become a veritable Petri dish for urban education reform. It was the only city where Congress paid private school tuition for some kids. About 40 percent of public school kids went to charter schools, also thanks to a law passed by Congress. So families constantly moved across the D.C. and Prince George (in Maryland) borders "shopping" for the best educational deal, private, public, or charter. For a generation of D.C. kids, this meant the end of the neighborhood school as their parents knew it. Their reality reflected fractured communities.

Their parents' generation shared rides on school buses, had city-sponsored mobile stages, and music and marching band programs in D.C. public schools. By the time the members of the younger generation had reached school age, many of these programs had been axed, and music instruction was inconsistent at best. This affected the sound of go-go. While the earlier go-go's nursing in marching band traditions made it more musical, the new bounce beat sound was more aggressive, less melodic, and had more in common, aesthetically speaking, with punk.

Embodying the Departed

For the generation of go-go fans who came of age during D.C.'s Murder Capital days, death was a major preoccupation. As the Dice told me: "I can't rap about having money or cars or model girlfriends—none of that stuff. I've lost so many people in my life, death is nothing. The simple fact, it's gonna happen today, or the next day." Much like newspaper headlines, RIP T-shirts break the news and express grief, tragedy, and loss—transforming individuals into walking, talking, and dancing obituaries. The first day I attended the practices for the INI Band in College Park, the whole band wore matching black RIP T-shirts with the newspaper photograph of LaKita Tolson, a nineteen-year-old young mother and nursing student killed while leaving a go-go the previous weekend in November 2005.

In LaKita's case, the newspaper had run a photo, but more often, the lives lost are relegated to a brief paragraph in the newspaper's metro section and have no photograph. In those cases, the instant photos taken at most go-go clubs come in handy for commemorative T-shirts. In 2004, I worked on a newspaper feature about one youth who had been killed leaving a go-go.[6] I contacted the police, but the case was still unsolved and the actual police report had gone missing. But when I went to the local T-shirt shop in Iverson Mall, I was able to choose from a selection of photos on file for sixteen-year-old Rod "Hot Rod" Valentine: pictures of him at the go-go, pictures of him at the prom. The shop's computer hard drive stored hundreds of other images of teenagers from the D.C. area. The owner told me he usually deleted the images after three months.

At shows, people in the audience often thrust RIP T-shirts toward the lead talker to have the dead acknowledged and remembered. In 2002, when I was working on an article about the Beat Your Feet dance movement at the Hot Shoppes,[7] an "all ages" go-go on Branch Avenue in Marlow Heights, Maryland, I ran into Marvin "Slush" Taylor, the nineteen-year-old rumored to be the dance's creator. When we saw him, Slush wore a "Happy Birthday" T-shirt for a lost friend that bore the latter's photo. The following week, Slush was gunned down in his car on his way home from leaving the Hot Shoppes. The week after, teenagers returned to the club with "RIP Slush" T-shirts. (In 2009, Slush's immortality gained when the Beat Ya Feet Kings, a go-go dance group, paid him tribute on MTV's *Randy Jackson Presents: America's Best Dance Crew*.)

Big G ended his show at the University of Maryland with an RIP shout out: "Rest in peace, Marcus 2-6-4": a kid named Marcus had died on 6 February 2004; the College Park performance took place on the second anniversary of his death. Sometimes lead talkers guide the crowd in even more elaborate tributes. During a performance in April 2006 at

the Phish Tea Café on H Street, Donnell Floyd, the lead talker of Familiar Faces (and a founding member of Rare Essence) led the crowd in a
chant for his former Rare Essence band mate Quentin "Footz" Davidson.
Footz was considered one of the greatest go-go drummers of all time,
known for his signature "One On One" drum intro, which the crowd prepared to hear with the chant "Put your hands in the air, y'all. Get ready
for Footz!" Footz was gunned down in 1994, devastating the go-go world.
Twelve years later at the Phish Tea Café, the crowd's chant had changed
only slightly. "We gon rock it for Footz!" the crowd repeated. "I don't
want to bring the mood down too much," Floyd told me later. "But sometimes you have to remind people that this can be a short stay. It can be a
long stay, it can be a short stay. Respect each other when you're partying.
If someone gets a little bit too drunk. If you talk about the people that
passed everyone once in a while, maybe it will click. That sometimes it's
OK just to try to avoid conflict."

Adaptation

From the beginning, go-go has been dominated by cover tunes or adaptations of current popular R&B and hip-hop Top 40 hits. Go-go artists
love to do covers as much as some people like to criticize them for it.
But this is how go-go has become the main gateway to pop culture for
young Washingtonians — and it is also a time-honored practice.[8] Western
practice tends to marginalize the art of adaptation, privileging artists who
compose scores over artists who perform and reinterpret those works.
But as Zora Neale Hurston famously said, the modification of ideas is
the definition of being black in America: "The Negro is a very original
being," she wrote in her essay "On Art and Such." "While he lives and
moves in the midst of a white civilization, everything that he touches is
re-interpreted for his own use."[9]

The roots of go-go's practice of adaptation began with Brown's childhood friend and the bandleader of Los Latinos, Joe Manley. Manley listened to Top 40 radio at his home in Fairmount Heights, Maryland, and
used the band to interpret that music through his own lens, one that reflected his Latino roots. Later, when Brown started his own band, the
Soul Searchers, he added percussion, congas, and timbales to the horns
and keyboards making the Latin sound. "I did a little talking, a little call
and response," Brown told me. And he carefully read the crowd at a club

called the Maverick Room at Fourth and Rhode Island Avenues in Northeast Washington, taking careful note of what made the bodies move. In 2010, he described to me how he tweaked the sound until he got just the right formula for Washington:

> When the beat caught on, they were dancing on the top of the tables and chairs. And so they took all the chairs and tables out. Sometimes I didn't even have to sing a song, just play that groove all night. My sound, that go-go ended up being a sound for the town, the country and [traveled] abroad. The other bands jumped right on it. I had four drummers before I got Ricky Wellman. He had great hands, great showmanship. I said, "this is the beat I want *boom-bom-chuck-a-boom*. . . ." All that funky percussion was laying on there, and he was rocking right with it. Now this band — they jammed so hard. And when Ricky was playing the beat, he said to me, "Hey Chuck, when I play, I feel so empty." I said, "that's because you've been playing that garbage." Before he was playing with a group called the Jaguars. They played too fast and they played too busy. I said, "The floor is jam-packed. You keep that empty feeling all night!"

The beat is a custom-made sound for which cowriting credits belong to the crowd at the Maverick Room. Generations of Washingtonians went on to experience popular music via go-go. Coming of age in the 1980s, the Community of Hope pastor Reverend Tony Lee told me in 2010 he liked hip-hop too. But he said he only experienced it "through the lens of go-go. Like 'Wild Wild West.' It was cool to hear [the rapper] Kool Moe Dee hit it. But when the [go-go] bands hit it, that was it."

Non-Western musical traditions are almost exclusively performance traditions. The jazz artists of the Harlem Renaissance era loved to adapt mainstream music as a way to "show up" the original composer. Later, John Coltrane completely transformed the classic Richard Rodgers and Oscar Hammerstein musical score for "My Favorite Things." As Henry Louis Gates Jr. explained in his theory of the signifying monkey, black artists are critics by definition, signifying on previous works of art.[10] Paul Gilroy has pointed out that in "sound system cultures" such as reggae and hip-hop, the role of the piece's composer is separate from "the equally important work of those who adapt and rework it so that it directly expresses the moment in which it is being consumed."[11]

Big G also defended the practice of adaptation in an interview in 2001 with the writer Bobbie Westmoreland: "I can free-style. Anybody can sit down and write a rap, but I can make one up off the top of my head. I can rap about what a person has on, what the ladies are doing, what's going on at the bar. I got some other things coming up that will make the city proud of me and make the haters hate me even more."[12]

And even better than *consuming* popular culture—an Ashlee Simpson hit, the latest by Jill Scott—go-go makes the local people and places in Washington, D.C., participants. Timely go-go adaptations of national hit songs tell the story of the local physical environment, peer networks, and history. And musically speaking, by revising cover tunes, go-go artists give their own take, or commentary, about how music should sound. The beat should be slower; there need to be more layers of percussion; throw in a conga riff there. In *how* they stray from the original lyrics, the musicians opine on the original message, signifying on the original writer and composer. So Brown playfully signifies on Duke Ellington by crooning: "It don't mean a thing if it ain't got that *go-go* swing!" In the moment of the live performance, the meaning of the song is transformed.

Like jazz and hip-hop, go-go, or its lead talker, uses several standard phrases to bridge freestyle compositions. As the African music scholar J. H. K. Nketia has noted, the repetitions of these verbal and musical phrases serve to emphasize the singer's point or to give him or her time to think of something new to say.[13] In jazz it could be a lick by the saxophonist Charlie Parker, in hip-hop it may be the phrase "Throw your hands in the air!" Go-go has several standard phrases, among them, "Tell me wh-wh-wh-where y'all from!," to which the audience responds with the names of crews, neighborhoods, or churches.

Roll Call

Call-and-response chants draw the geographical map of black Washington throughout a go-go performance. A large portion of go-go lyrics are shout-outs, or so-called calling-out spots, a trait common to hip-hop and influenced by Caribbean traditions. Typically before a show, the lead talker in go-go will circulate among the crowd, greeting patrons and collecting pieces of paper with their names or their neighborhood crew's names, nicknames, and blocks. Before the INI Band opened for Backyard Band at the University of Maryland, it set up a MySpace page for the event for fans to post names for the band to call out at the show. The talker uses the names as text for ad lib compositions, incorporating each name into a narrative or conducting a straight roll call.

I once saw Brown perform at a weekly show in 2001 at the Legend nightclub off Branch Avenue in Maryland. Long after the band had packed up, he stood onstage with his microphone, reading off the names of the people lined up to give him a piece of paper with their names. As Go-Go Nico told me, for many Washingtonians, a recording of them being shouted out is their "birthright." This idea was voiced in a series of articles in the *Washington Post* in the wake of the shooting death of a seventeen-year-old girl outside a Washington go-go club in January 2007. Four teenagers were asked to write about why they chose to "dance with danger at go-go clubs." One student, Alton McDougle, explained: "When my friends and I went to a go-go one night, we had a great time because it was my birthday. In the club the members of the band M.O.B. were singing, 'It's Your Birthday, Doo-Doo.' That's my nickname. They were recording, and they put me on the album. I was so happy!"[14]

Bodies Talking

For much of the 1990s and early 2000s, the typical go-go uniform consisted of expensive T-shirts and sweat suits with embroidered logos made by neighborhood-based and black-owned companies. But these seemingly basic clothes can say a lot. Washington's urban fashion industry became established as an offshoot of go-go in the early 1980s, starting with the Madness Connection on Georgia Avenue. Most neighborhoods in the District and Prince George's County have storefronts selling T-shirts and sweats bearing the corresponding logo, which tell what neighborhood the wearer is from. Madness was in uptown Northwest. SHOOTERS and ALLDAZ were in the Northeast. HOBO was across the Southeast Washington border. Aja Imani and Vusi Mchunu were lines based in Prince George County. Dozens of clothing lines operated at their height in the early 2000s, the stores comprising a massive network of storefronts where go-go concert tickets and PA tapes were often sold. Patrons typically wore their neighborhood brand to the go-gos and elsewhere to wordlessly indicate their localities.

Bodies are also used to tell stories through dances such as the Beat Your Feet, a dance created by followers of TCB, including Marvin "Slush" Taylor. The dance caught on in a big way at a now defunct warehouse district club in Washington called NuBoxx around 2000. At the end of the night, someone told the TCB lead singer Polo, aka Reggie Burwell, to sing the chant "Beat your feet, bitch!," inspired by lyrics from the Houston rapper Scarface. At that, the crowd of about two hundred youngsters detonated. They began to pair off, and fights appeared to erupt everywhere, according to an account written for *Tmottgogo* magazine by Richard O'Connor under a pen name.

> One minute I'm watching this guy and girl (probably no older than fifteen) just grooving with each other. The next minute he's taking swings at her, she's hitting him in the gut, he pulls out a whip and lashes her, she pulls out a knife and starts shankin' him, all the while neither one has missed a single beat of the music. She gets up, smacks him across the face two times. It didn't look like much of a hit but it must have been because his head turned right and then left. He recovers, gathers himself then leaps in the air while pulling his t-shirt up, then slam dunks her head under his t-shirt. After this they both re-gather themselves for the next mutual assault. Then I look around, and this scene is being repeated all over the place. I feel like I have walked into a bad science fiction movie where the whole world has gone mad. Imaginative scenes like this were played throughout the club by different groups of youngins, and man can they get creative. The best dancers can literally tell a story, or a joke through their moves.[15]

When I described the Beat Your Feet dance to Katrina Hazzard-Donald, a Rutgers sociologist and the author of *Jookin': The Rise of Social Dance Formations in African-American Culture* in an interview in 2002, she recognized the tropes immediately. "Oh, that's a dance play," she told me. It is the "highest popular aesthetic form in African American dance. When you get into a challenge, the only way that you can win is to engage in a dance play. . . . I'm drawing my gun and gunning you down. Walking the dog, that is a very old one."[16]

Of course, dance has been at the center of black expression for centuries,[17] beginning in Africa. This practice survived the Middle Passage and thrived on plantations, where dance and rebellion were intertwined. The African music scholar Nketia described a West African "dance drama" remarkably similar to Beat Your Feet in that participants act out a series of scenes. "The dramatic use of music and dance finds its highest expression in the dance drama—mimed actions incorporated into the dance or used as extensions of the dance proper," Nketia writes. "A dance drama may be based on many themes, without necessarily having a single coherent story line."[18]

What Do You Mean?

As in almost all black vernacular forms, it is hard to tell what is actually happening above the din of double talk and the mischief of the trickster. This is definitely the case in go-go, which also sometimes makes the story lines tough to follow. Such was the case with the Backyard Band hit "The Dippa." In 2003, the local mainstream news media had begun to report about increased problems with the hallucinogenic drug PCP,[19] which experts said began its resurgence in 2001, when a new format called "dippers" had been introduced, slang for cigarettes dipped in PCP. In 2001, "The Dippa" was a major local radio hit, and it had won the WPGC 95.5 FM "Battle of the Beats" so many times it had to be retired from the competition. The new form of the drug was growing in popularity just as it appeared in a popular song referencing it in the title. While working on a Washington Post profile of Big G, I asked him what responsibility "The Dippa" had in fueling demand for the drug.

Big G responded by getting up from the restaurant table where we were having our lunch and doing "The Dippa" dance: dipping his body side to side. He used his body to plead ignorance to the song's other meaning. Of course part of the dialectics in the black oral tradition is the ability to present two interpretations at once: one for authorities such as Washington Post reporters and a different one for live go-go audiences. Regardless of which interpretation one accepts, both spoke of real youth culture trends completely missed by mainstream news outlets in Washington, D.C.

Pulling the Stories out of the Pocket

The "Pocket" is a groove in the go-go performance in which the lead talker free-styles about what's happening, especially controversies — news most meaningful to the band and audience. This is the richest source of narratives, information, and history produced by go-go. "My man is back in the big chair!" Big G announced live onstage during one performance, to cheers and laughter from the audience. Implied, but not stated, was that his "man" was Marion Barry and that he was celebrating the politicians return to the city council in 2004, after his many brushes with the law. Also unsaid was that the "big chair" is a massive sculpture erected by a defunct furniture retailer that stands as a landmark in Anacostia, a neighborhood in D.C.'s Southeast. This is one of the blackest parts of the city, and it has been Barry's political base and the ward he represented in his comeback to public life after his nationally televised run-in with crack.

After Ronald Reagan's funeral in 2004, which caused a huge disruption to local Washington communities, Big G used the Pocket to proclaim that he had no tears for the former president. In the soul singer Raheem DeVaughn's live collaboration with Backyard Band in 2006, DeVaughn can be heard shouting loudly during a Pocket: "George Bush is some bullshit!" In highlighting these narratives, I do not mean to suggest a trend toward political content in go-go. Lornell and Stephenson are correct that go-go is party music and that the purpose is to have a good time, not make political commentary.

But go-go performances are so ubiquitous that it is impossible to make any definitive statements about what live go-go does or does not discuss. Some messages can be as political as a plea for black self-determination, as evidenced by the campaign to support the local black clothing industry in the District. But there are also messages as straightforward as "I'm here!" or bluesy ballads mourning that "my friend is gone."

As can be seen in the transcript of a classic Rare Essence performance in 1986, sometimes it takes years to have the proper perspective on what kinds of stories are told in the live go-go moment (see chapter 9). The narratives in go-go are abundant and rich, but they are what James Scott describes as "hidden transcripts," and one will have to work to find the meanings.[20] My goal is not to translate these narratives and fit them into more linear ones, as this automatically would lead to crossed messages and double meanings, which are always complicated by what is *not* said.

But the essence of go-go is the live show, which I have not done justice in my description here. The kids at KIPP were correct that it cannot be precisely translated into words — or into film, as the following chapter will show. It is live and direct. Simple. True. For lives (and deaths) that are often made invisible in the mainstream media, go-go rituals comfort and reassure the crowd that they exist, that they are part of a community, able to hear news that may not necessarily be black and white.

4 ★ Call and Response

Evolution, from the past to the present. That's where this whole thing comes from, Africa. Drums was used to talk from tribe to tribe. Call and response and that whole thing. So that's basically the foundation of go-go. . . . [On a visit to West Africa] I saw a lot of rhythmic congas and drums. A lot of call and response. They just don't call it "go-go." —DONNELL FLOYD, lead talker of Familiar Faces, October 2006

It is one of those hot, sticky summer days in Washington, when I, my mother, my six-year-old daughter, Maven, and my nine-year-old, call-me-a-preteen son named Maverick head out to D.C. Carnival, the annual Caribbean parade and festival on Georgia Avenue. Maven waves a red, green, and yellow flag from my parents' native Guyana, while Maverick sports a bracelet with the tiny green, black, and yellow flag of my husband's parents' native Jamaica. My son sulks as we make our way down to the football field set up with food vendors and concert stages. He wanted to stay at home, and it *is* hellishly hot. When I try to hold Maverick's hand to avoid being separated in the crowds, he pulls away from me: an early-onset teenager.

I ignore this as we cross Georgia Avenue near Howard University's campus, past the man of about fifty in a diaper hoisting a beer in one hand and an oxygen tank in another. We walk past the mud-splattered "mas'" (masquerade) camps representing

Sierra Leone and the ones representing Haiti. We pass the glittery peacock costumes, rows and rows of dancers.

We take seats before a mobile stage on Benjamin Banneker Academic High School field, which is filled with people waving umbrellas in colorful flags. A Jamaican emcee in a white tank top and jeans, a T-shirt tied on to his head, paces the stage. "I want one lady from Jamaica, another from Trinidad. Another Caribbean country, I wan dem come up on de stage. Real quick, real quick," he beckons. "Real quick, real quick." About a dozen women quickly scale the stage. A cheery soca harmony pipes out of the loud speakers as the emcee calls out their countries or cities as they step right up. Kingston! Trinidad! Panama! Guyana! Puerto Rico! Washington, D.C.! Belize!

One by one, the women take turns on center stage. The rumbling begins in their thighs and shoulders and moves like a precipitous earthquake. Rear ends jut out, sending ripples of cellulite into motion. One leg up. Headstands. Skinny hips shake on spin cycle. Butt flesh jiggles at the speed of popping corn.

My sixty-one-year-old mother, Serena, exchanges knowing looks with a woman sitting next to her who is about the same age. "That's my grandson over there," she tells the woman, pointing toward Maverick. His jaw drops as a woman drops into a push-up position and then grinds her hips against the stage. The women both sigh. "He'll be alright," the woman says in a West Indian lilt. "Yeah, he'll be alright," my mom agrees in her singsong voice. As we leave our seats to buy some food, my son clasps his hand on my shoulder; a peace offering. "I'm glad I came," he says. I bet he was.

When we get home, Maven reports her first trip to D.C. Carnival to our neighbor, a white, gay, emergency room doctor in his thirties. "There was B-U-T-T shaking," she says, her eyes growing big. "That's the best kind!" our neighbor responds cheerily.

Tweak the soundtrack a bit, and the scene could easily happen on any given night, at any go-go in Washington. You'd find the same frenzied movement. The same sweaty exuberance. The same overt sexuality commanded by a male gaze.[1] The same too-loud sound system that grinds melodies into gravel. And rhythm, lots of rhythm.

When people ask me about go-go and about how I could spend ten years thinking and writing about it as a journalist and an ethnographer, the best I can do is shrug: "It's a Caribbean thing."[2] Along with the black church, the Caribbean greatly influenced the go-go creator Chuck Brown. But the connection is more a state of mind. When I heard my first live go-go broadcast on the radio my freshman year at Howard University in 1994, my ears perked up in the same way they did when I first heard hip-hop emcee Melle Mel's show-stealing guest spot on Chaka Khan's "I Feel for You" at my Canadian elementary school. When I first experienced go-go live, my body began moving unconsciously, just like it did on a childhood visit to Guyana when I first heard soca music, with its staccato *jump*-up and *jump*-up rhythms.

What *was* that music?

Go-go, hip-hop, and soca (soul calypso) were born in the 1970s, when each place was celebrating hard-earned political freedoms. The music expressed the exuberance of creating something new. In the West Indies, it was emancipation from European colonial rule. In New York, it was the civil rights movement and emancipation from Jim Crow. In D.C., it was the birth of the Chocolate City. I was born in Canada in the mid-1970s and grew up in the United States, but the music always makes me feel at home. It's like the words on a sign I discovered with one of the roti vendors at the D.C. Carnival: "All ah we is one family."

Black music is not just entertainment. It is a conversation across time and space. The same ways of speaking appear and reappear throughout the African diaspora throughout time, geography, and context. Through a transatlantic call and response among Africa, the Americas, and Europe, these musical traditions have survived centuries of trauma, holocaust, slavery, and dislocation with remarkable resilience. As old forms die out, new combinations of the same components appear in their place. The riffs, rhythms, and repetition common to music throughout the African diaspora translate into social structures, according to the music scholar Ingrid Monson.[3] In Chocolate Cities, they also translate into political structures. This is what gives us a common identity.

But the root lies in Africa. In the past one hundred years, some aspects of West African musical tradition have remained intact; some have even intensified their authenticity. Still others metamorphosed into new traditions, as the Ghanaian-born musicologist Kofi Agawu writes in *Representing African Music*. All across the globe, they are created, tweaked, and forgotten every day.

Of course, by state of mind I do not mean a biological or genetic connection between everyone with African blood in his or her veins. I do not buy into any notions about racial authenticity. Many black people never hear the call. Many white people are the first to respond. Centuries of colonization, trade, and immigration on both sides of the Atlantic have made it impossible to have an undiluted African essence. Whether black music is played on the vast, culturally diverse continent of Africa itself or points West, it is by nature what Agawu describes as "irreducibly mixed, hybrid, syncretic, in-between, impure."[4] The traditional sound has been influenced by the events happening along the coast. It was influenced by the Europeans who carved up Africa. People and products moving back and forth across the Atlantic have carried this call and response. At many times it is hard to tell who is responding and who is calling. Or as Aretha Franklin put it, "who's zooming who."

But even in this post–[insert identity] moment, there is still a place for a bottom line: "Different groups possess sometimes-subconscious collective memories, which are frequently forged and maintained through a storytelling tradition, however difficult that may be to pin down, as well as through individual experience," writes Elizabeth Alexander.[5] By any measure, we are talking about exceedingly buoyant ritual communication forms—potent stuff.[6]

So, while go-go in the Chocolate City can be viewed as a strictly provincial experience, speaking to specific blocks and contained in the Washington Metropolitan area, the music is also in conversation with the black experience happening all over the world. It is Mardi Gras and jazz funerals in New Orleans. It is carnival in Trinidad and its many variations across the globe. It is the samba schools in Brazil. It is Santería in Cuba, juju in Nigeria. All around the world, black music and rituals tell a story of freedom, of life and of death.

Go-Go against the Grain

By the early 1970s, Brown had been dipping his cup into funk, blues, and gospel traditions. Disco was the rage, and so the guitarist was looking for a way to compete with his live band, the Soul Searchers. Brown was influenced by a childhood friend, Joe Manley, whose family immigrated to Washington in the 1960s from Latin America. Manley liked to listen to Top 40 radio and make salsa versions of popular songs with his band Los Latinos.[7] Brown enjoyed working with Manley's troupe, but he always felt the percussion was missing. So when he formed the Soul Searchers, he made sure to include congas, timbales, cowbells, and other layers of percussion to give the music spice. He played a little guitar and did a little talking to the audience. Brown hired and fired several drummers before he and Rick Wellman found the right formula to create the proper beat—the perfect blend of congas, rototoms, timbales, Ghanaian hand drums, and cowbells—that kept the bodies moving on the dance floor at the Maverick Room at Fourth and Rhode Island Avenues.

Wherever these rhythms appear and reappear throughout the world, they can always be traced back to West Africa. The early African music scholars J. H. Kwabena Nketia and Francis Bebey noted that traditional African drummers had a command of oral literature, history, and the bynames and praise names to be chanted during performances.[8] According to Michael J. C. Echeruo, in Victorian-era colonial Lagos, the drummers' job was to maintain the historical record.[9] Today the "talking drum" is still fundamental to contemporary Nigerian juju music (popular music rooted in Yoruba traditions). Talking drums mimic the sounds of human speech, telegraph messages, and serve as living historical documents. In modern African highlife music, traditional drumbeats are mixed in with song texts from conversations in buses, bars, churches, and schools. "Taken as a whole, these imaginatively composed texts provide a window onto the contemporary African mind," Agawu writes.[10] But even these musical traditions on Africa's west coast are in conversation with musical traditions across the ocean. Brazilians who immigrated to the Nigerian capital in the 1920s had an influence on the juju sound, according to a study by Christopher Alan Waterman.[11] Which came first? Who influenced whom? It is often hard to tell. Whatever its path to Washington, D.C., the beat drives go-go in layered, interlocking rhythms that would easily feel at home in Ivory Coast or Brazil. The name *go-go* was taken from the Smokey Robinson and the Miracles album *Going to a Go-Go*.

Brown's other primary influence was the black church. In the introduction to an album of 2007, *We're about the Business*, Brown explains how he admired the way Grover Washington adapted a gospel beat into something groovy, and he did him one further:

> I just had this feeling, that some of that old spiritual church music that we used to play in my church when I was a little boy. Real fast. You know what I'm saying? I heard Grover Washington come out with "Mr. Magic." He had that beat, only it was slower, groovy. It was slower,

it wasn't hyped up like church music. I said, "they used to play that at my church!"

So I decided to try it and started playing "Mr. Magic." From there, we started dropping down into the percussion. The same feeling I had with Los Latinos, I took the same percussion with me. So we started dropping that percussion and we had other ideas. The audience liked it. They liked the call and response. They liked the participation. You know, the band participating with the audience. And I was searching for a sound for the town.

Go-go can feel a lot like a Pentecostal church service. Both run for extended hours, and you never know when they will end. Neither erects a huge barrier between who is performing and who is watching. Both are heavy in call and response. In the beginning there was Brown, then generations of Washingtonians came after him that continued to make go-go a place, subject, and verb. And although it never fully crossed over into the mainstream for reasons I will explore shortly, go-go has always remained in dialogue with the residents of D.C., as well as with black music throughout the world.

Miles Davis was impressed when he first heard Brown's hit "Go-Go Swing," a funked-up version of the Duke Ellington classic "It Don't Mean a Thing." He especially admired the album's rhythm work, so he called Brown to ask if he could steal his drummer, Wellman. "He fell in love with Ricky when he heard that jazz song," Brown told me in September 2010. "I said, 'you welcome to that.' It was an honor. That is the same with any musician in my band. If something great happens for them I'm glad that I was able to give them that exposure. Miles Davis said to me, 'you a jazz player!' I said, 'I play blues, jazz, and gospel. I created this sound so I can eat. And everyone who plays in this band can eat.'"

Even more important than a sound, Brown also created a whole economy built on an ever-shifting constellation of local, independently owned clothing boutiques, music stores, and venues. Hundreds of musicians, graphic designers, club promoters, club owners, and security companies went on to eat off that sound.

Much like they do New Orleans brass bands, young black men dominate go-go bands. Most public high schools in the eastern part of D.C. and in neighboring Prince George's County have go-go bands, just as most high schools in New Orleans have brass bands. Both are natural outgrowths of the black high school marching band tradition in public schools. The schools help provide a steady supply of drum, horn, and trumpet players from every corner of the city with the skills to move their bodies with music. They are often the most visible manifestations of youth culture in both cities. Kids are into hip-hop in D.C. and in New Orleans too. But they do not have the same connection to, say, Jay-Z, as they have to the bands that play at their high school prom.

Like the blues and Nigerian juju, go-go also generally wears what Lornell and Stephenson call the "mantel of low-class or blue-collar music."[12] Some black D.C. private school kids may not be allowed to attend go-go clubs, but many of them go out of their way to have go-go come to them. Just as black student groups brought Backyard Band to the University of Maryland, College Park, similar groups brought go-go to the elite Sidwell Friends School, where the presidents Clinton and Obama sent their daughters. At many private high schools in D.C. where go-gos take place, a private student ID earned access to go-go parties at other private schools. "A lot of times people come from the underbellies of the city," Donnell Floyd, of Rare Essence and later of Familiar Faces, told me in October 2006. "A lot of times people come from the upper crusts of the city. We just like to bring everybody together. In one great big melting pot and enjoy each other's company."

Because the roll call is so integral to go-go, it can be considered a form of praise music. Nketia notes that a large part of the repertoire of Akan song texts consist of eulogies, praise songs, or boasting songs that reference the exploits of ancestor kings and the names of those defeated or captured in battle.[13] Like juju band captains, go-go lead talkers must identify people in the audience to put on display. But juju band captains are "sprayed," or have money thrown at them by the people they acknowledge during the performance. Go-go lead talkers are not paid directly; instead, they are rewarded by receipts at the door and by admission fees that rise dramatically over the course of the night. In 2010, some patrons paid as much as $100 at the door to bypass the main line and get in late. How late someone comes into the club speaks volumes about their status, and lead talkers know to acknowledge them accordingly when they walk in.

The (typically) male figure that presides over the music is called different things in different places. In traditional West African culture, he is called the griot, a professional musician, a troubadour who goes from village to village, peddling stories and collecting new ones. The griot knows all the town gossip and historical events, serving as a living archive of his people's traditions. In go-go a similar figure is called the lead talker. In hip-hop, it is the emcee or a rapper. In juju we have band captains. Whatever the name, the role is rooted in the ancient mythical Yoruba trickster figure called Esu-Elegbara. Esu figures prominently in the music of Nigeria, Benin, Brazil, Cuba, Haiti, and New Orleans, as Gates has explained in *The Signifying Monkey*. Gates notes that Esu's role is not just that of a messenger but also that of a "linguist" and "interpreter" of the wider world. In his study of hip-hop, William E. Smith describes Esu as the Yoruba deity who serves as the guardian of the crossroads between the spiritual realm and the physical world of humanity.[14]

Like modern network news, this "messenger" business is mostly a boys' club. *Divine Utterances*, Catherine Hagedorn's study of Cuban Santería, may provide one explanation for the exclusion of women. In her apprenticeship learning the *bata* drum, Hagedorn defied Santería drumming tradition. When she did gain the confidence of a teacher, she was told not to play the drum while menstruating: the drummers feared female reproductive power.[15]

Singing the News

Around the world and in different parts of history, black music has been the primary medium to deliver news. In 1950s South Africa, it was common for singers to make studio recordings ripped from the latest headlines, gossip, and controversies. Such songs often contained coded lyrics interpretable in many ways, which proved useful in a repressive political climate, as the ethnomusicologist Lara Allen states.[16] People could get away with criticizing the government in the form of songs, jokes, or gestures, whose true intended meanings could be emphasized during live performances. Similarly, Nigerian juju song texts told the story of the ebb and flow of the Nigerian oil economy in the 1970s. Sensitive political developments became encoded in popular song texts, making traditional drummers and singers in effect the "local newspapers and propaganda leaflets," finds Christopher Alan Waterman.[17]

A similar patchwork social history of black Americans existed in blues lyrics during the decades following emancipation. In *Blues Legacies and Black Feminism*, Angela Y. Davis notes, for example, that Bessie Smith's "Poor Man's Blues" preceded the stock market crash that ushered in the

Great Depression and that her release of "Backwater Blues" in 1927 co-incided with catastrophic floods around the Mississippi River, when six hundred thousand people, more than half of whom were black, lost their homes. Davis notes that the blues constantly contests the borders between reality and art. The songs' quiet allusions to real-life events made them accessible to working-class audiences. Blues music continues slavery traditions in which humor, satire, and irony are indirect means of protest because their targets were sure to misunderstand the intended meaning.

Public Enemy's Chuck D, born Carlton Ridenhour, explained this conception of rap music as news in his memoir, *Fight the Power*, of 1997:

> We worked to hijack the media and put it in our own form. That's originally how we came out. Initially, Rap was America's informal CNN because when Rap records came out, somebody far away could listen to a Rap record because it uses so many descriptive words and get a visual picture from what was being said. So a person that was coming up in Oakland would listen to a record from New York and get a visualization of what New York was all about. When rappers came out from Oakland and Los Angeles and they were visual with their words, people all over could get informed about black life in those areas without checking the news. Every time we checked for ourselves on the news they were locking us up anyway, so the interpretation coming from Rap was a lot clearer. That's why I call Rap the Black CNN.

According to Robin D. G. Kelley, in the early 1990s gangsta rap lyrics delivered a kind of "street ethnography" or "street journalism" of racist institutions and social practices, often told in first person.[18] Tricia Rose noted in *Black Noise* that "rappers' emphasis on posses and neighbor-hoods has brought the ghetto back into the public consciousness." "It satisfies poor young black people's profound need to have their territories acknowledged, recognized, and celebrated."[19] Simply naming individuals and places makes a powerful statement for communities often treated as invisible.

Nigerian juju tells the stories of specific personalities, institutions, and events during live performances.[20] Sometimes, to praise a juju patron, the band captain would denigrate his enemies. Feuds between juju stars were the subject of public gossip and sometimes extended over a series of recordings. Much as with hip-hop "beefs," which run the course of several albums, juju fans would feel compelled to buy the entire sequence of discs to keep up with the feud.

Personal Is Political

African-derived communication keeps the integrity of the individual and his or her personal voice, but it does so in the context of group activity, notes the black feminist scholar Patricia Hill Collins in her canonic book *Black Feminist Thought*. Black music genres such as the blues, for example, do not distinguish between a public and a private, the personal and the political, Davis found in her study of early blues women.[21] Through their songs, blues transformed collective memories of slavery into commentary on working-class black life. Davis argues that black oral culture plays an equivalent function to print media in Western culture, exceeding it, however. The blues created a cultural space uniting the community, a place to mediate discussions about taboo topics such as domestic violence.

In the extended groove of the go-go performance called the "Pocket" musicians make social commentary about events of local and international significance. In the 1980s, Washington was a booming and violent drug economy, and in a separate track, it saw the emergence of a prosperous black middle class. Opinions about events that rarely receive an ear in the mainstream media can be heard during go-go shows. In 2003, when health officials in the District of Columbia sought to encourage teens to test for HIV, they turned to members of the go-go community, who proved extremely effective at the task. Big G of Backyard Band worked with the health officials on safe-sex media campaigns aimed at teenagers. He traveled to area schools with the Health Department to teach kids about safe sex, and he did free performances at health fairs, where he took HIV tests onstage and encouraged the kids to do the same. "Kids just flock up to the area," the District public health adviser Deborah G. Rowe told me in 2003. "They go test. They get in line. He's like a commander." Cultural art forms as "folk media" are also used to disseminate vital information in rural Africa. There, government and development groups have employed the "folk media," "oramedia," or the "talking" drum in HIV prevention efforts, according to a study by Aaron Mushengyezi in 2003.[22]

Go-Go Global?

Typically cultural movements go in a few different directions. They can take off, as hip-hop left the Bronx, reggae left Kingston, and Motown left Detroit. Or they can die off, like disco. Then there are movements like go-go that do neither. How can that be?

Go-go has drawn the interest and investment of the music industry — most notably Island Records, which successfully globalized reggae and hip-hop. But its failure to replicate that business model with go-go in itself makes a powerful statement about the ability of black music traditions to resist commoditization. Whatever go-go may have lost in its failure to completely cross over, it has also gained a lot.

When reggae left Kingston, it busted open a market for "third world," usually black, music that did not previously exist. Among the first people to hear the call of this music was Chris Blackwell, a white, Jamaican-born, UK-educated music aficionado. Blackwell founded Island Records in Kingston in 1959 but moved its headquarters to London after Jamaica's independence in 1962. Blackwell became a bridge to reggae artists such as Jimmy Cliff and Bob Marley and the wider world. Intent on making Marley "a rock star, rather than a star on black American radio," Blackwell overdubbed white session musicians onto Marley's classic major-label debut "Catch a Fire."

When Island Records got into the movie business, it helped introduce a wider audience to the Caribbean artists they signed. Island Visual Art's film of 1972, *The Harder They Come*, a gritty tale of an aspiring singer in Kingston battling corruption, violence, and drugs, helped lay the foundation for reggae's international crossover commercial success. Rather than sanitizing the actors' heavy Jamaican patois, some versions of the film used subtitles, resulting in a rich, subtle — if slightly campy — portrait of island life. The soundtrack proved an instant classic; *The Harder They Come* not only launched Cliff's star but also primed an international audience for reggae music.

When hip-hop came along a decade later, it was a local Bronx thing, too — at first. But from the beginning, hip-hop reflected this ongoing call and response of black musical traditions. "The hip-hop scene had roots in Jamaica, inspired by the rapping style of Jamaican toasters, which was ironic in itself, as the Jamaican DJs had been inspired by American jocks broadcasting out of Miami in the late fifties," the British filmmaker and cultural historian Don Letts noted in his 2007 memoir *Culture Clash*.[23] The Jamaican-born deejay Kool Herc brought these traditions to the burned and decimated Bronx and laid the groundwork for the development of hip-hop.

Film proved a key bridge between hip-hop and larger, global audiences. The films of the early 1980s, including *Wild Style* (1983), *Breakin'* (1984), and *Beat Street* (1984), along with a steady stream of cable music videos, set the stage for hip-hop's international acceptance. When the vibrant films were shown around the world, and New York hip-hop artists got signed to major record labels, the party moved from the neighborhood and into the studio. Instead of hearing hip-hop created live at shows, fans began to hear it in cars, on home stereos, or on boomboxes on the street. Nelson George lamented in his 1998 book *Hip-Hop America* that recordings "killed the house-rocking mic." But this is also what helped hip-hop hop onto a global music network.

So it had been with reggae. But after Marley's death in 1981, Island Records sought to keep expanding its cultural empire. Blackwell signed King Sunny Ade, the best-known juju musician outside Nigeria in 1982. In 1984, Blackwell found another lead when he heard Brown's national hit "I Need Some Money" on New York City radio. Blackwell tracked down D.C.'s Max Kidd, the aspiring Berry Gordy of go-go, who invited him to a show in D.C. featuring artists from his label TTED. In a later interview, Blackwell shared his impressions of the show featuring Rare Essence, EU, Redds and the Boys, and Trouble Funk with Lornell and Stephenson:

> What I saw amazed me, there were about seven thousand kids dancing in this auditorium, really going wild; it was quite combustible. I had never heard any of the bands playing who had drawn this huge crowd.... It reminded me of Lagos where groove rules, but there were no songs really and therefore no radio potential. I thought the best way to break this music would be to make a movie recreating my experience. This had worked for me with the Perry Henzell film "The Harder They Come" and Jamaican music.[24]

Island joined with Kidd to give international distribution to TTED's roster of go-go artists. And in 1985, members of Island Records spent a summer in Washington, D.C., filming *Good to Go*, a gritty tale of violence, drugs, and corruption in journalism and government in a crime-ridden

U.S. capital. This was to be the vehicle to take go-go out of the District of Columbia. Things did not quite work out that way.

Not Good to Go

Blackwell knew the perfect person to direct the go-go film: a filmmaker named Don Letts. Although born in London, Letts had been inspired by the music and culture of his parents' native Jamaica his whole life. He was Marley's confidant and one of the earliest (pre-MTV) music video directors documenting the punk scene. In his memoir *Culture Clash* Letts described being connected to his identity through cultural traditions such as London's Notting Hill Carnival, which "blurred the lines between participant and spectator and quickly became a symbol of freedom":

> Over a million pleasure seekers every year cause a roadblock in the heart of London, oblivious to the Carnival's political, social and historical background. From its early days, it was controlled by the first Trinidadian settlers of Ladbroke Grove, but it was not long before all the Islands found a voice at Carnival. It was nearly hijacked by the Jamaican sound systems in the seventies and that's where I came in. . . . After an initial sound clash, a balance was struck. Reggae and Calypso provided a running commentary on current events. Journalism set to music. And if you can resist the smell of various foods on sale then you are a slimmer man than I.[25]

When Letts came to Washington, he immediately heard a similar call. "Go-go was truly a live experience with the most happening club action I've ever witnessed—period," Letts wrote. "The original intention was for me to direct Good to Go, but Audrey, who I had met a year previously, was pregnant with my first son, Jet. We had my daughter Amber seven years later. Anyway, to cut a long story short I ended up working second unit filming all the live performances of Trouble Funk, Chuck Brown and Redds & the Boys."[26]

The longer version of the story was a bit more complicated. Things had gotten off to an inauspicious start for the low-budget ($1 million) film when Blackwell's coproducers Sean Ferrer and Doug Dilge arrived in Washington flanked by bodyguards. "We heard it's a bunch of kids stoned on PCP dancing around," Dilge told the *Washington Post*.[27] "When the music stops, fights break out. If you're white you don't go into these scenes because you're in an incredibly dangerous situation. We come down here and we see that the go-go is really sort of community parties in different locations. Wherever people can rent, the party goes there."

As filming began, the racial politics on the set only got worse. While Letts said he left the set for family reasons, back in Washington people felt something more sinister at play. Vern Goff, an independent D.C.-based producer working on the project, was horrified at Letts's treatment on the set. "[The writer-director] Blaine Novak humiliated him, and convinced Chris Blackwell that Don was incompetent," Goff said.[28] "Blaine fashioned that film after his own distorted understanding of the go-go scene."

In a word, the results were bad. The plot was ripped from the headlines: a brutal rape-murder of a white nurse by drugged and crazed young black men. A corrupt cop convinces a white reporter (played by Art Garfunkel) to wrongly blame the incident on a go-go club, producing the headline that said go-go caused violence. A black music mogul—based on the real-life Kidd—fights to set the record straight. Many gunfights, concert scenes, crooked cops, and violent gangs follow. Innocent people are framed, the media censors the truth, and more gunfights happen. In the grand climax, the white newspaper reporter fights his way to the stage of a massive go-go show and tells the truth about what happened to a crowd of cheering go-go fans.

If you look at the film closely, and excavate beneath the relentless streams of gratuitous violence and bad acting, you might find some larger redeeming themes. The plot did seem to want to convey some truth about how the media and the police conspire to make black people appear scary. Yet in an interview with the *Washington Post*, Novak gave an even more ambitious goal: "To have a quality message: That white people must open their eyes to see the black community needs help and improvement."

Lornell and Stephenson snarked: "Blackwell, Dilge, et al. were in search of . . . a highly volatile mixture of street violence and niggers crazy on drugs, all highlighted by the blackest music outside of Lagos, Nigeria. . . . It was beginning to look like the 70s when blaxpoitation films like *Shaft* and *Cotton Comes to Harlem* were commonplace. If only Island had aimed so high!"[29] In his memoir Letts offered his own explanation for why the movie failed: "Go-Go did not translate well into film, which is not a put-down; if anything it is praise because there is something about it that is intangible. It is almost too hot for vinyl and definitely too hot for celluloid."

Novak was run out of town—he refused to even attend the D.C. premier. Black Washington was appalled at the movie's implied paternalism and racism, as were the critics. The movie tanked. Kidd's business fell apart. Suspicion against outsiders was poured into cement. Critics generally panned the movie and its campy plot but almost universally praised the musical sequences shot by Letts. The excitement and international interest helped create a fertile period for go-go in the mid-1980s. Brown, EU, Trouble Funk, and Rare Essence toured outside the District, and there was a brief go-go craze in London.

Ironically, another Blackwell investment in film ended up bearing more fruit for go-go. Island had signed on as a distributor for *She's Gotta Have It*, the independently produced film by a young director named Spike Lee. At a party in 1986 that Island threw to celebrate the Washington premier for this film, Blackwell arranged for EU to perform. Lee, the son of a jazzman, was impressed. "Them go-go bands, they can play three hours straight, non-stop, serious funk. They're bad. I said to myself at the party, 'I gotta use them in my movie,'" Lee later recalled in his book *Uplift the Race*.

Lee's second feature, also backed by Island, was *School Daze*, a musical set at a historically black university that explored color and class divisions on campus as the school debated whether to participate in sanctions against apartheid-era South Africa. At the last minute, Island ran into money problems and worried about whether Lee was capable of handling the sprawling, expensive project, dropping it altogether.[30] Columbia Pictures quickly picked up the project, and Lee followed through on his plans to use go-go in the film. The Splash Jam scene featured a campus party to which students could only be admitted if they wore beach gear. Lee hired the young bassist Marcus Miller to write "Da Butt" and the go-go band EU to perform it. "Even before I set Marcus up to write the song, I had made up the dance," Lee later recalled. "I've always wanted to start a dance. . . . All of us got into a debate about how we should handle this call-and-response bit where people from different states yell 'We got da butt.' We never did get that together." Lee borrowed the chorus from one of his favorite films, the *Wizard of Oz*. "Oh we oh, oh oh, oh we oh we oh, oh oh." And the result was "Da Butt":

Walked in this place surprised to see
A big girl gettin' busy, just rockin' to the go-go beat

The way she shook her booty sho' looked good to me
I said, "Come here, big girl, won't you rock my world
Show that dance to me." She was

Doin' the butt. Hey pretty, pretty
When you get that notion, put your backfield in motion, hey
Doin' the butt. Hey sexy, sexy Ain't nothing wrong, if you
wanna do the butt all night long.

"Da Butt" became a hit, topping the R&B charts and reaching number thirty-five on the Billboard Hot 100. Go-go purists have never fully embraced the song as true go-go. But even interpreted through Lee's black middle-class, Brooklyn-born lens, go-go could be seen for the jubilant, joyous percussive bacchanal more closely recognizable to Washingtonians. The less pathological view of a Chocolate City turned out to be more artistically and commercially successful. No one remembers *Good to Go* (also known as *Short Fuse*). *School Daze*, on the other hand, remains an iconic portrait of black music and life in the 1980s.

Island Records' gambit did not work with juju either. In 1984, the company dropped juju superstar King Sunny Ade because of poor record sales. Ade's 1983 album, "intended for export and tailored to suit Western context, tastes and attention spans, scored a modest success in the United States and Europe." But, "it soon became apparent that King Sunny Ade was not going to take over the role of the late Bob Marley in the world exotic popular music market. Subsequent releases sold fewer copies, and Ade was dropped by Island in 1984."[31] (Ade was later picked up by a record label in the United States and continues to headline massive tours around the world.) Island had much more success globalizing the Irish pop group U2.

So it went with go-go. Aside from brief flashes of national media attention and crossover record sales by individuals such as Brown, Trouble Funk, DJ Kool, EU, and the rapper Wale, the live show is still king. Washingtonians are still eating off Brown's sound. Go-go is still a mom and pop business, a community-based art form serving the nation's capital. Go-go survived its brushes with cultural imperialism in part because the economy of the Chocolate City is strong enough to support it.

For all the obsessive talk I hear on the go-go scene about "going national," I am not convinced people really want it to happen. A pop-friendly format necessarily changes the music from something that can be defined as go-go. The difference is between creating music to connect with an audience through their iPods and aiming to connect with an audience face-to-face. And more important, go-go is still big business. Instead of going to New York or Los Angeles or London to the corporate music structure and the lawyers, agents, and press handlers that run it, those dollars stay and circulate in the black community of Washington, D.C. It is like Bruce Brown, a D.C. filmmaker whose two features, *Streetwise* (1998) and *Divided City* (2004), successfully and organically integrated go-go, told me in 2003: if go-go went national, "a lot of people would lose their jobs."

And paradoxically, go-go has gained much by staying against the grain. Just as Jürgen Habermas feared something got lost in the transition of the public sphere from coffee house to mass media, so it was when the black public sphere moved to recordings, radio, and music videos. And as yet another technological shift rocks the music industry with the rise of the Internet, live is still where the action is.

With the rise of piracy on the Internet, it became dramatically less profitable to make musical recordings that could be easily copied and distributed among fans. A whole generation of music fans believes it is optional to pay for the latest record release. However, that generation has no qualms about paying top dollar to see its favorite music stars in concert. Everyone from artists on the rise to megastars such as Jay-Z, Beyonce, and Madonna have gone back on the road. Speaking to a *London Telegraph* reporter in 2009 at the fiftieth anniversary of Island Records, Blackwell, then seventy-two, predicted that music would return to the days when a hit record was more advertising for live appearances. "I think the new artists and new talent, and new characters like myself, will thrive in that kind of business," he told a London reporter. "They can build up their own company, which is based on touring. So you bring the new act out with you. That's exactly how it was in the early days."[32]

Go-go's business model stayed against the grain long enough to come back into style. In the process it also remained deeply engaged in responding to this enduring transatlantic call and response. As Letts wrote: "Go-go was the ultimate black tribal rebel sound in Washington, home of the White House and the capital of America. People tried to demonise the whole scene saying it was all about drugs, but in reality that was only a small part of it. . . . The bottom line is: you don't know the complete story of contemporary black music if you don't know Go-Go."[33]

The Rebirth

If a singular theme unites the black experience and its cultural rituals across the globe, it is a preoccupation with notions of freedom and death. In go-go the RIP shout-outs and T-shirts make for one contemporary example, jazz funerals in New Orleans another. When slaves sang Negro spirituals, freedom and death were twin themes with double meanings. It is never clear until the moment of live performance whether they are celebrating death or freedom. "Amidst the terror of slavery, where bodily and spiritual freedoms were readily distinguished along lines suggested by Christianity—if not African cosmology—death was often understood as an escape from worldly suffering," Gilroy explains in *Against the Race*.[34]

This is the case on both sides of the Atlantic Ocean, as Joseph Roach explains in his book *Cities of the Dead*. Roach studied how a live theater tradition in London, as well as New Orleans traditions such as Mardi Gras and jazz funerals, allow participants to use "orature" to remember the past and reimagine the future. By invoking long-gone spirits during live performances, participants are not just mourning or remembering the departed. Through performance and song, their bodies become "performed effigies" used to bring those who have moved on to the spiritual world back to life. These rituals allow ancestors to live on through a specially nominated medium or surrogate such as an actor, a dancer, a priest, a street masker, a statesman, a celebrity, a freak, or a child, Roach writes. These traditions push the boundaries of circum-Atlantic identities across race, time, and space. They create a "genealogy of the past" as the living remember, reenact, and improvise a collective memory. Music constitutes a channel between the past and the future, a bridge between death and life.[35]

My husband, Rudolph McGann Jr., grew up steeped in the rituals of St. Luke's Episcopal Church of New Orleans, a black church first established in 1855 and located in the heart of the Tremé, one of the oldest black neighborhoods in the country. When the neighborhood was originally established decades before the Civil War, a mix of citizens, free and enslaved, descendants of Africa and Europe, some fleeing revolution in Haiti, gathered there to cook up the magic that New Orleans culture is known for today.

Weeks after our children experienced their first D.C. Carnival, we came to St. Luke's for a home-going service for my departed mother-in-law, Beverley Hyacinth "Bev" McGann. Over time, the Tremé had gone the way of many Chocolate Cities and was allowed to wither on the vine. When we traveled there for the funeral in the summer of 2010, some of its historic shotgun houses had not been restored since Hurricane Katrina, and some of the ones still standing looked better loved than others. And next door to St. Luke's, I was appalled to see that students at John McDonough High School were expected to learn with plywood-covered windows, surrounded by yellow tape and barbed wire.

St. Luke's had not been full since Hurricane Katrina scattered its members from Atlanta to Idaho. But on the day of Bev's funeral, the vestibule was at capacity with mourners from Bev's native Jamaica, Canada, and from throughout the United States, all of them wanting to send her "home" in style. After the eulogies, a feast awaited us — including two sets of red beans and rice, one cooked in traditional Jamaican, one cooked in traditional New Orleans style. But first we followed the booming horns of the Society Brass Band of New Orleans outside St. Luke's for a second line procession down North Dorgenois. My daughter Maven held hands with her godsister Griffin. I cleaved to my mother as we marched behind my son Maverick, who carried an urn of his grandmother's ashes. He marched behind his grandfather Rudy Sr., whose hands clasped an urn carrying the rest of his wife's ashes. My husband hoisted a massive framed photograph of his mother as we danced and marched down the streets of the Tremé.

An older black man carrying a white poodle joined the second line as we turned at Governor Nicholls. "When the Saints Go Marching In" played in honor of Bev's beloved Saints. They had just won the Super Bowl after a lifetime of being derided as the "Aints." The cancer did not take Bev before she saw the day New Orleans held a jazz funeral for those wretched, cursed Aints. Bev's friends threw up parasols and white handkerchiefs to the rhythm. Older black couples sitting on their porches cheered us as we danced by.

When we turned off Esplanade and a door flew open revealing a white face, I thought I was seeing things through my tears. Then a few steps later another white man opened another door, snapping photos of us marching by. I finally believed my eyes when I saw a white couple walk out of their porch with a blond baby in tow. It was not a sight that I — or the former mayor of New Orleans Ray Nagin — expected to see. But Bev always had.

Despite its tragedies, she believed New Orleans had a chance at a new beginning. "It's a cleansing," she had told me.

The Society Brass Band wrapped up its final song. Were we celebrating death or freedom? My smiling husband raised a hand to the crowd. "The party's not over," he exulted. "Let's eat!"

The Lead Talkers

Chuck Brown, the Godfather of Go-Go in 2010, developed the sound through a call and response with the crowd at the Maverick Room, a club in Northeast Washington. "I created this sound so I can eat. And everyone who plays in this band can eat," Chuck told me.
© Jeffrey MacMillan, *The Washington Post*

Fans reached out for Ralph Anwar Glover, aka Ghenghis, aka Big G, aka the Ghetto Prince, who was the lead talker of the Backyard Band and a popular radio personality. His life history—part Tupac, part Marley, part Fela—represented a generation that came of age in the early 1990s. © Marvin Joseph, *The Washington Post*

The author and Big G after a Black History Month performance at the University of Maryland, College Park, in 2006. One of my UMD students told me about the show taking place on campus. In his back pocket was a rolled-up copy of the script for the final season of HBO's *The Wire*, in which he played the character Slim Charles. Photo by Natalie Hopkinson

Donnell Floyd, an alumnus of Rare Essence, looked dapper at the Go-Go Awards at Constitution Hall in 2006. Photo by Natalie Hopkinson

The INI Band was a go-go and reggae fusion band comprising University of Maryland, College Park, students, primarily of Caribbean descent. They used MySpace at this 2006 campus performance to gather the names of fans to shout out during the show. Photo by Natalie Hopkinson

On 4 April 1968, people had gathered in Washington to participate in Martin Luther King's Poor People's March on the Mall. This aerial view shows the riots that erupted in the city's black neighborhoods on the news of King's assassination in Memphis. © *Washington Post* file photo

Safeway supermarket at Fourteenth Street and Park Road in April 1968. © Stephen Northup, *The Washington Post*

April 1968: When the smoke cleared on H Street, only storefronts remained standing. The strip was still struggling to rebuild forty years later, when Go-Go Nico's music store opened on that corner. © Matthew Lewis, *The Washington Post*

Black Body Politic

Little Benny strolled on the red carpet outside Constitution Hall for the first annual WKYS Go-Go Awards in 2006. Four years later, he would die in his sleep the morning after sharing the stage with his mentor, go-go creator Chuck Brown. Photo by Natalie Hopkinson

In June 2010, nearly six thousand mourners filled the Walter E. Washington Convention Center for the funeral of the go-go star Little Benny. © Mark Abramson, *The Washington Post*

Adrian Fenty, the mayor of Washington, D.C., speaking at Little Benny's funeral. © Mark Abramson, *The Washington Post*

The former Junkyard Band member Mikey Strong pays his respects to Little Benny in June 2010. © Thomas Sayers Ellis

All the Way Live

Backyard Band fans thrust an RIP T-shirt up to get a shout-out for a departed fan, "Shake."
© Marvin Joseph, *The Washington Post*

2K9 club near U Street in February 2003. There is usually a "Polaroid" corner at every go-go
to commemorate the moment. © Marvin Joseph, *The Washington Post*

In 2002, the "all-ages" crowd at the Hot Shoppes, a go-go on Route 5/Branch Avenue in Prince George's County, scream into the microphone. In go-go, the audience is part of the band. By the early 2000s a majority of go-gos took place outside the city in Maryland. © Marvin Joseph, *The Washington Post*

In 2002, then sixteen-year-old Donté Brooks, master of the Beat Your Feet dance, joined the band Fatal Attraction onstage at the Hot Shoppes. Far right is vocalist Wayne Mills, then eighteen. © Marvin Joseph, *The Washington Post*

Andrea Stevens, then nineteen, beat her feet at the Hot Shoppes in 2002. © Marvin Joseph, *The Washington Post*

While circled by a crowd of teens, Isaac "Shank" Marshall, then nineteen, performed the Beat Your Feet dance on the floor at the Hot Shoppes in 2002. © Marvin Joseph, *The Washington Post*

The Departed

In early 2004, sixteen-year-old Roderick Valentine was shot and killed after leaving a go-go show. His mother, Gwendolyn Valentine (right) and brother, Michael McDonald, wear RIP T-shirts. Police could not find the police report when I inquired about the murder investigation, but a store at Iverson Mall did have his photo on record, where I was able to custom-order my own HOT ROD RIP T-shirt. © *Washington Post* file photo

Sadly, Marvin "Slush" Taylor, the inventor of the Beat Your Feet dance, was killed when leaving a go-go days after this photo was printed in the *Washington Post*. On the far right is Randy Danson, then eighteen. © Marvin Joseph, *The Washington Post*

Terrance Brown, thirty-one, was killed at Club U on 13 February 2005, ending more than a decade of go-gos at the government building. © Family photo, reprinted courtesy of the *Washington Post*

Fat Rodney's son represented his slain father at the Go-Go Awards in 2006. Photo by Natalie Hopkinson

Fashion

In the early 2000s, wearing expensive sportswear by your neighborhood black designer was almost mandatory when attending the go-go. Here is the designer Vusi Mchunu with one of his creations at his store in 2003. © Michael Williamson, *The Washington Post*

The mascot for HOBO (Helping Our Brothas Out), the clothing line located just across the Southeast Washington border in Maryland, which was ubiquitous at go-gos in the early 2000s. Photo by Natalie Hopkinson

The Unity Clothing Association hired a lawyer, organized a boycott, and distributed fliers like these all across town to maintain black ownership of D.C. fashion lines. © *Washington Post* file photo

In the summer of 2004, the go-go promoter and activist Ronald "Mo" Moten founded the Unity Clothing Association, which comprised black D.C. designers, to fight back against a new upstart line by a Korean manufacturer. © *Washington Post* file photo

Aside from the outstanding music sequences shot by the black British director Don Letts, this film by Island Pictures of 1986, *Good to Go*, designed to bring go-go to the mainstream, was a commercial and artistic failure.

Spike Lee's interpretation of go-go depicted in the film *School Daze* (1988), viewed through his middle-class, Brooklyn-born lens, was much more recognizable to Washingtonians than *Good to Go*.

The Archive

Go-Go Nico talks about his collection of thousands of live go-go recordings from the H Street store he managed, iHip-Hop and Go-Go Factory. Photo by Natalie Hopkinson

A detail from Go-Go Nico's collection. Photo by Natalie Hopkinson

A close-up of the sign for iHip-Hop and Go-Go Factory, the now defunct store located near Tenth and H Streets. Photo by Natalie Hopkinson

On Easter Sunday 2006, Tony Lee opened his church, Community of Hope, by renting Legend, a go-go club near Route 5. © *Washington Post* file photo

Days before they were evicted in 2002, Samantha and Ken Moore sit in the Complex, a fitness club they had turned into a gospel go-go club on Route 5 in Marlow Heights. © Debra G. Lindsey, *The Washington Post*

On Martin Luther King Day in 2010, hundreds flocked to the Haiti Relief Benefit Concert at Tony Lee's Community of Hope church on Route 5. Photo by Natalie Hopkinson

5 ★ The Archive

VIII "Tapes" for Nico Hobson
We made copies,
Refusing to trade the ones
With our names on them . . .
"Make me a copy,"
Carmichael said
The day after his brother's murder
A way of remembering
Holding on
. . . . Attention
Care.
Respect.
—THOMAS SAYERS ELLIS, *The Maverick Room*

Dancing Lady

It is a crisp, blue, Saturday morning in March 2006, and the busy H Street corridor is jumping with the grit and rhythms of city life. Cars swoosh past the string of stores housed in century-old attached buildings: chicken and check-cashing joints, a Muslim shop selling oils and Egyptology books, barbershops, beauty shops, several liquor stores, and sleek new bars trying to come through. The chilly air outside is filled with laughter, the wail of sirens, the steps of families strolling, and playful banter among strangers and street peddlers. Outside the iHip-Hop and Go-Go Factory, a huge speaker sitting on the sidewalk blasts music to entice people to come inside the store, which opened just a few weeks before. It works — maybe a bit too well.

A cocoa-skinned woman in her forties wearing clean jeans and a sweatshirt stands on the sidewalk on the other side of the glass door, dancing wildly to the medley of go-go and R&B. Her eyes stare vacantly. Her movements are fast yet clumsy, and she misses the beat more than she catches it. She is in her own world. Discussion in the store quickly turns into a parlor game about what substance the woman is on. Is it alcohol, or "that diesel — " or is it PCP, the drug also known as Love Boat, buck-naked, LB, or boat that has had a huge impact, for the worse, on the go-go scene.

"That *is* the buck-naked," "Go-Go" Nico, the store manager, diagnoses. "The boat'll do it to you," a customer agrees. Maybe she is high. Maybe she is mentally ill, or both. Whatever her mind's state, it is clear that this woman has spent a lot of time studying BET. About an hour into the performance, she discards her winter coat. She drops to the ground, grinding her hips against the concrete. Passersby stop, gawk, and then keep stepping. A boy of about ten approaches on his bike. He has picked up a good amount of speed, heading straight toward the woman as she jiggles her body around the sidewalk. "Move, dumbass," the kid screams at her, and deep, hearty laughter fills the store.

I conducted several hours of ethnographic interviews with "Dancing Woman" in my peripheral view. She comes to dance on most Saturdays. While Go-Go Nico shared his life story in the spring of 2006, she danced on the other side of the glass behind him, as if performing accompaniment. Nico's life story unfolds on the street, in go-gos, in the military service. Race, class, drugs, violence, and the street are recurring themes. Since the early 1990s, Nico has been a major go-go collector who has sold music in all kinds of venues, from the streets, to his tricked-out van and vending stand with flashing lights, to independent music stores like this one.

The H Street store where Nico works as a manager is nicely appointed with wood laminate floors and flat-screen monitors playing DVDs. Shelf space in the rear bursts with go-go recordings from as far back as 1979 — recorded at long-shuttered places like the Howard Theatre, the local jail, parks, and various high schools in Prince George's County and the District. The front section consists mostly of five-dollar mix CDs of the latest hip-hop. Under the glass case immediately as you walk into the store is a collection of the latest go-go CDs, mostly live recordings of bands such as Rare Essence, TCB, and Backyard Band. There is a remote lock and alarm system that Nico never feels the need to use. He has dedicated most of his adult life to archiving and preserving thousands of live go-go recordings, which he keeps locked in temperature-controlled storage. Being in the store is fine, but he prefers the world on the other side of the glass. The street, he says, is his "element."

Nico works here six days a week after working the 3:30 A.M. to 11 A.M. shift as a cook at Ben's Chili Bowl, the legendary chili dog spot on U Street. His importance to the go-go community, as Thomas Sayers Ellis's ode to Nico excerpted in the chapter epigraph indicates, transcends whatever place he happens to sell his wares. The former Rare Essence saxophonist and Familiar Faces frontman Donnell Floyd explained Nico's role in the community like this: "He's kind of like a historian. He's the guy, kind of like Box in [the 2002 film] *Brown Sugar*. He keeps track of who's doing what. He was writing for a little while. He's always a good person to talk to in terms of his overall perspective of the go-go community."

Lornell and Stephenson describe PA tapes as "generally unauthorized recordings; essentially bootleg recordings (usually compact discs rather than tapes these days) recorded from the sound mix directly off the Public Address soundboard at a live performance. These master tapes are sold to one of the local entrepreneurs, who then duplicates the tapes either digitally onto a compact disc or onto an analog audio tape."[1] "Because these entrepreneurs operate on the fringes of the recording industry, usually deal in cash, and generally have no written contracts," they continue, "the world of go-go P.A. tapes remains murky and few are willing to talk about this aspect of go-go."

Live performances are the essence of go-go. Yet the PAS play a critical auxiliary role in sustaining the go-go information economy. (Lornell and Stephenson also note the parallel to the trade of tapes of live juju performances in Nigeria.[2]) The contents of these stores—and Nico's personal collection—provide a rich archive of the history and culture of black Washington. As its chief curator, so does Nico.

I first met Nico in 2003. I was working on a *Washington Post* article about the go-go DVD craze. It discussed the proliferation of neighborhood amateur filmmakers recording local occurrences and selling them using low-cost digital production technology that preceded YouTube.

Nico was working at Mad T's Record shop located near the U Street corridor (directly across the street from the Reeves Center), where he set up
a go-go aisle based on his collection of recordings. When I caught up with
him again in early 2006, he was working the early morning shift cooking
at Ben's Chili Bowl. He agreed to meet me at a new go-go and hip-hop
record store that had just opened on H Street. So in February 2006, I
went down to H Street to check it out.

Nico was generally leery of outsiders to the scene. He said he had
helped two young white filmmakers who were students at Georgetown
University who had made a documentary on go-go called *The Pocket*. But
Nico resented that he and many people on the scene were unable to see
the debut screening and never got a copy of the documentary itself. (Several months later, I dug up my own press copy and gave it to him.) Nico
agreed to be a part of my project, and we have become friends over the
years.

Off the Books

Mom and pop stores such as the one on H Street once existed in every
quadrant of the District, as well as in many aging strip malls in Prince
George's County. These areas were slated to be rebuilt as black businesses
following the riots of 1968. In the 2000s the city and private investors
finally got around to it. During the lean decades while neighborhood residents rebuilt the burnt retail corridors, the go-go economy filled with informal economic arrangements that stayed off the IRS grid: everything
from a network of geographically dispersed clothing lines to graphic
shops that create event fliers and press T-shirts.

Elliot Liebow's classic ethnography of 1967, *Tally's Corner*, which
looked at black men living in Washington's Shaw neighborhood in the
1960s, described how record shops, along with carryouts, had recently
joined taverns, pool halls, liquor stores, corner groceries, rooming houses,
secondhand stores, credit houses, pawn shops, and storefront churches
as part of a "distinctive complex of urban institutions" adapted to the
changing needs, limited choices, and eclectic tastes of inner-city residents. Hylan Lewis notes in his introduction to *Tally's Corner* that these
serve more than their outward functions: "Among other things they may
serve as informal communication centers, forums, places to display and
assess talents and staging areas for a range of activities, legal, illegal and

extralegal. And although they exist in the heart of the city, they are like outpost institutions—gathering places for outsiders in the center of the city." These are the gathering places referred to here as the public sphere, which rely heavily on "face-to-face relationships of the personal network."

Off the Books, Sudhir Venkatesh's ethnography of an urban Chicago community, described the informal economy's relationship to the rest of the city. Underground economies are part of a "parallel urban world" that developed mirror institutions to the mainstream. After the civil rights era forced integration and housing opportunities outside of urban centers, blight reigned and the alternate economy set up as a function of segregation continued to thrive. For those left behind, the underground economy quickly became a primary economy as buying off-the-books goods turned into a mode of survival. Venkatesh writes:

> The entrepreneurs are foundations of the community operating in a very different public sphere, exempt from yellow pages listings and business cards: they can be found in homes, on designated alleyways and street corners, and in bars and restaurants. Whether one is starting or sustaining a business, "underground" institutions provide a backbone for all aspects of local enterprise, from loans and credit to advertisement. The cash economy abuts a world where trading and payment occur through verbal promises, in-kind payments, and barter.[3]

Mark Anthony Neal in *What the Music Said* notes that this postindustrial underground economy also provided a source of patronage for the arts. One of the few black patrons of the Harlem Renaissance was the West Indian numbers runner Casper Holstein, who helped finance the Urban League's literary awards in 1926 from his profits. Across the Atlantic in Nigeria, a similar "nocturnal economy" has thrived around juju music, which has ebbed and flowed with the patronage of the oil economy. Economic factors, ranging from international oil prices to conflicts between captains and band boys, are a crucial aspect of urban Yoruba musical practice. This process has led to the emergence of the first millionaire juju stars, Waterman writes:

> As the rich got richer, so the stars they patronized rose higher. . . . Well-placed band captains were able to accumulate theretofore unheard of amounts of cash for investment in musical and nonmusical enterprises (e.g. recording labels, hotels, construction firms, mill companies). In addition, those with contacts among the high elite gained

access to smuggled electronic equipment, which, if bought within Nigeria, would have been exorbitantly expensive. The size of most popular bands increased from around ten performers in the mid-1960s to fifteen or more in the mid-1970s.[4]

In the United States, two factors similarly impacted the nature of the informal economy of the black public sphere in the post–civil rights era. The first was the intensity of the economic collapse of the industrial urban economy, which produced mass unemployment. The second was the emergence of crack, perhaps the most destructive element to emerge within the contemporary black life. And for H Street (like U Street) it was the riots of 1968.

A Public Sphere

CUSTOMER: You got BMG?
[*Nico hands him the* CD]
CUSTOMER: This not a bootleg copy, is it?
NICO: We don't sell bootleg.
CUSTOMER: Sorry about that.
NICO: It's not a problem. I'm glad you asked. That way I could answer.

Nico has sold live go-go recordings, also known as PAs, around Hains Point, other federal parks, and outside schools. He has sold outside Chinese food takeout spots frequented by drug dealers until the wee hours of the morning. He has navigated dueling drug turfs and been caught in the cross hairs of drug enforcement agents who twice mistook him for a dealer. He has confronted imposters selling tapes under his name and fought them hand to hand. For the record, Nico has never been a bootlegger: "It really bothered me to dub somebody else's work to sell it. The kind of business I'm in, it's kind of crazy to have a conscience, but I did."

Building the business was a painstaking process. By the time he started out in the early 1990s, he had already had a complicated life. He had been estranged from his mother, lived in a foster home, reconciled with an absent father, parted ways with his father, and then spent a few months as a homeless high school student. He did a three-year stint in the military. While he was away, go-go sustained him. He kept up with the world back home through recordings, the radio, and concerts, much in the way Chuck D meant when he described rap as a "Black CNN."

On his return to D.C., a broken vertebra forced him to leave his job as a cook at a law firm. So he began wandering the city with a boombox and a rolling suitcase filled with PA tapes. Nico eventually got a license, then slowly built up the business and his reputation: "I got a little small table. I graduated to building a stand. We built this outrageous stand built with a car speaker system. It was state of the art for the time. BET, City Paper [all did features on him]. Matter of fact, *Spin* magazine put me in as if you want to [hear go-go music]. I'm not even a store. They said, come see Nico's tapes at Twelfth and F. It got to be real big . . . from '93 to 2000. So that's seven years." Nico said when he pulled up in his tricked-out Ford Aerostar van, or his other weekly car rentals, customers used to come to him "like I was the ice cream man."

> I liked being outside. I loved it. Actually more so than [being inside]. . . . We used to order snowsuits from an outerwear company. They were professional snowsuits. Like you would see guys working on manholes. They were for working at thirty below. We'd be hot. Everybody out there freezing, these body suits from head to toe. We were straight. All we needed was some gloves and a hat. We could be butt-naked under them joints and be straight.

Nico became a phenomenon. He was making "oodles and oodles of money"—between five hundred and a thousand dollars per day, money he now wishes he had invested in a home instead of renting flashy cars and "living fast." In 2001, he ran into "the drama." On his way to a show he was promoting in Virginia, a fire tore through his van, ruining his inventory of thousands of tapes. Luckily, he still had the master recordings in storage. But losing his entire inventory was a blow from which it took years to recover. He had several less than satisfying experiences selling wholesale and working in other independent music stores. He had been working at Ben's Chili Bowl for the past three years, where he occasionally sold recordings on the side.

At the time Nico and I talked, he was on the verge of turning forty. I asked him if he could get a license today in spite of the push from city officials to limit street-vending licenses. "Yeah!" he said without hesitation. "In a minute! In a minute. I'm telling you." He reentered the scene in February 2006 after being hired by the owner of the iHip-Hop and Go-Go Factory to manage his second retail store in the District. The owner, Derrick, also owned the clothing store Planet Chocolate City located on Georgia Avenue.

Back in 2005, Nico operated at a time when the business model for the PA industry had begun to shift. I asked him about a *Washington City Paper* article published the previous fall, which talked about why go-go bands were deciding to release fewer live recordings. Bands had told the reporter that fans and bootleggers alike were too often pirating the recordings and that they felt exploited by the whole industry. Live releases, once a weekly affair for most go-go bands, were trickling down to once or twice a year among the most popular bands. They had begun to cut out middlemen like Nico. Naturally, Nico believed it to be a mistake:

> Back when they were putting out tapes every week, it was a more profitable game for everybody. It made their shows hotter. But I guess now, people still go to the shows. Shows always going to be the bloodline of the city, of go-go. People want to hear their name. Why you think the lead talker of the show calling out the names of the crews all night? People want to hear their names! That's why they got signs up, and hand-signs, they want to hear their name. So in order to hear it, other than just hear it that time that night. They want to hear it on a tape or a CD. So if it don't come out, they disappointed. So you are disappointing your clientele.

A Shrinking Black Space on H Street

A black lesbian couple walk into the H Street store. They pick up a couple of CDs that they had ordered and now they are looking for something else to buy. Nico suggests the latest CD by the major-label R&B artist Christina Milian. One of the women balks. "She's from the area," Nico points out, alluding to the early years that the Jersey-born singer of Afro-Cuban descent spent living in Waldorf, Maryland. "She from the *white* part," the customer says. "This about to be the white part too!" Nico replies, gesturing around him and the gentrifying street beyond the glass wall.

Nico has seen the change at Ben's Chili Bowl, where he works his other job. The restaurant stands as an iconic symbol of black resilience for staying open after race riots of 1968. Ten years ago, U Street felt similar to H Street. Today, though, it is filled with exorbitantly priced luxury housing and hip new restaurants. Ben's Chili Bowl remains a proud symbol of black Washington, but today has equal numbers of white and black patrons. It is no longer a "black space."

At an early age, Nico decided that he preferred being in "black spaces." When Nico was thirteen, he refused to follow his mother to a job in very white Alaska—most certainly out of his black element. He decided to stay in Washington and fend for himself: "I think what really changed my life was going into a foster home—actually a shelter home. And then some white folks wanted to adopt me. But I refused. I wanted a black family. . . . Yeah, they wanted to keep me. I said, 'Naw, that's alright.' I didn't want to be raised listening to Foreigner, Journey, and Def Leopard all my life." Race and music have shaped virtually every aspect of his life. Washington has been overwhelmingly black for all of Nico's thirty-nine years. His contacts with white culture were limited.

In Washington, white spaces and black spaces have each been constructed separately and linked to disproportionate levels of power, according to the cultural anthropologist Tanya Y. Price.[5] This political reality has had palpable effects on the psyche of black Washington. Price believes the cause of many of the city's social ills stem from the colonial relationship with the federal government and the historical ambivalence that that institution has had with the city's majority black residents. She describes the psychological barriers erected around the "white spaces" associated with federal Washington and the "black spaces" that comprise most residential areas.

Liebow described Washington, D.C.'s unique racial exchange that took place in the 1960s.[6] The city has been a principal stopping place for blacks moving up the Eastern Seaboard out of the Carolinas, Virginia, Alabama, and Georgia. He noted that in 1963, Washington was the only major U.S. city with more blacks than whites living in it. He noted the exchange between them during the work week: "The city gives up Negro women to the suburbs where they work as domestics, and receives, in exchange, white white-collar men. At the end of the workday, city and suburbs reclaim their own."

At the time of my research on H Street in 2006, the corridor was in the beginning stages of gentrification, and this fact was a popular subtext to discussions in and around the store. When I went across the street to the Cluck-U Chicken for a lunch break, I found the owner, Bernard Gibson, tongue-lashing his employees to give me better service. A petition sat near the register, asking the community to support his battle with the local Advisory Neighborhood Commission (ANC) that wanted to withdraw his license because it was not a "sit-down" restaurant, as the zoning certificate allowed, but a fast-food joint. It seemed strange that an ANC would target a business, especially one so immaculately kept and that in fact offered chinaware and table service for patrons. I assumed there was something else to it, so I ordered my food and ate without signing it.

A few weeks later, an article in the *Washington Post* confirmed Gibson's account of the battle: "H Street in Northeast Washington is a strip trying to shed its bedraggled past and become a gleaming urban paradise," the article said.[7] Property values in the area have taken off, as detailed in countless media accounts. The developer Jim Abdo recently spent $27 million to buy the old Capital Children's Museum seven blocks from the music store. Abdo planned to restore the buildings of 1870 that once housed a convent to create 480 housing units, most of them upscale condos. The Atlas Theater, built in 1938 and located on H Street, was being restored as a performing-arts center.

The perceived encroachment by gentrifiers provided a constant subtext to many of the discussions in the music store. Gibson stopped by one day to chat in hushed tones. Nico's offhanded comment to the customer reflected the widespread feeling of the inevitable. That a "black" space could collide with a "white" one without one of them collapsing seemed almost inconceivable.

Meeting of the Public Spheres, Part 1

I joined Nico as he celebrated his fortieth birthday in October 2006 at another club on H Street called Phish Tea Café, where the go-go band Familiar Faces had a regular Wednesday night gig. I brought my DVD camcorder and digital camera to record the show. Several months earlier I had told Nico about a white master's student in folklore who called himself Funkmaster J and had been blogging with detailed information about all the Familiar Faces shows. I was pleased to finally meet him in person. Nico was automatically suspicious of J. As soon as we walked outside, Nico grilled Jordan, a thirty-something white man, about his intentions. He seemed peeved that this outsider was using the Internet as a forum to represent the go-go community.

> NICO: Right. But if you gon' do a blog, and you trying to reach, obviously millions of people. Why would you keep it in first-person?
> JORDAN: But I'm not trying to reach . . . that was never my intention.
> NICO: But I mean, that's what it's *doing*, right?

JORDAN: Yeah, but that was never my intention.

NICO: Why wouldn't it be your intention, if . . . you blogging, you're online, so anybody can see what you're doing. Reason why I ask you that is because go-go is a fragile art right now. And reason being, because it has only itself to stand on. Nobody is trying to support it. Other than the people that's involved in it. Patrons and the artists. Alright. Outside of that, there's a lot of detractors. So I personally, not calling myself the go-go police, . . . but I personally am questioning anybody who has any type of . . . I take that back. Not saying you have them, but, anybody who possibly might have alternative motives. Because I've dealt with those types of people. And it's been detrimental to the art itself.

On his blog the next day, Funkmaster J mentioned meeting Nico and me. He had the following take on the exchange:

> I talked for a while with Natalie and Nico, one of her two colleagues. He asked me a number of questions about my blog saying, "GoGo is really fragile right now (which I know and is a shame) and I've known a lot of whites who have said they were trying to help GoGo and have hurt it." I found some of his questions a little strange like, "Why did you decide to write the blog in first person?" I understand his concern, it's a damned shame that authorities are trying to eliminate GoGo.

All communities police the symbolic boundaries that surround them. However, this exchange also represents the collusion of cultural codes. A communication took place, but several signals crossed. For Nico, it was suspicion about Jordan's intentions and motives behind writing authoritatively in the public sphere about a community of which Nico did not consider him a member. The grilling he gave to Jordan was no different from the one he gave me before agreeing to be a part of my project.

During the encounter, I put down the video camera and I tried to ease the tension. Nico said to me, with a little bit of annoyance, "I'm doing this for you!" I told Nico that it was OK, that I did not see Jordan as a rival but a colleague. In recounting the incident on his blog, Jordan automatically inserted the racial subtext that might have been implied but that Nico never brought up directly. He also assumed Nico was talking about "white authorities" who were trying to eliminate go-go, but Nico was actually alluding to other outsiders who had sought to portray go-go in the public realm. A few of the best-known examples are the British man Chris Blackwell of Island Records, whose film *Good to Go* of 1986 was considered an insulting depiction of the go-go community and of D.C. as a whole. The other example was the two white makers of *The Pocket*, whose story I mentioned earlier.

Meeting of the Public Spheres, Part 2

About midway through my several sessions with Nico, my ethnomusicology professor, Jonathan Dueck, agreed to have a meeting with Nico at the University of Maryland's Clarice Smith Performing Arts Center. I wanted us to talk about the process of digitizing Nico's archive, as well as get some advice for pursuing grant funding to make the collection available to scholars. Dueck invited another doctoral student, who has done extensive archival work for the Smithsonian, to advise us in this process. I hoped to be able to get Nico some funding to do the important cultural archival work he had already been financing on his own as a way to give greater visibility to go-go and provide access to primary source materials. I saw this as a way to give back for the many hours he spent helping me on my project.

Walking alongside Nico into the vast arts complex with thirty-plus-foot ceilings, I realized how white my daytime world was. There were really only young white kids milling around. I experienced a similar culture shock when I first started going to go-gos, or even when I first arrived in D.C. as a college freshman. It was a reminder of all these cultural worlds sharing the same space. Nico actually lived just a few miles away in Mount Rainier. If he could experience this culture shock, he could relate to what it is like for me to move in and out of go-go, a psychological and cultural boundary I cross every day.

When we got into the ethnomusicology lab with sound and other kinds of engineering equipment, Dueck offered Nico a seat near the door. Nico declined, explaining that he never sat with his back to the door, and took another seat. When we realized that we had left something in the car, Nico looked over at me pleadingly to walk with him back to his car to retrieve it. When Nico arrived at his silver suv, he grabbed a bandana to put on top of his braids. "I didn't realize I was looking that rough," Nico told me with a laugh.

When we got back to the ethnomusicology lab, Nico pointed out all the equipment that he was already familiar with. When the audio expert quizzed him about how he was storing his master copies and what kind of techniques he was using to copy them, we realized that Nico had already been archiving his go-go music using best practices for all these years. This with no formal training.

We initially meant to speak for thirty minutes, but much to both my and Nico's delight, the four of us talked for nearly three hours. As I was walking Nico out to his car, we talked about next steps. I passed on the pointers that Dueck had given about grant writing, building a budget, and the like. I told him I viewed go-go as a cultural artifact for D.C. and for the lives and people that live in it, and he agreed. "Go-go's not like other music," Nico said. "It *is* what's happening."

The next time I arrived at the H Street store, I had to chuckle at the sight of Go-Go Nico, aka Nico the Go-goologist. He had made a big show of not sitting with his back facing the door at the university. Now he was sitting in a leather swiveling chair with his back to the floor-to-ceiling glass doors facing H Street and the ghost of the dancing lady—asleep.

Oral History

Even if not another single go-go performance is recorded, Nico's collection already contains thousands of tapes, forming a rich archive of events, controversies, people, lives, and deaths that have occurred during the past twenty-five years. Nico's status as the chief historian and archivist of go-go highlights the nature of this particular black public sphere. Nico's archive updates earlier African-derived expressive forms by storing cultural capital in the oral tradition. Nico's collection contains a social history and narrative not readily accessible at the District of Columbia public library, the D.C. Historical Society, or the Smithsonian Institution. Each recording in Nico's collection is carefully documented and labeled. On the back wall of the store, customers could pick up recordings of the show on 26 June 1991, at which the rappers Ice Cube and Yo-Yo performed with Junkyard Band at Triples nightclub. There was also the show recorded when the Northeast Groovers performed at Lorton penitentiary. There was the oft-cited classic show of Rare Essence on 9 July 1985 at the Panorama Room, known to most as "The Fight Joint." The recording captured a physical altercation between the lead talker and the bass player, throughout which the band continued to play.

Customers can also buy the show recorded on 5 May 1994, the night that changed the go-go sound forever. Big G, the lead talker of Backyard Band, had just been released from jail after a several-months-long hiatus. He returned that night to the stage with a hero's welcome and initiated a new generation of go-go bands, who followed the Backyard Band in the rap-influenced "gangsta" go-go genre. Then there is a show that three years later also represented a watershed for the city and for go-go. Backyard Band was playing. Big G instructed club bouncers to throw out a fan who was causing trouble. The fan went outside and shot the off-duty police officer Brian Gibson, killing him on 4 February 1997. It was a critical moment in the mediation of go-go, cementing its reputation as an incubator for violence. The Ibex, a club located in the Petworth neighborhood in Northwest Washington, was thereafter closed (and early in 2006, it was renovated into luxury lofts).

Other recordings captured the key debates and controversies that captivated black neighborhoods in the city. There was a series of battles between rappers, while Rare Essence played in the background in 1988. Fat Rodney, a reputed drug dealer, battled against a rapper known as DC Scorpio, a strident opponent of drugs. A series of recordings chronicle their onstage battles, which mirrored the battles going on in the streets of Washington.

> NICO: Rodney used to kill him. Because Rodney was street. Scorpio had a lot of scripted kinds of things that he used to say that was really wack for real. . . . [Later on] Fat Rodney got killed. As a matter of fact, he got killed coming out of the go-go. I do have that tape. I never put it on CD. 6-9-1989. He was coming out of a go-go. They gunned him down. As he was coming out.
>
> NATALIE: What about DC Scorpio, what happened to him?
>
> NICO: Actually he came back. He came back in '90, '89. He was gone for a couple years, said he went to college or something. He tried to make a return, but he wasn't the same. He never came out with another hit record. Rap had changed. . . . A couple years back, he put out a full-release rap album that didn't do nothing. It was promoted to do something, but nobody was feeling Scorpio. He could actually rap, but it was the content of the rap.
>
> NATALIE: People thought it was corny?
>
> NICO: Yeah. [*laughs*] And the wild thing about it, he tried to come back with this rap album, he tried to come back hard.
>
> NATALIE: Yeah, they usually do.

On the Move

Nico and I still hope to have a portion of his collection preserved in perpetuity in an archive. Until then, the collection will live on at places like the H Street store, in neighborhoods depicted by the local media as an urban wasteland. Even if not another go-go is ever recorded, this collection will be there forever, maintained by people like Nico and countless others quietly amassing archives of these cultural artifacts in private collections all over the city — and beyond.

By the spring of 2007 — a year after we had first met — Nico had undergone some major changes. He had married and had joined the staff of *Take Me Out to the Go-Go* magazine, where he wrote a column called "Nico's Niche, by Nico the Gogo-Ologist." He had also left his job as the manager of the H Street store to move his collection to a music store located at Iverson Mall, in Prince George's County, and had started working with a go-go band named Suttle Thoughts. For the first time, he lived and worked outside the District of Columbia city limits, where the black public sphere is continually shifting. He had also left his job at Ben's Chili Bowl. As for most of the rest of the go-go community, including live performance venues and mom and pop stores, his reality has shifted outside the District. He was regretful but excited about his future at Iverson Mall, which he said was a "very high-profile" location.

On one of my last visits to the store on H Street in the spring of 2006, a customer who looked to be in his late forties or early fifties walked in. He asked Nico if he had any old-school Rare Essence, "anything from '80 to '85."

> NICO: It's not like this is my whole collection right here. I got a lot of stuff. For me to put everything on CD, I would have to take a year out of my life.
>
> CUSTOMER: All right, there is one in particular I'm looking for. Luther with Rare Essence in '91. Hitting that Luke, "I Wanna Hit It Good to You." Mike and Luther. Know what I'm talking about?"
>
> NICO: That was '89 or '90. . . . Definitely that was '90.
>
> CUSTOMER: Got that up there?
>
> NICO: I got that on tape. I know I got that on tape. It wasn't that significant a show to me . . .
>
> CUSTOMER: You got Highland in '92?

NICO: I was just telling her [Natalie] about that show. That was the first time they had gotten back together in years! Funk, Benny, Jungle Boogie, even DC was there.

CUSTOMER: For real? I don't mean to interrupt you, man.

NICO: That's all right. This is business, baby. We gon' take care of business. You all right. You here, I'ma take care of you. Anything else you looking for?

6 ★ The Boondocks

"Go-go" is broad—the musical title. But you got different links. You got crime. You got regular stuff. Then you got neighborhood issues. It's like where all the neighborhoods meet each other. We only meet because of the go-go. That's the meeting place. —GRANDVIEW RON, 2006

"So this is it." I steer my beat-up SUV around a bend on a suburban Maryland block filled with seventies-era ranch and modest two-story homes, struck by how similar it felt to the working- to middle-class suburban spaces where I went to high school. "Plenty of trees and grass," I say, teasing. "Woods and deer and shit," Grandview Ron says.[1] He is directing the tour from the passenger seat, wearing a gray sweatshirt with "Canin Sport" embroidered in the D.C. style. His puffy jacket is superfluous on this unseasonable, seventy-degree December day. A teardrop tattoo hovers below one eye; another tattoo reads "GANGSTERISM."

A massive satellite dish sits on one lawn. "Yeah, that's Mr. Al's house. He don't play around. He a preacher. Mr. America." Then he spots it. "That's my house right there. The one they locked me up in."

Grandview Ron's mother lived in the house during his freshman year in college, when he sold weed to an undercover agent on campus. The feds raided the house in the investigation of what a local newspaper described as a "four month inquiry investigation of drug selling" on the college campus. After the raid, Ron's horrified mother, a schools administrator he lists as "SuperChristian" in his cell phone, was so embarrassed that she left the state for a while. She came back to the neighborhood after things had cooled off.

"My next house was this gray one," Grandview Ron continues. "Some Spanish people live there now. You know how you have the stereotypical cars and playing guitars and shit? I took my daughter there, and she says, 'Daddy, why they got their cars parked in the grass?'" Next stop on the tour: a basketball court shut down by "bourgie-ass neighbors," who complained about too much congregation and loud noise. Ron points out graffiti tags spray-painted on street signs nestled in the woods. We get out of the car at a corner convenience store; I notice two bullet holes in a window reflecting images of leafless trees. Inside, he greets the store clerk by name. Outside, he points out the trash bin where dealers keep their stash. Ron explains he is welcome at the store because he and his crew provide protection.[2] Less than a mile away, we pull up to a bridge in a wooded area shut down to traffic. "We can't run through the woods no more," Ron explains. "The police drive on the grass. They drive on the grass and chase everyone to the back."

Ron was born in the late 1970s and is a second-generation native of Prince George's County. The suburb is a shadow Chocolate City. The county and go-go developed along parallel tracks, and in fact, when Chuck Brown moved to the D.C. area as a child, his family lived in the modest D.C. border town of Fairmont Heights, Maryland. Prince George's later became known as the wealthiest jurisdiction in the United States with a majority-black population.[3] Ron's father, who manages a recreation center, grew up on a farm in the county before integration. Back then it was majority white and known as a rural, somewhat backward place with trigger-happy cops and streets named for the tobacco crops that flourished there.

When the Civil Rights Act ended legal residential segregation, Prince George's became the suburb of choice for black Washingtonians of means, sparking development throughout the county in the 1970s. Thanks to the influx of upwardly mobile black families, when Prince George's County became majority-black, it also raised the county's socioeconomic status and income level. It is a massive, geographically diverse place. In one area you might find farmland. In other spaces you might find well-tended lawns, "not-having-it" block associations, and green golf courses — all the trappings of any middle-class suburb in the United States. Then there are older, depressed communities that sit on the eastern border with Washington, D.C. Because of its family, business, and political ties with the nation's capital, the county is sometimes referred to as D.C.'s ninth ward.

Ron grew up in a generation in which many believed that "go-go is life." His community also stands as an enormous symbol of black success. It is the richest black county "in the *country*," Ron said. "Hard to believe till you go out of town. You go out of town and you be like, 'damn, look at this.'" As Ron's generation became adults, the county began to experience another demographic shift. Thanks to the stability of high-paying federal government and contracting jobs, the Washington region started ranking among the most expensive in the country. The region rode the historic nationwide housing boom of the early 2000s that never fully busted. Prince George's was affected by the foreclosure crisis, but it remained one of the few places in the region that still had affordable housing and broad swaths of land. As D.C. continued to gentrify, many working-class and poor people, often Latino and black — began to settle in Prince George's. These first-tier suburbs where blacks first moved in the 1970s were being filled with Latino families.

In a county concerned with its image of black uplift, officials took pains to appear sensitive and welcoming to these newcomers. But it also kept a close eye on property values and on maintaining a tax base capable of meeting the demand on police, school, and other services. Prince George's officials often battled with officials from the District of Columbia to see who could be the toughest on go-go and its sometimes-rowdy young crowds. Both jurisdictions did this while balancing the legal rights of property owners, who rarely passed up an opportunity to make money in the thriving go-go market. Go-go clubs were constantly moving back and forth across the District of Columbia line into Prince George's. Many clubs went farther and farther into the mostly white, semirural Charles County in southern Maryland.

As the post–civil rights generation came of age, Prince George's County was caught between what the sociologist Mary Patillo-McCoy in her classic book *Black Picket Fences* called "the privilege and peril of the black middle class." While black middle-class suburbs are wealthier than average municipalities in the United States, they are overburdened with their share of historic, racial, and socioeconomic baggage.

The United States remains largely segregated. Middle-class black communities have filled the gap between affluent white communities and neighborhoods where poor black people live. Compared to wealthy, majority-white, middle-class Washington suburbs such as Fairfax, Virginia, and Montgomery, Maryland, Prince George's disproportionately faced crime, dilapidated housing, and social disorder in deteriorating, poor neighborhoods that continued to grow in its direction. The segregated middle-class black neighborhoods also have easier access to criminal networks. In her late 1990s study of an affluent black Chicago community, Patillo-McCoy has described the resulting tensions it caused for the post–civil rights generation:

> The in-between position of the black middle class sets up a certain crossroads for its youth. This peculiar limbo begins to explain the disparate outcomes for otherwise similar young people in Groveland. The right and wrong paths are in easy reach of the neighborhood youth. Working adults are models of success. Some parents even work two jobs. . . . But at the same time the rebellious nature of adolescence inevitably makes the wrong path a strong temptation, and there is no shortage of showy drug dealers and cocky gang members who make dabbling in deviance look fun.[4]

Ron loved to throw eggs at the county's bourgeois image of itself. He laughed good-naturedly when I joked that Grandview was a real-life incarnation of the cable animated series *The Boondocks*, created by Aaron Mc-Gruder, who also grew up in suburban Washington and went to college in Prince George's County. The *Boondocks* character Riley lived in a green, idyllic suburban community, yet he coveted the thugged-out lifestyle he imagined happening in the "'hood." On our tour, Ron explained why he and his friends called one of the county's most prestigious upper-middle-class housing developments "Pakistan": "They call it Pakistan because they don't got no stores. No form of life back here except fucking woods and houses and trees and deer. You look around and see nothing but big-ass suburban houses [in] which everybody's dream live out. But look behind the scenes, this is a high criminal area with my youngins. All the niggas around here steal cars, smoke weed and sleep with people daughters all day long."

In the past decade, I have interviewed countless go-go fans of Ron's generation. Many of these Washington-area natives came from my personal middle- and upper-middle-class black networks and still have warm memories about going to go-gos sponsored by the black student unions at private schools. I attended Howard University with many of them, and I have taught some of them journalism at the University of Maryland, College Park. Most maintained strong emotional ties to go-go while pursuing productive lives. But go-go became less central to their identities and daily lives as they moved to other areas and as college and work exposed them to larger social networks.

Then there was Ron. Although dramatically atypical, Ron's life history proves instructive in several ways. First, it shows how the geography of the Chocolate City is mapped onto the live go-go performance. Ron's life also speaks to the vulnerabilities that even relatively privileged young people who grow up in the Chocolate City uniquely face. As a whole, white Washington-area teenagers do not live with the unintended consequences of how residential and school desegregation policies were implemented. And while white teenagers have higher levels of illegal drug use than their black peers, they do not generally have the same unforgiving encounters with the criminal justice system. Racial disparities in arrests exist throughout the country, but the D.C. numbers are instructive. For instance, in a study he conducted in 2010, the criminal justice professor Jon Gettman found that 12.2 percent of black Washingtonians said they had smoked in the last year, compared to 10.5 percent of whites. Yet even adjusting for population, black residents were eight times as likely to be arrested for weed as white smokers were.[5]

Ron's story might be even more hilarious than that of the satirical Riley character—except that he is dead serious. Ron's college dalliance with selling weed in college was a first-time offense; he ended up serving five years in federal prison. When he entered the penitentiary at age eighteen, Ron might have had to imagine what thug life might be like. But when he left prison at age twenty-three, he was a well-schooled criminal with the networks he needed to scale that particular ladder.

At the time he gave me the tour of his Grandview neighborhood, he had just spent nearly a year in the county jail awaiting trial for the murder of a twenty-five-year-old man. The victim was an acquaintance who worked in the same Prince George's shopping mall, where they both had retail jobs. At the time he was killed in a drive-by shooting outside a go-go club, Ron's acquaintance was trying to make peace between two neighborhood groups arguing outside. If Ron knew anything about who pulled the trigger that night, he never told me, and he never told authorities. A jury eventually acquitted Ron, but the murder still haunted him.

Ron was one of the first contacts I made on the go-go scene in 2001 when he held a short-lived job selling music in an independent store in Prince George's. Ron started following my work in newspapers while he was in prison. We linked up a few times over the years when I covered arts and leisure for the *Washington Post*. I could always count on Ron to tell me the latest styles and hot new go-go bands on the scene.

When the *Washington Post* published an excerpt from my first book in the fall of 2006, Ron sent a handwritten letter to me via the newspaper's downtown Washington, D.C., office offering his congratulations. By then I was back in graduate school working on an ethnography of go-go music, so I quickly made arrangements to meet him at one of Prince George's gleaming new upscale shopping centers. Our conversation started out with coffee at 10 A.M., stretched across a chicken-and-waffles lunch, and ended after 4 P.M. after a tour of his community. Through Ron's lens, I viewed an alternate reality to what most of Prince George's residents experience. Violence is ugly — chocolate, vanilla, Middle Eastern — whatever the flavor. Around the world, behind a loss of human life you will likely find a complicated mixture of fragile male egos, battles over turf, and good, old-fashioned capitalism.

"Go-Go Is Life"

I include here an edited transcript of my conversation with Ron while touring his Grandview. He talked about how geography dictated his life trajectory and about his fears about how both hip-hop and immigration were shaping go-go and the county's future. And he talked about his regrets.

They Schools

RON: [I went to] a magnet school. That was the worst thing they could have ever done. They sent kids away from their neighborhood school. It worked for some people. But it caused a lot of neighborhood beefs. That's how I started getting into neighborhood problems. My first day of school, seventh grade, we got off the bus. They say, "where y'all from." I was like, "I'm from Grandview." They say, "I don't like y'all." I was like, damn, I don't know anybody yet. We got into a fight.

The backstory is that the older boys who already went down

there, they was beefing. I didn't know that. That's when I first realized there was a bigger world outside Grandview. I didn't realize
that people didn't like us. You start defending your own cliques—
your friends, basically. So the decision by some dickhead at the
school board caused half the homicides in P.G. County. But they
don't think like that. Now they do what? They return kids back to
their neighborhood schools.[6]

NATALIE: Did you have to test into the school to get in?

RON: It was real big amongst the parents. I remember my mom going
to a bunch of meetings. My bus ride was like an hour and half, every
morning. That shit was retarded. All of us from the central part of
the county banded together against all of them from the southern
part of the county. We was outnumbered. We had two buses, they
had like seven.

NATALIE: What was the racial mix?

RON: It was at least 60–40, a majority-black school. They bused the
black kids to the white neighborhood. They said it was for school
testing, but really it was segregation shit. At the time [the Southern
Prince George's city] was majority-white. Now it's like half and half.
Didn't make sense to us, but made sense to some pencil pusher.

NATALIE: Did the white people fight too?

RON: Very rarely. We very rarely saw them. We had a couple of
Eminems. The cool people hung with us. The rest of them had their
little rocker clicks. That rock-and-roll shit. They were in school, but
you never really knew they were there. They were invisible. The
white girls, some of the white girls that was more, experimental,
they were experimenting with black boys, fucking the black boys.
The rest of them, you ain't see them until they came around the
hallways. That is another product of integration.

NATALIE: Why did you say math was "white people shit"?

RON: That's what they called it among the blacks. They had "white
people" classes and "regular" classes. Now they call it AP honors.
They had TAG [Talented and Gifted] classes.[7] It was a good school,
though. It was just a long-ass bus ride. It was in the middle of the
cornfields and shit. It was amplified because we would ride the same
buses with the high school kids. It was supposed to be different
buses with different age groups. But that twelfth-grade knucklehead
would be like, "rep the hood!"

All my schools were good. It wasn't no "ghetto urban, fucked-up" school. My vice principal said I got a problem with authority figures from an early age. My mother used to repeat that shit like every day, every time I got in trouble. I don't think it would have mattered where I went. Every pack of puppies there is an alpha male. I'm the alpha male. The problem is when one alpha male meets another alpha male. Either it's going to be cool, or it's going to be beef.

NATALIE: You went to Grandview High School. What was that like?

RON: Grandview was fun. It was like a fashion show. And the main rival was Greenwood.[8] That was established since the eighties. Grandview didn't like Greenwood. When I went back to the neighborhood school for high school, it was like, damn, everybody was more advanced. Where I went to middle school, it was like the country, nobody was smoking weed that I knew about. At [this school] it was the thing to do. I would say it was kind of like going from Carolina to D.C. You come up here, it's faster, more shit going on. But I'm a fast learner, though. I adapt.

NATALIE: You were a fast learner—what about the academic part?

RON: My grades were always good. I was on honor roll since first grade. My senior year, I had a 3.86. I was known for that amongst my peers. I was still down, but I always did my work. My focus at the time was establishing a reputation. I fought at the first football game my freshman year. That's how I started getting called Grandview Ron. I fought my man. For him it was over a girl. For me it was he disrespected me. The other people were like, "Where is that boy from Grandview, Ron. That li'l youngin from Grandview named Ron that was fighting that day." So people started saying, "Ron from Grandview." Then they switched it around eventually, became "Grandview Ron."

In elementary school, I liked to read. Even now, in prison, at home, I just read a book. I think that came from my father. When he was at home, used to read the paper all the time. So now I try to read the paper for my daughter. Hopefully she'll pick up. My father used to read the paper every morning. And my mother too.

Higher Learning

RON: I went to the college my mother made me go, [a state school]—the black one. I graduated high school in May, went to school in

August. I got locked up December 10. Drug trafficking, posses-
sion, distribution. Put this down: It was nothing but getting money.
There was a drug culture already there. Marijuana trade was already
there. It was crazy. It was people walking up asking me, "Where the
trees at?" It was already an established culture down there. Put this
down: college, everybody smoke and drinks. Definitely, everybody
smokes weed. That's why I said it was a gold mine. It turns entrepreneurs into drug hustlers, because there is a market there. The
American way. Capitalism. If you ask for it, you can get it. And I did
very well. Eighteen years old, making like $400–500 a day.

They got a tradition down there. They do a drug sweep before
finals. We was freshman. We didn't know that shit. The upper class-
man who we were cool with, he told us, "You better leave before
finals." We didn't listen. They still do that to this day. My whole
squad got caught. It was on TV.[9] It was the biggest thing in the town.
"Local college students running the drug trade."

Between you and me, the University of Maryland [College Park]
is one of the biggest drug markets in P.G. County. Because the white
people got excess money and they get high like a motherfucker. But
they don't ever focus on that because it's the white people. I know
a rack of people sell up there. That's where we got our pills from. I
couldn't get the pills around my neighborhood.

NATALIE: That's where you first got your what?

RON: Ecstasy pills. College kids only one knew how to make them.
The actual recipe is on the Internet, but who the fuck know how to
do it? We went to [College Park] Maryland for that reason. That's
where we made our first, we call it plug, but that's our connect. University of Maryland in 2000. We ain't even know what ecstasy pills
was. Most of the drugs are white people drugs and they come to the
blacks later.

One of my homegirls went to school in Syracuse while I was in
prison. When she came back, she came around. "Where the pills?"
What pills? "Ecstasy pills." Like huh? I'm supposed to be knowl-
edgeable about this shit. I'm like where in the hell is the pills at?
Asked around, they like, "That's some white boy shit." So where
white people be at? University of Maryland.

We go to Maryland. Post up. Mingling, but we was doing the
stereotype. "Y'all got the weed?" Yeah we got the weed. But we ask-

ing where the pills at. White people like, "Are you the police?" We like, what the fuck are you talking about? I got a gun on me. We ain't no fucking police. She went and got the white boy. The white boy like, "Are you the police? You know you have to tell us." So we about to beat this nigga up, like you disrespecting us. He got all nervous and shit. We are like, where are the fucking pills at? We got drugs and guns. Where are the fucking pills at? That's how we found him. White Boy Matt.

Think about it, Len Bias died of coke.[10] Think about it. Let's go back to '85–86. Cocaine was big back then. White people had cocaine money. At the [University of] Maryland, you never go to court. Whoever got Maryland money locked down, you getting paid. Colleges are basically the drug markets that people try to find. It's less violence than the street shit. The robbery shit ain't gonna be that much. You ain't gotta worry about getting killed for real. College is basically a free-trade zone.

Geography of Grandview Ron

RON: Most of my age group is either locked up or they kinda like, moved away. So all the youngins that's repping our neighborhood actually live in Grandview Woods. It's kind of like we've become a brand. You gon start seeing graffiti and shit. You'll know where you at. I see the signs.

It's a trail takes you to the high school. The trail was a robbery trail. I almost got robbed twice — by niggas from my own way! "Oh my bad, I didn't know that was you!" Dickhead. Dumb dick. All through there is trails right there. They just fenced this in.

Roll your window down real quick. Hey! Stu! [*yells out the window; turns back to me*] High as a kite. Look at this shit. [*Turns back to Stu*] I gotta holla at you later on. Turn that shit down. I gotta holler at you later on.

STU: [*takes off earphone*] Yeah? I'm about to go get my check and shit.

RON: I got something for you. Holler at me later on. Four o'clock, young.

[*We pull up to a bridge in a wooded area*]

RON: We used to hustle at this bridge. Sad shit, but niggas is thugging for no reason. Sad shit. We actually got recruits from other neighborhoods. Other subdivisions. We got ten subdivisions. And each subdivision got five knuckleheads. That's fifty motherfuckas. They all come through here. That's my man Fat Boy in that truck. Everybody come through Grandview. Everybody who aspires to be a criminal come through [the convenience store]. You got niggas who hustle and you got niggas who rob. The robbin' niggas they pretty much the lazy ones who can't hustle.

Grandview, traditionally, this is the boondocks. But we have a lot of drug dealers who live out there. You grew up in the city, "urban environment." This is nothing to you. These are the older starter houses.

NATALIE: They look like they were built in the seventies. So this was always black?

RON: Predominantly. It was built from scratch for black people. White people bought too. Some still live here. Make this left, I'll show you the big houses. To all the people who ain't from this area this looks nice, middle class. To us, we consider ourselves the undesirables live up here. The kids right here, they be worse than the ones from Southeast D.C. They feel they have something to prove. In your mind, you're like, "Dog, I'm gangster. Just because your parents don't make as much as mine, don't make you tougher."

We got different subdivisions. Mind you, this is an upper-middleclass neighborhood. They used to call that shit Rumblewood when I was in high school. We used to fight all the time. There is a high number of rollers around here. Cause there is nothing to do. This long-ass highway and you got ducks and shit over here. This shit is so peaceful. No bullshit. But the niggas around here would never look at it as being nice. When you are a young kid, you be trying to be from the 'hood. I don't know, it's like the parents want to be rich and the kids want to be motherfucking gangsters.

NATALIE: *The Boondocks*!

RON: *The Boondocks* is a good concept for my neighborhood. Yes it is. And this is coming from me. It's like a disconnect. The parents say [they don't want drug traffic], but it be they kids doing the shit. I'm trying to tell you, half the people who've been calling my phone since I've been here with you are from [this wealthy subdivision]. This is what they come home to, but they come around our way. So who bring the crime where? We not bringing it to y'all. You'll bringing it to our neighborhood.

Look at that shit, you got flocks of deer. That shit do look like the fucking *Boondocks*. No bullshit. Now that I think about it. You are in the *Boondocks* actual cartoon, in reality. Life imitating art . . .

NATALIE: You said this is Grandview, but this is really Mitchellville, isn't it?

RON: Mitchellville has cache too, but you can't go to a go-go say you from Mitchellville. You say you from Grandview. And like, specifically Grandview Woods.

NATALIE: Yeah, 'cause that's what I'm gonna start calling you, is "Mitchellville Ron" . . . now that I know the truth . . .

RON: Hey . . . I'm so cool wouldn't even faze me. I make Mitchellville popular. But naw, the cache. This is what they actually have going on amongst the youngins. Like, we actually be in the go-go and the niggas from around my way will fight the other subdivision because they say they from Grandview Woods. I don't really agree with that shit because the deeper we are the better. But it's actually happened. What they do now? They say, Grandview Stars. They just say they a "star," which means, they from Grandview, but they not affiliated with the Woods.

So I'm saying like, the Woods is the biggest crew in Grandview. But we are not the only one. The biggest clique, the Grandview residents, they called "Grandview Stars." We might be at a go-go. They might be like, "All my Grandview Stars here tonight." But then we come in there. They say, "The Woods in the house." So it's kind of like, we overrun everybody else when we get there. But it's actually not that many of us. Less than twenty.

NATALIE: So most of the kids you are talking about, the bourgie people kids. Do they just grow out of it?

RON: Most of these niggas, they hang right here. But this is what you call the typical Boondocks. They just be out here thugging for nothing. You'll see a group of young niggas with big jackets and scull caps on, smoking weed or something. But they bored, nothing to do. Average people might think it's an illegal activity. But it is really because niggas don't have nothing to do. So they just stand outside.

NATALIE: [*laughing*] Acting like they doing something.

RON: They might be out there smoke some weed. And people like calling the police. [*high-pitched voice imitates concerned citizen*] "They are outside selling drugs. I smell marijuana." And police come through and start pressing them. But once you get a record you gotta become a criminal.

[*We pull up to a high-rise tower where the novelist Connie Briscoe lived while doing research for her novel,* P.G. County.][11]

RON: Hey, my goal, I want to live at the top of that bitch and just be king of the world.

[*We pull up to a strip mall around the corner from the tower.*]

RON: Certain neighborhoods just ain't going to accept certain shit. See now how they got security. See that's brown right there [private security guard]. They basically made that a no-trade zone. You can't come around there. So they stand over there now, but this was one of my first spots when I first started that capitalist block captain shit.

I didn't start doing that shit until I came home. I went to college and started getting into capitalist shit. My mind frame got back on that money when I came home for Christmas. In high school, I was just fighting everybody. I just was on some, representing Grandview.

NATALIE: But weren't they doing a lot of capitalism when you were in high school?

RON: But I wasn't in that clique. I would just beat niggas up. I lived with my mother.

NATALIE: You live with your mother now . . .

RON: But I'm grown, I gotta pay my own bills. It's silly, but it's separate. Back then, my team was smoking weed, smoking dippers. But weren't selling it. The older boys were selling out the store. It guess it was like an internship. You can't really get a name for yourself. You can't get out here and try to protect your capitalist ventures if you don't have a name for yourself coming up as a hardbody. Somebody who ain't going for nothing. How do you establish that? You gotta start knocking niggas in they head. Establishing that you ain't to be messed with. So if you do get a package, you can keep your pack.

Before I got promoted, I never really wanted to leave Grandview. You see how big this area is? This will make you rich, just having control of this area. Imagine . . .

NATALIE: So who is your clientele?

RON: I'm just dealing with the plants. Most of the smokers work because they gotta buy the weed. It be old people coming out, the parents. Daytime, you get the teenagers who cut school. Construction

workers who come in the morning time. From four through like
eight, it be a rush because everyone coming home from work. All
the workers come home, get that shit, then go in the house. Then it
be dead again nine through one or two in the morning. It's money.
It's capital. It's the same thing, it's capitalism.

NATALIE: So you don't get any people from outside Grandview?

RON: Like Redskins games? It's nothing but white people coming in.
We kill shit with them niggas. You see the Virginia tags. Redskins
games, they pull up man. They ask for everything. White people get
high on damn near anything.

   It's like playing chess. You gotta plan your strategy. My strategy
in this particular neighborhood was the [convenience store]. Now
that I got promoted I ain't gotta be there no more. Now I gotta
worry about seeing the whole county instead of just one area.

NATALIE: Then that gets dangerous.

RON: Whole life dangerous. You can go to jail just riding around in a
car around here. You gotta pick your poison. I done been to jail over
a dub of weed. I did five years for a dub bag of weed. I can get five
years for ten pounds.

Go-Go Is Life

NATALIE: How big is your go-go collection? How many PAs do you
have?

RON: CD-wise, I used to have hundreds and hundreds of tapes. But
when I got locked up, I wasn't around to keep track of all that shit.
Some of my CDs are at my brother's house. Some of the actual tapes
that I kept is in a box. But I lost them when [his mother] moved.

NATALIE: Which PAs mean the most to you?

RON: The ones we get put on the most. The ones from like '93. Whatever put my name on the most. That was the thing when I was
younger. "They said my name, youngin! They said my name!" We
go home, go to school, and play that shit over and over again. That
was before I got recognized. That was when I was coming up when
I was trying to get my name out there.

NATALIE: Which bands put you on the most?

RON: All of 'em. Except for like, the only band that don't give us love,
like, that is Backyard Band. But all the young bands. CCB put us
on like real heavy. The mid-level band like TCB, Raw Image, UCB.
Backyard put us on, but it's like, you gotta work the most for Back-

yard to put you on. Everybody else, you come in the door, and they like, "What's up with y'all."

NATALIE: What do you mean "work"?

RON: All that hollering and shit. Go to the front, hollering. Throwing up signs and shit. That's the shit I used to do when I was younger. When I used to go see Junkyard, Northeast Groovers. But I feel now, I done already, put us on the map so much. Ain't gotta do that shit. That's one reason why we don't go see that band like that every week. Typically you only go see the bands that you fuck with or that gon' show you love. Backyard, don't get me wrong, they'll put us on. Backyard, each band got the people they gon' put on off the top of they head. We ain't one of the neighborhoods they call off the top of they head with Backyard. Other bands we are.

Go-go didn't start the crews. The term *crews* came from the media. I never really heard that shit called a crew. Anywhere you go in the country you are going to have neighborhoods. Say I'm from so and so. The go-go managers say, "Barry Farms in here." Or "Kentland in here." But they never called it the "Kentland crew" until they read it and seen it in the paper.

MS-13 is a gang—to the paper.[12] To them it's prolly a brotherhood of Salvadorian motherfuckers who stood together when they came over here from back home. That's not a gang. They start calling themselves a gang once y'all [the media] start calling them a gang. MS-13 got big, not because they recruiting, it's because y'all dumb motherfuckas started putting it in the news every day. Salvadorian motherfuckers that don't live nowhere near that shit that claim MS-13. So it's like, y'all advertise the gangs in the paper and the TV.

NATALIE: What is the future of go-go?

RON: You could write a whole book on this shit. "BET Niggas." D.C./P.G. County always had a unique style, slang, our own way. But we becoming modernized with this BET shit, the videos. Right now, around my way, or any neighborhood in the county, they always say, that "son" shit. "Son, son, son." It's, "What's up, young." "Yo" is Baltimore. "Yo" to me is Baltimore niggas. I smack someone say that shit. I don't like that shit.

That's not because niggas moved. It's because of cable. BET has changed the whole game around. All these young girls around here live and die for Li'l Wayne. Li'l Wayne got the tattoos I got. I earned mine.[13] That nigga ain't . . . Li'l Wayne say he's a kingpin at twelve, thirteen years old, that ain't possible. And he's a rapper.

NATALIE: So how does this come back to go-go?

RON: I'm about to come back to it. Ima flip all this shit around in one second. Like Li'l Wayne. They reppin' Bloods [gang] now. You look at the videos, they reppin' that red. You got people in my area, right here, repping Bloods and Crips now. All of P.G. County, different areas reppin' the gangs. Before you never had them in Maryland. You had different cliques, but it was never B&C [Bloods and Crips] That's not us. We don't do that gang shit.

So as far as how that relates to go-go. What is happening now, it's a sad story for P.G. County. In a lot of neighborhoods, you got certain members becoming actual Bloods and Crips in P.G. County. They don't understand, when you lock up people my age, the "ringleaders," niggas controlling all the youngins, who keep the shit peaceful, you letting the youngins jive, like grow up on TV.

If I become a Crip, my whole neighborhood tomorrow becomes a Crip. That shit be on the news tomorrow. I choose not to lead them down that path. What's gon' happen when the whole county turns blue and red? They start shooting each other for colors? The shit about to get real wicked, next five to ten years.[14] I hope I'll be aged out this shit.

Same way with that MS-13 shit. It's getting bigger and bigger now. Because what? They been advertising it, and they keep making it everyday news, MS-13, they making it like that's the big thing to be. We call it amigos. You see amigo nigga, you think, they MS-13. But they all not MS-13. But that gang shit, it wouldn't be so big if you would stop promoting it. You got people who live nowhere near the urban areas, but they claiming MS-13.

I predict one day you gon' be going to go-gos and they'll be saying Bloods and Crips in that shit. I went to a go-go one time, in Hyattsville, they calling out MS-13.

NATALIE: What?!

RON: "MS-13 in the house!" Niggas was like, "What the fuck!"

NATALIE: Are you kidding me?

RON: On my daughter. I swear to God. Niggas just looking around like, "What the fuck? MS-13?" A lot of Spanish niggas in our area.[15] They

Spanish, but they under the black culture. You go through River-dale, Hyattsville, Langley Park, they dress like us, talk like us. They still Spanish. They got they own culture. But black culture overrides all the other cultures in the county. It's like, even L.A., the "gang capital," they got they own brown pride, but they style of dress, our style of dress intermingle out there. Out here, we the dominant cul-ture, they follow the blacks.

Riverdale west side is Hispanic. It's nothing but gang shit all on the walls. Even the amigos out there, they still dress like, "What's up, young." They might say "Holmes." That's like that L.A. shit, but they Spanish and they rep there, but they basically black Spanish niggas. Like Black-tinos.

It was an incident in Langley Park at a go-go.[16] This is a watershed moment. It was basically like a baby race war was about to hap-pen. Langley Park used to be all black and the Caribbean people, African. Spanish people took it over. They had a go-go—basically a black event—and the Mexican, Salvadoran, the amigos prolly wanted to check out a party in their neighborhood. And something happened, the blacks start arguing with the amigos. One of 'em got stabbed. They made it seem like it was gang related. The blacks that I know took it as, "These niggas jive overstepping their bounds with that gang shit." The black people came together on some unity shit.

You gotta look for signs of things. The sign is, P.G. County going to have a race relations problem in a couple years. They have one now, but it's going to be gunplay for real. Right now, niggas ain't going around saying "fuck the amigos"—yet. That will happen. Right now you ain't gotta worry about going through a neighbor-hood [worried about colors]. That's my biggest fear. It becomes L.A. or some shit.

NATALIE: OK, so . . .

RON: How that linked to go-go? Eventually they going to be going to the go-gos. That was the first time I heard MS-13 in a go-go.

Technically that 'hood is no longer black no more. If it's a club that has rock and roll, and it's in my neighborhood, I'm going to try to go see it. It's my neighborhood. I wanna see what the fuck is going on. I told you, I heard, "We got MS-13 in the house." It wasn't like they was on the dance floor, repping that shit. But it was surpris-ing like, damn, we actually heard that shit.

Go-go is like, broad—the musical title. But you got different links to the shit. You got crime. You got regular stuff, then you got neighborhood issues. It's like where all the neighborhoods meet each other. We only meet because of the go-go. That's the meeting place. Go-go is like the meeting place for all the young males that have problems with themselves, with life, self-esteem.

No bullshit. There's been times I really just didn't give a shit about living. I go to a go-go and start something with somebody because I know there is going to be another nigga in there who I can push and he can push me back. I just be mad at the world. It's like routine. Go-go is life. It's our identity, P.G. County/D.C. crew. We play our music, let everyone know, that's us right here. We from D.C., nigga, P.G. County area.

They'll play house [music] to let them know they from Baltimore. You identify with the music. I play go-go, not because I want to hear it, but because I want everyone to know I'm from up this way. This is my identity thing. Let everybody know what it is. Y'all motherfuckas going to know where I'm coming from.

NATALIE: So what about the music? Where does that come in?

RON: Now that I'm older I go for the music. I say, "They crankin', they rockin'." But most time you go, because you with your crew, you trying to party, you trying to get put on, meet some girls. You don't give a damn who playing. It's just this area we grew up in. If I was down South, I'd prolly be going to some hole in the wall somewhere. Other people got clubs. This area, most niggas I know, never go to the clubs, H2O, all that. Them shits is like the bourgie clubs. If I called my niggas right now, eight to ten of them be like, "We going to the go-go." You would never hear, "We're going to [upscale downtown D.C. clubs] Love, we're going to Platinum."

Go-go is never going to die because people will always have musical talent and play instruments. It's kind of like a big ass loop. Basically it's the same shit going on. Same niggas doing the same shit.

[*Phone rings again*]. I jive like realize its four o'clock. Niggas going crazy. It's a cycle right now. The go-go bands I grew up with are getting older. The bands that was playing when I was younger don't play no more. The big thing with the young bands is this shit called the bounce beat. Fast-ass rototom shit. That's prolly something that you heard of when you started doing your research. That's what all the younger bands like. When I came up . . . I keep talking like I'm thirty-something.

NATALIE: [*laughs*]

RON: We like congos. Whoo-de-woot-toot. They like rototoms. That's a more aggressive style of music, which makes the youngins do more aggressive type shit. The music controls the environment. Slower music calms you down. If you hype, what they do? People get hype because of the music. So like, the rototom music, the youngins, they hear that hype shit, they dancing all crazy. That's just the style of music right now.

You gon' have clubs forever. This is how it usually works from my experience. When D.C. gets hot, the clubs they come to Maryland. When Maryland gets hot, they go back to D.C. So it's never really going to stop. There is always going to be somebody trying to make money on go-gos.

People always gon' make money on clubs. But as far as the shows, I think it's too many damn bands. Who are you going to see? Essence, Backyard, Familiar Faces, TCB. Or the little kids go see all them little ass alphabet bands. I can't keep track of them mother-fuckers. It be thirty of them every week. There is always more bands summertime, springtime because everybody home from school. Then the wintertime, it kind of tighten up. I won't go see no band who ain't going to be around in the springtime. I ain't gon' waste my money if y'all ain't gonna be around later on.

NATALIE: So you feel like you are making an investment?

RON: In the band, yeah. If I go see a certain band, it's because they start to know my face, know my name, reppin' my hood, stuff like that. They know my face now, so if I come in the go-go, "Oh, Grandview in the house. Grandview Woods in here. My nigga Ron." That's how bands work. The more you see, the more they show you love. Spend your time and money to go see them.

I see myself getting more focused on what I'm supposed to do and so forth. It's gotta be more than life than going to the go-go and being known for being a neighborhood star. If you get money, you buy a building, like this [*he points toward the Mchunu clothing bou-tique.*]

NATALIE: Like Vusi Mchunu.

RON: Oh, yeah. I didn't know his name was Mchunu. That's his first name? African or something?

NATALIE: Hmm Hmm. South African. But he grew up here in P.G. County.[17]

RON: So that's like, my mind frame has to change. That shit. I graduated to the top of the level. It's like damn, what else is there to do? My name ringing bells. I'm known through the jail and prison system. I can come home. It's like you get more props for the worst shit ever in history. It's jive ironic. Like my reputation got bigger because of [the murder]—and the fact that I ain't tell. Supposed to be death before dishonor. Before you dishonor somebody, you would rather die. A lot of people don't understand that shit. That's why so many people be getting attacked, retaliation. A lot of shit in P.G. County is retaliation. That witness intimidation shit. They don't ever make it into the papers. They might say it's a robbery or a drug deal. But it be because somebody told. Or some kinfolk. Can't get the brother so get him.

NATALIE: But it's not always guaranteed that you get the right person. I mean, I just feel like, you have to decide what kind of life you want to have.

RON: I've already seen the outcome of what's going on. My goal is to get off the track before the train hits the wall. That's the question that everybody has to face. This type of lifestyle choice, you got two directions. You go to jail or you gon' die. One of the motherfucking forks in the road. The key is, can you get off the train before it happens? That's the biggest question that everyone has to ask themselves. That's my constant battle. When do you stop? When is enough enough? But me, this my last go 'round. However it go. I feel like right now, I spent my whole life trying to get here.

Now it's here, I gotta take advantage of it. Six months from now, I should have five figures somewhere, easy. Thirty days from now I'm not going to be driving that [*he points to his beat-up sedan*]. The money gon' come. I'm in poverty. I prolly have less than $1,000 to my name.

NATALIE: But do you know what? You're free, though.

RON: Yeah, but you're not free in your mind. It's the mental battle that everybody gotta deal with.

NATALIE: It's the mental battle. You are here in the richest black county in the country. This is the richest. I mean, this is the best that black people are doing in the whole country. So you can't tell me that there is not other . . .

RON: Something else going on.

NATALIE: What's wild is that we're on this tour and you are talking about alternate realities, the same space. This is the nation's capital, capital of the world, basically. And we are in the same space but we had different realities . . .

RON: Two blocks from the White House, drug deals.

NATALIE: But it is all in our mind. We just gotta get out of this mental slavery.

RON: I embody all the dilemmas of black society in one person.

NATALIE: In one drive . . .

RON: [*laughs*]

NATALIE: In one day . . . [*laughs*]

RON: [*laughs*] You done went from the highs to the lows, to Goddamn.

NATALIE: I look at you and obviously you were very, you are very bright, able to even . . .

RON: I've been corrupted. That prison fucks you up.

NATALIE: But you still have a chance. You still have a choice and an opportunity. I keep thinking about [the twenty-five-year-old killed outside the go-go].

RON: Yeah, that shit was a blow. That shit was a cold blow.

NATALIE: And then I think about my own son.

RON: It could happen to any one of us. What I did learn from that? Now, I promote no more drive-bys. Get out the car if you going to do some shit. That drive-by shit, that shit's fucked up. Cause you can get anybody. You are literally aiming at a crowd full of people on a sidewalk.

It's all part of the lifestyle. The daily battle with your feelings and your thoughts. You could go out today, die tomorrow. You never know when it's your last. You gotta plan ahead, but act like it's your last. People who don't plan to fail, they fail to plan. And with that . . .

Grandview Ron and I have not spoken since. A few months after his tour, he was pulled over by a Virginia State Trooper with five pounds of marijuana, seventy ecstasy pills, a nine-millimeter pistol, a .38 caliber handgun, and a scale. A jury convicted him on drug and weapons charges. He is currently serving a seven-year sentence in a federal prison on the East Coast. It's his first time living outside of the state of Maryland.

7 ★ Redemption Song

We are going to emancipate ourselves from mental slavery because
whilst others might free the body, none but ourselves can free the mind.
—MARCUS GARVEY, 1921

For kids growing up across Washington's Southeast border in the 1960s, visiting the mall was a bit
like taking a trip to the Pearly Gates. That is where
you bought your freshest new Chuck Taylor All
Stars shoes, your first taffeta prom dress, your first
stilettos. It's the place you met your first love, had
your first kiss, cried over your first breakup. It was
your first taste of freedom. So it was when Iverson
Mall, the D.C.-area's first air-conditioned, indoor
shopping mall, opened on Branch Avenue in 1967.
As the slogan said, "Springtime Is Forever at Iverson
Mall." Chuck Fraley holds memories of the community around Iverson Mall so dear that he created an
Internet shrine to the space and time in history.[1] "We
are the ghosts of Marlow Heights who walk among
its inheritors," the site announces. The apparitions of
Branch Avenue appear in photos and text: The bru-
nette in pastel green polyester, standing in front of
a groovy swag lamp and orange curtains. The tow-
headed Unger boys—one wearing a red Silver Hill

Boys Club T-shirt. And whatever happened to the Andrattis? They had a horse named Bonnie.

Just a mile from D.C.'s Southeast border, the 1960s-era youth who congregated around Branch Avenue also had some rough edges. In elementary school, Fraley was introduced to a gang called the Grits, who were also known as Blocks (as opposed to Preps and Mods), Fraley recalled. Grits wore slicked-back, greased hair and their own style of construction worker–type trousers that they called Macs. They wore short-sleeved nylon T-shirts in garish lime green or yellow—and they had a redneck swagger. They were tough-guy characters reminiscent of the 1973 film *American Graffiti*. They cuffed their pants up to show off colored shoe-strings on their Chucks—not tied but with the laces dangling. But you really weren't a true Grit, Fraley wrote, unless you had a "Peters" windbreaker embroidered at the breast pocket with a heart or a pair of dice and a couple of names.

Fraley realized the Grits had stopped being underground one day when, while visiting Montgomery Ward store in Iverson Mall, he heard an announcement piped over the PA system. "Shoppers, we have Macs available in the boys department!" Grits had gone "almost mainstream," Fraley recalled. This watered it down a bit compared to previous generations of "hardcore" P.G. County Grits:

> These new Grits were paper ones really (myself included), because it was more a fad than a way of life [as it was] for the "real" Grits. By becoming a Grit, a boy could adopt a "bad" attitude and get some perceived respect from the neighborhood or school. But if you talked the talk but didn't walk the walk, eventually somebody would put you in your place. I know, because I thought I was a "bad dude," getting into fights and such, until one day a classmate picked a fight with me before school, right in front of everyone. Got the crap beat out of me! But I also remember the "head" Grit at Stoddert [school] then, Bill Arnold, turned around and knocked the other boy silly. I guess by me being a former Grit, Bill took some pity on me and did something to give me some "get back." Thanks, Bill!

"There was nothing fancy about Marlow Heights," Fraley told a *Washington Post* reporter.[2] "It was pretty much a working-class community, but it was made up of some very hardworking, honest people who had few pretensions but great outlooks on life." Would Fraley, then fifty, want to go back to that time? "No. I wouldn't want to stay in 1968 forever, but to be truthful, yes, sometimes I wish I was in Miss Doyle's fifth-grade classroom again, looking at the clock and seeing that it was 1:30 and soon I could run home and watch 'Dark Shadows' or something."

That idyllic, sepia-toned picture—with few black faces in it—all shattered with the civil rights movement. Racial tensions ran high as the region's large black population began to agitate for more access to housing and schools. Washington, D.C., exploded on the day in 1968 that Martin Luther King Jr. was assassinated in Memphis. In the aftermath of King's death, black Washingtonians literally burned segregated black retail strips like U Street and H Street to a crisp. They wanted to escape their black neighborhoods, where they were held captive by real-estate agents and racial covenants as though under quarantine. They did not want to go to "black" stores, black restaurants, black theaters. They wanted the white picket fence. They wanted the mall. They wanted the American Dream. And in Prince George's County they got it. And as Prince George's population tilted black, it became better educated and had more money to spend than Fraley's generation.

But a strange thing happened at places like Iverson Mall. One by one, major chain stores began to flee between the late 1970s and the early 1980s. The Gap and Montgomery Ward left. Galaxy Furniture Store shut down. Woodward and Lorthrop went bankrupt. The mall's once cutting-edge, modern sixties architecture began to deteriorate. With the rise of crack in the 1980s, guns started being run back and forth across the D.C. border. What major retailers remained became spooked at crime reports of shootings in the Iverson Mall parking lot. Headline after headline spoke of armed robberies and drive-by murders on the once idyllic Branch Avenue.

Even with those challenges, the crowd had much more money to spend than Fraley's earlier cohort. Wasn't their money green? In 1999, the *Washington Post* published a lengthy investigation of the struggles to attract quality retail in Prince George's County malls. It found that the average household income in the county ranked higher than state and national averages, and the outside-the-Beltway section of Prince George's County had more residents and higher household incomes than majority-white communities in Howard County to the north, as well as Loudoun and Prince William Counties in Virginia. It continued:

> Millionaires now have homes in many Prince George's communities, most notably Mitchellville. Despite these trends, a growing num-

ber of residents, developers and county officials say the number and quality of retailers does not match the county's demographics. And some say there are hints of racial discrimination in many retailers' decisions, whether it's bypassing the county or simply offering lesser merchandise. "I think we've known for some time that there is what appears to be substantial economic red-lining taking place in the retail community," said the County Council member Thomas R. Hendershot (D–New Carrollton). "The kind of shopping opportunities our residents want — Macy's and Nordstrom — have refused to locate in Prince George's County. . . . My own belief is that it has to do with the fact that the majority of residents in Prince George's County are African American."[3]

In 1999 I began spending time in Prince George's as a journalist, covering the local arts scene and youth culture in general; I found myself returning to Iverson Mall and Branch Avenue (also known as Route 5) over and over again. Forty years earlier, I might have been interviewing Fraley and the Grits. Instead, youth culture now was driven by go-go, which along this strip was not "almost mainstream" but *the* dominant economic and cultural force. All along Branch Avenue, go-go music and its fashion, dances, and entrepreneurs told the news: the Chocolate City was alive and well — in suburbia.

Iverson Mall had no Border's or Barnes and Noble to sell books. Instead, you bought your literature at Karibu Books, the largest chain of black bookstores in the country, all located in Prince George's County and owned by black D.C. natives, which hosted everyone from Maya Angelou to Toni Morrison and Walter Mosely.[4] There was no Tower Records or Best Buy. But you could buy the latest go-go and hip-hop releases at an independent, black-owned chain called PA Palace. A few blocks down Branch Avenue you could stop at the old Hot Shoppes restaurant, possibly finding teenagers creating the latest innovation in black dance.

Across the street from Iverson, you could find the Complex, a fifty-three-thousand-square-foot skeleton of an abandoned health and fitness club, where two lost souls of the night experienced a religious conversion via go-go music. Wander down the halls of Iverson Mall, and you could witness the birth of the Unity Clothing Association, which came together to ensure that the multimillion-dollar industry of D.C.-based urban wear stayed in black hands. You could see the award-winning Iverson Mall Walkers, a group of black seniors, seventeen hundred strong, who walked and line-danced their way to better health. Around the corner, there was Chuck Brown's weekly gig at the Legend nightclub.

And in the carcass of Iverson Mall's Galaxy Furniture store, in 2010 you would find Reverend Tony Lee leading his Community of Hope AME Church, a place where seventeen hundred members danced to go-go, hip-hop, and gospel rhythms, which gave them spiritual sustenance and faith in the unseen.

It was not the Pearly Gates as the old-timers had imagined them, but it provided deliverance just the same. Iverson Mall was considerably shabbier than an older generation would remember. But in many ways Branch Avenue had become the cultural beating heart of the new Chocolate City, where black people lived, died, danced, sang, prayed. The *Washington Post* wrote of early U Street, "Old Jim Crow shaped its earliest existence, creating rigid rules of engagement, but also, perversely, carving out a niche where black folks could be. African Americans didn't have a place to go, so they made their own. And they owned it."[5] The following scenes and character sketches took place along Branch Avenue in Prince George's in the first decade of the twenty-first century. Separate and not equal, the same as it ever was.

RIP Hot Rod, 2004

Sixteen-year-old Roderick "Hot Rod" Valentine had been dead for well over three months, but that day, I was in luck. Had I come to Iverson Mall a few days later, the images of the slain junior at D.C.'s H. D. Woodson Senior High would have been gone, much like the police report that has been lost in bureaucratic limbo, any witnesses who saw anything, or the outrage over "another senseless tragedy."

For now, there's still time. I drop $26 on the counter at Variety clothing store, and the owner Jas Singh flips through a binder until he finds the Valentine designs: there's Hot Rod, crouched down in a red jumpsuit with two middle fingers extended, framed by the words "R.I.P. Hot Rod" and the dates of his birth and death. There he is again, surrounded by three of his boys, all playfully cocking invisible guns for the camera. There's the teenager posing at homecoming with various finger gestures, accompanied by the phrases "In Loving Memory" and "Hot Rod, We Miss You."

I can pick one image and Singh will heat-press it onto a T-shirt for me.

Within hours of Valentine's death on 8 February, dozens of his classmates did and wore them to school. What is the proper way to mourn a life interrupted? Bereaved parents of the Victorian era pressed photographs of their dead babies lying in coffins onto postcards. Ancient Mexican townsfolk feasted, drank mescal, and burned incense when dead children's souls arrived each 1 November for the Day of the Dead. Around here, people buy RIP T-shirts. "It's like you know when somebody gets killed in D.C., it's going to be some shirts made," says Roderick's nineteen-year-old brother, Michael McDonald. "It's like a doctor hitting your knee. It's just a reflex."

Michael used to joke that his face was "too pretty to be on somebody's T-shirt." Then his little brother got shot—in the face—on a street in Northeast D.C. after a dispute at a go-go club. Now Michael has seven RIP T-shirts that bear a painful resemblance to his own face.

Beat Your Feet, 2002

Every Friday from 8 P.M. to around 3 A.M. at the New Hot Cafe—located in a strip mall off Maryland's Branch Avenue—two lines of teenagers form: one for girls and one for guys. Even before they walk past the off-duty cops cruising the parking lot shared with a Giant, Sonny's Barbershop, a nail salon, and a dollar store, they empty their pockets of all banned items. The pile on the sidewalk will include cell phones, pagers, pencils, pens, eyeliner, lipstick, cigarettes, matches, lighters, and chewing gum. In one line, young men in cornrows and dreadlocks crouch down to unlace their shoes. The ladies, wearing mostly tight jeans and skimpy tops, step out of clunky sandals and knee-high boots. An agent slaps the shoes to make sure there are no false bottoms holding shanks or other weapons. And the teens show the soles of their feet to prove nothing is taped there. A female guard performs a full-body pat-down on the young women, and a male guard searches the young men for weapons. The security officers also make small talk with the patrons, just to see if they might be hiding something in their mouths. For good measure off-duty police officers cruise the parking lot, running tags.

Once security has ensured that the New Hot Cafe is safer than any airport in the United States, girls pay a $10 cover, guys $15. The dance floor throbs in sync with TCB as the band members pound the timbales, congas, and rototoms and the sound roars through massive speakers, vibrating club windows and taking total command of the room. Hundreds of bodies answer the percussion in near darkness. Young women, hands on the floor, jiggle their flesh against whoever is standing behind them. The guys wander through the club rubbing themselves against random rear ends, gliding from partner to partner.

In the corner beside a bar stocked with generic soda and plastic Kool-Aid bottles, about twenty dancers drift into a circle. Two sixteen-year-olds, Donté Brooks and Charles Holcomb, are in the middle. They leap into the air with each beat, to return crashing onto the parquet dance floor. Their feet do not stop as Holcomb takes off his belt, ties it around his neck, and yanks it in the air. The feet remain in motion as Brooks grabs the belt and walks Holcomb across the circle like a dog. The feet pound as the young men knot their T-shirts and switch across the dance floor with an effeminate gait.

Tit for tat, they continue in this vein, acting out a procession of scenes for what seems like twenty minutes: Holcomb "baptizes" Brooks with water; Brooks's body trembles as with the spirit of the Holy Ghost. Holcomb casts a fishing pole behind him; Brooks grabs the pole, now a machete, and stabs Holcomb in the chest. Holcomb hoists a machine gun and pumps Brooks full of bullets; Brooks falls to the dance floor, his lifeless body twitching to the beat. For this, Holcomb has no answer. The crowd declares Brooks the winner, and the circle vanishes as quickly as it formed.

Most of the basic movements in black popular dance have been recycled throughout the years, popping up every twenty years or so under a new name. Beat Your Feet is no exception. Toward the middle of the twentieth century, black social dance split into two factions: the upwardly mobile African American elites that often frowned on those dance traditions seen as backward, and the black working class that kept patronizing blues-based establishments such as juke joints, after-hours clubs, membership clubs, and the like well into the 1960s.[6]

The latter looked a lot like contemporary go-gos. Heavy security hovered, and police were often called—sometimes too late—to prevent a killing. Some proprietors required their patrons to check their weapons at the door. But black dance traditions thrived in this environment. "These forms are ancient," the sociologist then known as Katrina Hazzard-Donald told me in a 2002 interview. "We are talking thousands of years here."

The Complex, 2002

Ken and Samantha Moore knew that some people see go-go as the devil's music. They knew its history, the violence associated with it. They knew that the Prince George's County police had linked go-go to half a dozen slayings in the summer of 2002 and had declared war on the row of clubs along Route 5 and in other parts of the county. And they knew this: that for some, the idea of gospel go-go was simply ludicrous, blasphemous even. But they were not buying it. "All music started with God first," Samantha says. "The angels in Heaven worshiped him with music. . . . Why can't we praise God in go-go music?"

They did not agree with the ministers who tried literally to pull the plug on gospel go-go in its infancy a decade ago. You have to reach people where they are, and a lot of kids in the Washington area love go-go. It's like Ken told patrons of the Complex one night when things were getting too rowdy: "If you want to fight, this is the place you need to be. If you want to have sex, this is the place you need to be. If you want to get high, this is the place you need to be." The Moores wanted trouble to walk through their doors. They wanted troubled souls to walk in and cleansed souls to walk out. Salvation can happen in a second, or it can take years, they say. It isn't a predictable thing—and, as the Moores will gladly testify, it certainly isn't pretty.

In the summer of 2002, when I met with Ken, then thirty-seven, and his wife, Samantha, who was in her twenties, they waved off menus at Jasper's restaurant in Largo. They had four more hours before their daily fast ended. They were allowed liquids, so Ken nursed a glass of water. Samantha sipped from a vanilla milkshake. Just two years earlier, Ken would not have dared sit as he did then, his back to the door and flanked by just one adoring woman. In his earlier life, he never traveled with an entourage of fewer than a dozen people—business associates, hangers-on, and women, lots of women.

That day, the balding, stocky man with curly red hair wore wire-rimmed glasses held together by tape. Under the table, he held hands with Samantha, a shapely woman with red highlights in her long, bouncy curls. He used to be known as Icy Ice. She was Pleazure. He ran several businesses, including a crew of exotic dancers—Daddies Girlz—a porn web site, and a number of go-go bands. His biggest moneymaker, though, was the Icebox, an all-ages go-go club in Northeast Washington. She was an exotic dancer with the group EWC (Entertainment with Class), known for its elaborate costumes and stylish stage shows. And Pleazure was the queen bee, the winner of numerous contests, among them "Miss Buns" and "Rumpshaker of D.C."

The first time she saw her future husband, he was running around in his Northwest Washington strip club, 1919, smacking dancers on the rear. "Who is this freak?" she thought to herself. "His hair was all over his head. He was running around freaking on them, and he wasn't even tipping." She had agreed to work at the club for a few nights for extra money. Backstage, Ice laid his hand on her famous posterior. "I thought, 'I am the Rumpshaker of D.C., this is so beneath me.' But I needed the money," Samantha laughed.

Soon, though, the two learned they had more in common than the world of adult entertainment. Both had grown up without fathers, had started their street lives as teenagers, and shared a similar sense of humor. "I got her number off the bathroom wall," Ken joked. "He was funny," Samantha snapped back—"and funny-looking." Then Ken turned serious. "Everyone at some point meets their match," he says. "I was looking for a relationship. I would run with women, but I had nobody that could settle me down." "I tamed you," Samantha said, throwing an invisible lasso at her husband.

By the end of the summer of 2000, Samantha was working full-time for her boyfriend, and he had given up his stable of lovers—mostly. They moved in together. That summer Ice also started working on a big business deal. The Icebox, the Northeast D.C. club that had for years packed in thousands of teenagers, paying between $5 and $50 admission three nights each week, had finally been closed because of City Code violations. So the entrepreneur took his savings—he says it was $1.6 million—and along with some business partners leased the Complex, a former fitness club.

He saw too many dollar signs to fully consider just what it really would cost to keep the enormous structure operating. The building, right next to the Skate Palace, was past its prime. But it had fifty-three thousand square feet, a pool, racquetball courts, an indoor track, even a movie theater. For months he poured tens of thousands of dollars into renovations. In the meantime, the Complex became a gathering place for friends and business associates. Ice took pictures for the porn web site there. The strippers, including Pleazure, would use the racquetball courts to practice routines. In time, they believed, the Complex would become the area's biggest and most lucrative go-go club ever — right there on Route 5. Right there in Prince George's County. "It was going to be the world's largest party spot," Ken said.

The couple had been together for about a year when Bishop Donald Downing started coming around. The leader of Heart to Heart Christian Center, Ken's sister's church in Fort Washington, Maryland, wanted Ken's help packaging a gospel CD. "I walked in and saw all those children of darkness, as we call them," recalls Downing, a man with his own worldly past as an R&B singer in the 1960s and 1970s. He knew to keep his indignation to himself — and to wait. Each time Downing visited the Complex, Ice and Pleazure seemed to have more and more questions. "They were just like starving people," Downing says. "Truthfully, I've never seen a couple more hungry for God."

Pleazure, who had spent years dancing, was weary. "I was so young, but I had already seen so much," she says. Dancers being stalked and killed. Girls getting locked up, raped, robbed, beaten. The alcoholism, drug abuse, degradation, the humiliation, the misery — all had taken their toll. Ice looked back on all the times that friends and associates had died in his arms. He was tired of sleepless nights, of always watching his back. "I had been down some very dark alleys," Ken says now. "I was just doing so many things. I had pretty much experienced everything. It just got old."

The day Ice's sister became a minister at the nondenominational Heart to Heart Christian Center, the couple went to church for the ceremony. They returned to the fourteen-year-old church for several Sundays after that. At the service on 8 July 2001, Downing asked if any of those present wanted to pledge their lives to God. Pleazure felt her hand rising. She looked over, and Ice's hand was already in the air. Two weeks later, they were baptized. A week after that, they had their marriage license. "God worked fast for us," Ken says. "He delivered us from lust, smoking cigarettes, drinking, getting high, and it all happened immediately. All I can attribute that to is the receiving of the Holy Ghost."

Samantha quit the life first. "Once you get rid of those dancing boots, that's when you know a dancer has retired," she says. It took a few weeks longer for Ken, who puzzled his colleagues at the strip club many nights as he sat reading his Bible at the bar.

Next he dissolved or signed over to business partners control of all his former companies. Ken and Samantha married that October. For Ken's birthday party in November, the couple decided to open up the Complex for a "Holy Ghost Workout," a big party featuring several of the area's leading gospel go-go bands.

The young people who came partied hard just like at a regular go-go, except they did not have to pass through metal detectors, did not face invasive security searches, did not hear dueling neighborhood crews competing over who could shout their names the loudest—a go-go tradition that too often can end in violence. Instead, bands called out the names of various churches. The Moores decided to repeat the Holy Ghost Workout every Saturday after that.

The day his sister, Margo Valentine, came to bless the building, Ken cried. The Complex had completed a conversion of its own.

The lead rapper of the Submission Band, Damont "TWO" Wood, was on the mike, firing up the crowd like a boxing promoter at ringside: "Let's get ready to praise God!" The bass groove, congas, drums, and cowbells detonated from the stage, and there was an explosion of movement among the crowd of about three hundred at the Complex in February. Many of the revelers had been dropped off by church vans or their parents.

"Tell me wh-wh-where y'all from!" Woods sang. "Wh-wh-where y'all from?" "Ebenezer!" some in the audience screamed out. "Faith City!" shouted others. "Tabernacle!" The band would pause for a Beat Your Feet dance contest onstage and for regular "altar calls," in which young people marched to the stage to pledge their lives to God.

The scene would repeat every Saturday for months, with gospel go-go bands from the entire area. Soon the Complex would become a gospel hot spot. But soon things began to change.

Maybe, the Moores think now, they fell victim to their own success. Word spread that the gospel go-go bands at the Complex "cranked," and more kids started coming, kids who had not already been "saved"—just as the couple had hoped. They would find kids who smelled of marijuana or alcohol. Fights became a problem, like at the other go-gos. Samantha and Ken reluctantly agreed to install a metal detector and to hire more security. It was beginning to look more and more like too many other scenes along Route 5. But the Moores were still believers. They saw that some of the kids mocked the whole idea of the Complex, but they listened to those who called the club their church and meant it. They were dealing with kids "most people are scared of," Ken says.

But they were also going through their savings fast. Soon, financial problems began to overwhelm them. Ken's business partners, who had not shared in his religious conversion, pulled out soon after the Complex became a gospel go-go. The Moores had been going it alone. There was rent, heating and gas bills, leaky roofs, staff to be paid. When the sound system finally went that June, they knew the end had come. In July 2002, the Complex was served with an eviction notice.

"Every dollar I made from every company I owned is in this place," Ken told me in 2002, sitting in one of the Complex's cavernous rooms. He and Samantha were staying with relatives for the time being. Ken had experience in food service management, he said, and Samantha had trained as a beautician. But the Moores were convinced that they had found their calling. "God has told us that this is the place," Samantha said. Their days were spent fasting and praying, attending church, and trying to figure out a way to revive their vision. "People are going to be shocked," they said, "when God finds a way to reopen the Complex." As Ken told me: "What's too hard for God?"

Unity Clothing Association, 2004

When Visionz urban clothing opened its doors at Iverson Mall in January 2004, the line looked a lot like the other thirty or so D.C.-based sportswear brands commanding upward of $100 a T-shirt, with the same quality and workmanship — only it cost a lot less. Helped by endorsements from the popular black comedian Billy the Kid — who at one point claimed to be a co-owner — the line became instantly ubiquitous on basketball courts, at clubs, and on the street. What buyers did not know was that the real force behind the line — the vision behind Visionz — was Jung Won Kang, a Korean-born entrepreneur who had been manufacturing most of the black-owned companies' clothes out of his factory in nearby northern Virginia for years.

At the rate Visionz was going, the area's black T-shirt designers figured it was only a matter of time before Kang would put them out of business. "We got two things in this town, urban wear and go-go," says Steve Briscoe, owner of Xtra Ordinary Clothes on St. Barnabas Road. "This is our culture, this is our identity." So the Unity Clothing Association was hastily formed, and it immediately set about "educating" the public about Visionz's true ownership through a flood of fliers at clubs, basketball courts, and at Iverson Mall. "There is already a carryout and liquor store in every black community run by Asians," the fliers pleaded. "How long will we let them RAPE the Urban community? Wake Up! Don't be Bamboozled or Hoodwinked!" The association spent thousands for a community picnic outside a club in Capitol Heights and broadcast its message through community bullhorns like the go-go talkers and the street basketball commentators, giving out hundreds of T-shirts with the words "Visionz: Asian Wear" inside a red circle and slash. The association also entreated the public to "support your local black business," helpfully listing nearly two dozen black-owned companies.

That was not all. The association leaned on Kang's two black pitchmen—Billy the Kid and Polo, the leader of the go-go band TCB. For those who had already bought Visionz clothes, they offered amnesty: customers could exchange Kang's Visionz brand T-shirt for a black-owned line, free of charge, "just like a gun buy-back program." "We are hoping that Mr. Kang will just go back to making clothes," said Ronald "Mo" Moten, the community activist and concert promoter tapped to lead the Unity Clothing Association. "He'll realize what he did was wrong, and we can continue having a good relationship."

Kang, however, had no such plans. In fact he had planned to open another location, at Springfield Mall. He said the Visionz storefronts were just "sample stores," part of a plan to ultimately take his company national. "If Mr. Kang wanted to take over D.C., we would have done it already," said Daniel Montgomery, a design consultant for Visionz's parent company, East Coast Inc. "They should have a little bit more faith in somebody they've been dealing with for a long time. Mr. Kang doesn't undercut people. Mr. Kang is open, he's honest."

This drew a lot of shaking heads across town. I crossed back over the D.C. line, where inside the back office of a Georgia Avenue storefront, the figurative granddaddies of Washington's urban clothing scene, the originators who perfected "out the trunk" commerce in the early 1980s, were shaking their heads. "We've been doing this for twenty years, feeding our kids and grandkids," said Ty Johnson, the fifty-two-year-old co-founder of Universal Madness, his silver hair in cornrows, perched on a desk beside his partner, Eddie Van.

They introduced a generation of Washingtonians to the ultimate legitimate business hustle, creating a blueprint for building a clothing brand, a method that has not changed much since: Buy a bunch of T-shirt designs from young artists with an eye to the streets. Peddle them at clubs and concerts out of your van. Get the hottest go-go bands to wear them. Set up a storefront in your neighborhood. Count your money. "Ty and Eddie were like uncles to me," said Billy the Kid, who peddled Madness at his high school and his Southeast neighborhood. "They showed me how to stay out of the street."

As other entrepreneurs joined the Madness-inspired T-shirt gold rush, Johnson and Van established a wholesale division, Absolut Images, run by Billy the Kid's sister, Joann Robinson. The company silk-screened mono-grammed T-shirts alongside the logos of the many companies that suc-cessfully followed the blueprint. But their reign ended in 1995, when John-son and Van were jailed on drug charges. By then, the game had begun to change anyway. Kids wanted T-shirts with elaborate embroidered de-signs. That was around the time Kang began going door to door to differ-ent shops, offering his embroidery services from the basement of his Vir-ginia home. "He would pick up the merchandise and deliver it to the store owners on the same day, which was unheard of," said Robert "Shooters Rob" George, the owner of three SHOOTERS stores in the D.C. area and Baltimore.

Kang soon mastered the popular puff embroidery style and eventually opened a factory to meet demand. A few years later, he opened another factory in Huntington Beach, California, where the T-shirts were cut and sewn, allowing black designers to eliminate another step. "He was a one-stop shop," George claimed. In the Washington market, a cultural island where styles change on a weekly basis, Kang quickly became indispens-able. His company, East Coast, provided a custom-made product with-out the high minimum orders required by many overseas suppliers. By the late 1990s, Kang had become the go-to man for product, and almost everyone on the scene has used him at some point. Some of the bigger companies, such as the popular HOBO line, which employs ten full-time tailors in its own factory, have weaned themselves from Kang in recent years. Some of them have tried to use other tailors, but none are as flexible and capable of producing high-quality output in volume. Those who do not use Kang find it hard to compete. Van and Johnson, whose Madness line remained popular, went to Kang too, starting in 1999. "I knew from day one what he was trying to do," Johnson said. "He got his Visionz from our visions." Van agreed: "That's where it came from, our eyes."

Johnson said the Unity Clothing Association better get its act together, because the threat was serious, "because Mr. Kang—he's a baaaaad man," as Van said. Added Johnson: "He's a genius."

When I caught up with Kang in the office of his Virginia factory, he sat on a black leather couch, silver snaking through his slightly thinning hair, his expression stoic. Far from being a maven of urban style, he looked like any other fifty-two-year-old suburban dad with a short-sleeved polo shirt tucked into black slacks. A photo of him, his stay-at-home wife, and two teenage sons hung on the wall, along with watercolors of Korean landscapes. He spent most of his adult life in the apparel business. One of five children, the son of a doctor and a homemaker, Kang took his first job at a T-shirt and underwear factory right out of college. In 1991 he moved to the United States, where he had family and his two small sons could get a better education. The vision for his own clothing line first emerged in 1993, when he went to a trade show in New York and saw sportswear decorated with elaborate embroidery. He tried several of his own lines, but none really took off. The manufacturing side of his company, however, did—enough to move out of his basement, open two factories, and eventually employ nearly thirty people. "His clients were growing, so he felt the need to study this business more," Montgomery said. "As word got around and his clients grew, he had to focus on them."

By the summer of 2003, Kang began to run into financial problems. He stopped taking orders from smaller companies and told the bigger storefront customers that he would be coming out with his own line, one he ultimately wanted to expand into Georgia and the Carolinas. He leased a storefront in Iverson Mall. He hired Billy the Kid, whom he had known for years from his work on the clothing scene and who by then was fast making a name for himself in the city as a comedian. Billy the Kid became his top seller. This time, Kang's line took off. He was surprised when one of the anti-Asian fliers, bearing names of his embroidery clients, made its way to the factory, but he "understands what some of the customers on that flier are saying," Montgomery said, speaking to fears that Kang's line might flood the market.

At the moment, outside his office door, a loud hum echoes through the five-thousand-square-foot factory where forty-two sewing machines run simultaneously. It is a run for ALLDAZ, one of several clients who, though they are part of the Unity Clothing Association, continue to patronize him. "He believes he has good customers that come to him still," Montgomery says. "As long as he has his own vision and his own goals, this won't be a hindrance in the future." Then Visionz will have to do it without the help of its star salesman, who informed the company two weeks ago he was leaving for California to pursue his career as an actor and comedian. "Now he's gone Hollywood," Montgomery says, and Kang beams a proud smile.

When I caught up with Billy the Kid a few days later, he was, in fact, sitting some three thousand miles east of L.A. in a booth at Cranberry's restaurant in Forestville, Maryland. "Yeah, I told them I was going to California," he shrugged. "I'm not about to burn my bridges. I have no problems with Kang." Bald and plump, the comedian wore a plain white T-shirt with a Visionz logo on it, a diamond-encrusted stud flashing from his left ear. When Kang offered the thirty-three-year-old with three daughters a job with Visionz a few months ago, it seemed like a good way to pass the time when he was not hosting local go-go shows or traveling for stand-up comedy gigs. "A Korean offered us free clothing and money," Billy the Kid says. "What's easier than that? It was nothing but a business opportunity." Billy the Kid grew up in the clothing game while living in the public housing complex of Barry Farms, and he had worked or repped for all the major clothing lines at one time or another, especially Madness and HOBO. He knew exactly how to increase his sales and performance-related bonus.

He would call his friend at Nike and ask him what the colors for the new sneakers would be the following week, then tell Kang what colors to bring to complete the outfit. He got Polo to wear the clothes and do in-store CD signings for TCB; he had friends in the other go-go bands wear them. He told customers at the Iverson store, where he worked part time, that he and Polo owned Visionz—with the disclaimer "for commission purposes only." "You got ten kids coming in with a pocketful of money," he says. "'This TCB's clothing line?' 'Yeeeup.' 'Who the Chinese people?' 'That's my connect.'" But after the fliers and phone calls, "it was starting to get hostile. My sugar is going up and down, my diabetes flaring up. You can't be an angry comedian. Crazy, ain't it? Over some clothes. I had less problems selling drugs." So he gave in. His agent worked up a contract with the Unity Clothing Association. He would be paid $375 a week and host all the events sponsored by the association and its affiliates. He has seventeen gigs lined up this year alone. Polo got a similar financial arrangement. "They gave me a Michael Jordan deal," Billy the Kid says. "It let me know how important I was to the cause."

Just a few months earlier, sitting down for dinner together would have been unthinkable. As one of the participants around the table at Jasper's restaurant in Largo observed, "Half of us wouldn't trust each other in the street." But they were all there: representing uptown and Northeast, Southeast and Maryland, more than thirty of them, all owners of Washington-area storefronts meeting as the newly chartered Unity Clothing Association. "The power that this symbolizes is unmatched," claimed Pamela Crockett, an attorney tapped to be the association's consigliere. "In the history of recorded thought, this has never been done by people like us."

"This right here is a nuclear bomb," agreed Harold Redd, the owner of Squash All Beefs clothing store. "They never wanted a group of black men, the trendsetters, to get together. Let us all get paid off this power." Feasting together as brothers, they saw nothing but possibilities. They could incorporate, take it national. Start registering voters in the stores. The meeting adjourned with a prayer and a word of gratitude for the man who was not invited, the one who made the dinner possible. "I want to thank Mr. Kang for bringing all of us here together," said the HOBO shop owner John E. Day, dangling a toothpick between his lips. "It took a while."

Community of Hope, 2010

On 12 January 2010, a catastrophic earthquake devastated the island of Haiti, killing more than two hundred thousand people and making nearly a million Haitians homeless. On 18 January 2010, on the lower level of Iverson Mall, where the Galaxy Furniture store once stood, a stage, lights, and a PA system were set up for the Haiti Relief Benefit Concert. The room was filled with teenagers and young adults off from work and school for the holiday honoring Martin Luther King Jr.'s birthday. Dre "Mayday" Hines, the twenty-two-year-old lead talker of Peculiar People, gripped a microphone and paced back and forth across the stage in jeans and a crisp white T-shirt. A full-service go-go band stood behind him, ready for him to give the cue. But first, he explained what the song was about:

> I know everybody got our issues. That's how I know we can all relate to them over there. You hear me? I know we're not strangers to pain. I know we're not strangers to a struggle. We're saying, look. It's horrible what happened over there. But look, with God, you can make it

through anything. So look, in this next song, man, we're talking about dancing through our struggle. We don't run from the storms. We learn and grow in them. We're dancing in the rain over here. We're dancing through the struggle and our pain.

It was a message to which Reverend Tony Lee could relate as he looked proudly at the crowd assembled at his church. He was a bit of a storm-chaser himself. As soon as he saw the images of devastation that came across the television screen, he knew what he had to do. Thanks to both his religious training at Union Theological Seminary and his life as a veteran of D.C.'s Murder Capital days, he had come to learn a few things about how to cope with tragedy. For the past ten years, he averaged one eulogy per month. Roughly half of them were for young people who had died of unnatural causes. As terrible as that was, he remembered a time that was much worse. Like in high school in the 1980s, when he had opened the paper every morning to see who had been killed the night before. Or when he was in seminary in New York and almost quit because he had to keep coming back to D.C. for funerals. One semester, he had to return seven times:

> I've buried more friends than I have fingers and toes to count. And by friends, I don't mean acquaintances. I mean people who ate dinner at my mama's table.
>
> I realized I was effective at helping people through grief because I'd grieved so much. Murder in D.C. had become normative. Normative—but not acceptable. One of my friends said I'm a professional eulogist. Because I've been on the side of grieving, in a family's most painful moment, I consider it an honor that I would be the one that can hopefully bring comfort to them. Part of my role as a minister is to be able to stand in the gap to help them to get on the other side. If you don't do that well, the cycle of violence will continue. . . . That's why I felt compelled to start the Community of Hope where it is. Really we want to be in a space where you can find that hope. To be able to find that redemption.

Lee had been a believer in go-go since 1979, when a sixth grader friend slipped in a tape of Trouble Funk. When he heard the synthesizer riff whizz *jooooong-joooong*, he asked, "What is that?" His friend answered: "Oh, that's a juju stick." Lee laughed, recalling the memory over dinner at Graces Restaurant at National Harbor. In 2010, the latter was one of four new upscale shopping centers that had popped up in Prince George's County since the *Washington Post* had done its investigation about redlining in the county. Lee wore jeans and a black T-shirt with the SHOOTERS logo. His hair was braided in neat cornrows that snaked down his back.

As he was growing up in Southeast Washington and later in Fort Washington, Maryland, Lee's parents (his father worked in the Air Force and his mother was a school nurse at Ballou High School) did not allow him to go to the clubs. But go-go came to him, through city-sponsored mobile stages. He watched live bands in summer camp. After the family moved to Prince George's County, and he got his driver's license, he became known for packing twelve people into his tiny Ford Grenada to shows.

So that is why, after he graduated from the University of Maryland, College Park, and got his master's degree from seminary, he thought it only natural to start a go-go band called Ghetto 4 Christ. When the band tried to practice one day at a Christian studio, the managers cut off the power and delivered a stern lecture. "It was the go-go, the *movement of the bodies*," Lee recalled. "He sat us down and told us it wasn't of God."

Like Samantha and Ken Moore, whose efforts he supported, Lee was not buying it. He had spent his whole life in the Chocolate City, on both sides of the D.C./Prince George's border, where there is little contact with white people. Tensions over class become very clear when they are not blurred or confused by the overlapping issues related to the history of racism. Lee believed, then as he does now, that much of the negativity directed against go-go music stems from deep-seated class issues. "Go-go is an easy scapegoat," Lee said. "People won't always be honest about the class warfare that is taking place. Instead of doing what needs to be done to help people with regard to public policy, they think the answer is to displace a whole class of people. It's thinly disguised generational and class warfare."

Throughout his career, Lee has straddled the three worlds that collide in the Chocolate City: the bourgeois elite, the working class, and the young people of all classes whose lives intersect at schools, churches, and go-gos. Lee began his career as a youth minister at Ebenezer AME, the wealthy, powerful, and politically connected seventeen-thousand-member-strong church in Prince George's led by two progressive and intellectual powerhouses, the pastors Grainger Browning Jr. and Jo Ann Browning. The church's path tracks that of the Chocolate City as a whole. It was founded in 1856, when thirteen "colored members" left Mt. Zion

Methodist Episcopal Church in Georgetown because of discrimination and segregation. They wanted to "establish a church by colored folks with colored pastors where they would worship in dignity, spirit and truth."[7] They worshiped at their Georgetown location at 2727 O Street for more than a century. By 1983, few black people remained in Georgetown, and that was reflected in the membership of just seventeen members. So the church sold the Georgetown building and relocated to Prince George's County, where it was reborn into a political and economic powerhouse.

When Lee became Ebenezer's youth minister in 1999, he immediately put the church's $1 million budget for youth programs to use. He supported a whole generation of gospel go-go bands at a time when many church elders objected. On Easter Sunday 2006, with the blessing of Ebenezer, Lee went out on his own and started Community of Hope Church. The inaugural service made local headlines because of its location: the Legend nightclub, known for hosting go-gos and popular stripper nights. Lee covered the liquor bottles with white sheets, ignored whatever ungodly substances made his shoes stick to the stage, and preached the first sermon at Community of Hope.

Within nine months, the congregation outgrew the space. At first, Lee tried to lease the still vacant Complex building, fulfilling the prophecy of the Moores. But when negotiations fell through, he looked to Iverson Mall across the street, perhaps an even more high-profile space everyone knew how to get to. By the summer of 2010, the Community of Hope had seventeen hundred members, ranging from Pulitzer Prize–winning writers and professionals to former strippers and drug dealers. Each New Year's Eve service, the church screens thousands for HIV. Community of Hope regularly hosts gospel and secular go-go bands at the church for fundraisers and health screenings. In addition to the neo-Pentecostal sermons, both hip-hop and go-go are incorporated into the services. Lee also hosts the Sunday morning gospel shows for WPGC, a popular FM radio station. The Community of Hope is the meeting place of the sacred and the secular, the young and the old, the square and the hip, the church and the street.

The benefit show on Martin Luther King Day featured both gospel go-go bands such as Peculiar People and secular bands such as Backyard Band. At the end of the night Lee had collected $5,000 to send to Haiti for relief efforts. The crowd at the concert exploded as the Peculiar People lead talker Mayday launched the crowd favorite "Dance in the Rain." The

song had an aggressive, hard edge, and fans threw up parasols while dancing along to a message that connected the struggle across the black diaspora. "We don't run from the rain, we learn through it. We gon' sing this
song so loud that they can hear us all the way in Haiti," Mayday said, jab-
bing his left index finger toward the islands across the water.

Clouds are rolling into my life
It's getting darker faster outside
When the raindrops fall,
Cold as ice but I'm not surprised

I refuse to travel inside
Overlook the beauty God shines
Cause if I go, I'll miss
The rainbow that's created from this

I'll
Just
Dance
In
The rain

8 ★ Mr. Obama's Washington, D.C.

My father was a white and my mother was black. Them call me half-caste or whatever. Me don't dip on nobody's side. Me don't dip on the black man's side nor the white man's side. Me dip on God's side, the one who create me and cause me to come from black and white. —BOB MARLEY

My ancestors were constantly on the move. They came from Africa and Pakistan, India, Europe, and parts of the Caribbean. They joined with nomadic Amerindian peoples, settled in Guyana, and then emigrated to Canada, where I was born. Since my family moved to the United States when I was almost ten years old, I have been an avid student of two strange species: American White People and American Black People.

I had just moved to suburban Indianapolis in 1986 when I casually mentioned to my first black friend, January, that I listened to the Top 40 rock music radio station WZPL. She was incredulous. No, you're supposed to listen to the black station, WTLC! I was the only black person in my "gifted and talented" classes, the new girl who spoke fluent French and English with a Canadian accent at a time when immigrants were rare in Indiana. At middle school, I wandered aimlessly, awkwardly around the lunchroom looking for somewhere to sit. Eventually the black kids bused in from the city claimed me, even though we were not neighbors and they probably found me strange.

Meanwhile, at our home in suburban Beech Grove, Indiana, the epithets, threats, and terrorism hurled at me and my siblings on the streets from white people only reinforced the message: This is America; stay in your lane and keep it moving. On another move to Florida, where I graduated high school, I found more of the same. You could add in large numbers of Haitian and Latino immigrants in their own section of the "black" side of the school cafeteria, but otherwise there was basically the same racial caste system in place.

Then I arrived in Washington, D.C., this alternate universe in the nation's capital where everyone I encountered was black. Howard University's curriculum, framed through the lens of the African diaspora, proved a revelation. It completely inverted the world order as I had learned and experienced it, tilting it definitely to the east. Living in D.C. after graduation, I quickly fell into step with the rhythms of the Chocolate City, where this expat not only found a "home" but also joined a conversation that had been going on for millennia.[1] I exchanged greetings with everyone I encountered on the street—from D.C. natives to other black transplants from Addis Ababa to Itta Bena. Even if I had never met them before, they knew me, and I knew them.

In 1995, during the Million Man March it was *we doing this for you, Sis.* Skip to 1998 at my first D.C. apartment, and it was the neighborhood bum/building superintendent: *can you believe your landlady asked me to do that?* In the late 1990s, as gentrification picked up speed, the most popular topic on the street was the increase in late-night white-people sightings: *you know they coming, right?* In 2004, I picked up the same thread with the grocery store clerk: *why we couldn't get fresh produce when WE lived here?* In 2008, it was ending the conversation at Ben's Chili Bowl with an eye roll: *now you KNOW white people ain't voting for nobody named Barack Hussein Obama!*

I lived happily in the Chocolate City, wearing my own hard-earned racial cynicism like an itchy blanket. I only began to loosen my grip on it when I watched Barack Obama's victory speech through tears. I could hear the black church in the crests and waves of his voice as he paid tribute to his black wife and daughters in front of him—and to the deceased white grandparents behind him. There in Chicago on 4 November 2008, he announced the response to his audacious call to the United States:

If there is anyone out there who still doubts that America is a place where all things are possible; who still wonders if the dream of our founders is alive in our time; who still questions the power of our democracy, tonight is your answer. It's the answer told by lines that stretched around schools and churches in numbers this nation has never seen; by people who waited three hours and four hours, many for the very first time in their lives, because they believed that this time must be different; that their voice could be that difference. It's the answer spoken by young and old, rich and poor, Democrat and Republican, black, white, Hispanic, Asian, Native American, gay, straight, disabled and not disabled—Americans who sent a message to the world that we have never been a collection of Red States and Blue States: we are, and always will be, the United States of America. It's the answer that led those who have been told for so long by so many to be cynical, and fearful, and doubtful of what we can achieve to put their hands on the arc of history and bend it once more toward the hope of a better day. It's been a long time coming, but tonight, because of what we did on this day, in this election, at this defining moment, change has come to America.

There is no getting over world history and its endless game of racial musical chairs, the dusty carcasses of white victors and blacks defeated. But on that cold November day, in that defining moment, I realized that I did not know American White People at all.

All of this is to say that I am still scratching my head, trying hard to make sense of Mr. Obama's Washington, D.C. Obama's arrival coincided with some powerful forces in the urban United States, the dismantling of public housing and a general return of what Richard Florida called the "creative class" to the cities.[2] Even before the Obamas came to town, D.C. was the most diverse it had been in a generation. The tax base was up, allowing the city to make countless improvements in city services. Crumbling, centuries-old school buildings were repaired, and new ones came up from the ground. Parks were revitalized; trash was picked up more regularly. The violent crime rate hovered the lowest it had since the 1950s. The fires of 1968 were finally being put out (or perhaps displaced).

Change is hard. It is impossible to overstate the profound psychological adjustments that the capital city's new purple and gray reality requires. In the summer of 2010, hundreds of thousands of anti-Obama Tea Party

protestors—most of them white—traveled to Washington from all corners of the United States on the anniversary of Martin Luther King's "I
Have a Dream" speech. As they gathered on the National Mall, they announced a message of muddled anger whose logic I strained to follow.
But the emotional truth I heard was a longing to return to a time they felt
was more comfortable, safe, and secure. In the 1770s, whether power was
centered in London or in Philadelphia, the white patriarchal world order
was clear. This new purple and gray reality? Not so much.

On a much smaller scale, with the death of the Chocolate City, I could
relate to their slightly unhinged *something-ain't-right* feeling. Just as I was
caught off guard by the sightings of white people in New Orleans' historically black Tremé neighborhood, the corners in which white people
can now be seen in D.C. constantly disorient me. It feels like an entirely
different city than the one I arrived in as a seventeen-year-old in 1994. As
Chuck Brown told me, "I remember the time when the only white people
you saw on U Street was the police!"

Where am I? Who am I? Huh?

And then, there is the issue of that *White* House. It took me about a
year to believe that I would not wake up from a dream narrated by George
Clinton and P-Funk. That it was really Barack, Michelle, Sasha, Malia,
and Grandma Robinson chilling at 1600 Pennsylvania Avenue. *President
Barack Hussein Obama.* I felt the same sense of vertigo when the National
Mall finally became integrated by a thirty-feet-tall white-stone sculpture
of Martin Luther King Jr. on 16 October 2011, the anniversary of the Million Man March. The Tea Partiers were feeling nostalgic about the "good"
old days of white privilege. Some days, walking the streets of Washington,
a colder place where people do not exchange greetings, I feel nostalgic for
the "good" old days of black privilege that Clinton crooned about in his
classic song of 1976, "Chocolate City":

> And when they come to march on ya
> Tell 'em to make sure they got their James Brown pass
> And don't be surprised if Ali is in the White House
> Reverend Ike, Secretary of the Treasure
> Richard Pryor, Minister of Education
> Stevie Wonder, Secretary of FINE arts
> And Miss Aretha Franklin, the First Lady
> Are you out there, C.C.?

A chocolate city is no dream
It's my piece of the rock and I dig you, C.C.

This black privilege had its ultimate manifestation in go-go music. Having your own dedicated music industry is a luxury few other cities can afford, let alone a cash-strapped urban center like D.C. Wherever you lived in the United States, depending on how you worked it, segregation might have worked really well, or it could have worked really badly. For better or worse, it was just the way things were.

Now, the Chocolate City is dying. That it gave way to Mr. Obama's Washington is no coincidence; it's poetic justice. The same change in attitudes that caused a generation of whites to release their fears and return to the urban centers their parents fled a generation ago is the one that allowed millions of white Americans, in the quiet sanctity of a voting booth, to vote for a black man. Where change ultimately leads may be unknown, but hope is faith that the direction is always forward. The world is flat—it always has been. Constant change is just the way things are.

★　　★　　★　　★　　★　　★　　★　　★　　★

Habermas believed that public spheres in their most ideal form constituted a physical space, places where people can meet and exchange ideas face to face. There is no better place to see this theory in action than in Washington, D.C.: on the House and Senate floors, at the memorials for the Vietnam and the Second World Wars on the National Mall, in the Smithsonian museums—and in the go-go clubs. These physical places are repositories of our national collective memory and the nexus of debate for the pressing issues of the day, whether they concern national governance, education, policy, slavery, poverty, or civil rights. The country's racially fraught history is the reason why the Chocolate City arose at this same intersection. Washington and D.C., go-go and "mainstream" music public spheres appear separate and diametrically opposed. In reality, however, they overlap. Federal Washington and black D.C. are two sides of the proverbial coin.

It is because of the symbolic importance of the District of Columbia that it often serves as a laboratory for social innovation—and for issues of race and justice. That is why Martin Luther King planned to use the city as a backdrop for his aborted Poor People's March on the National Mall in 1968. King had prepared to gather thousands of people in Washington in the wake of a string of uprisings in urban centers that had exploded into fiery and sometimes violent racial rebellions. King never lived to see the plan of the march come to fruition because he was assassinated in April 1968. Following his death, an angry crowd of residents of the District of Columbia looted and burned stores in black neighborhoods, destroying the economic infrastructure in the black city within a city, violently rejecting segregation. These demonstrations devastated a community already reeling from middle-class suburban flight, which had both blackened and impoverished the city's core.

The violence and mayhem that erupted following King's death set the physical stage for the birth of go-go. The rebellion of 1968 reflected a distinctly consumerist, capitalistic, and hedonistic rage. The go-go scene filled a power vacuum, bringing together a steady crowd of Washingtonians in and around the city's core for fellowship, communion, and the expression of a postriot, post–civil rights movement urban reality. This new musical form helped bring new life to the charred urban core.

Those who demanded that blacks rebuild the city after the riots only partly delivered on this promise of a prosperous Chocolate City. Black elected leaders governed a greatly diminished tax base and a physically depressed, riot-scarred infrastructure with limited access to development funding. Transportation policies were hostile to it. Businesses had little access to capital. Go-go flourished both because of and in spite of the decades of adversity that preceded the riots and intensified after them. Go-go established musical spaces in the ruins of social upheaval: in crumbling historic performance spaces such as the Howard Theatre, in hole-in-the wall nightclubs such as the Maverick Room; in backyards, community centers, and parks.

Postindustrial, postsegregation socioeconomic conditions gave rise to a parallel underground economy in the District of Columbia. The brutal jousting over drug profits showed U.S. capitalism at its most ruthless and bloody. The go-go underground economy quickly became a primary economy for many black urban dwellers. Go-go music and merchandise became a hot commodity. Much like its historical antecedents—blues clubs, rent parties, juke joints, and early jazz communities in New York—it functioned at the center of the black public sphere. Go-go lived both because of and despite these adverse conditions. Thus the spectacle of a government building moonlighting as a go-go became not only possible but went largely unnoticed by the mainstream media. Club U embodied the arts-based, mixed-use development strategies that would later be adopted all over the world by the "creative class." But the city's rejection of Club U demonstrates how race and class often determine what policy-makers define as "art."

The Migration

In chapter 2, I demonstrated how within this municipal body, a single, bloody Washington intersection located at the corner of Fourteenth and U Streets came to serve as the historical, ritual, and spiritual center of black Washington, and constituted a publicly owned sphere. I examined the moment in 2005 when more blood was spilled at this sacred intersec-tion. The debate about the murder of Terrance Brown and the future of Club U became another historical instance in which this specific physical space came to function as a proxy for race relations and the larger socio-political shifts going on in the city. In that chapter, I also made a case for black Washington as the political and cultural capital of black America, in part due to its unique positioning in the history of slavery and the city's federal and colonial governance structure. The city's structure and history have had mixed implications for blacks living there. Various White House administrations helped promote the cause of black self-determination to varying degrees, yet as a whole, the city emerged as a privileged place for blacks, with high levels of black homeownership, education, and employ-ment compared to other urban centers. The presence of the historically black Howard University also contributed to the city's status as a Choco-late City.

The debate about the future of Club U exposed yet another seismic shift in the District of Columbia: by the mid-2000s black residents no longer constituted the majority of property owners in the city. The city was reversing its course, a correction taking place in urban centers across the United States. White, well-to-do residents returned to the U Street corridor, leading to another rebirth of the business strip following the de-pressed "normal" of D.C's "Murder Capital" days. Thus the end of Club U told the larger tale of gentrification. It sounded the death knell for the Chocolate City, as black enterprise migrated into the eastern suburbs in Prince George's County. In chapter 7 I showed how those migrating found culture's heart beating along Branch Avenue in Marlow Heights.

I made a similar point about the migration of the black public sphere in chapter 5, which recounts the life history of Go-Go Nico. The various stages of Nico's life chronicle the larger structural transformation of Washington's black public sphere as it went into economic decline and an off-the-books economy took root. Throughout his life, Nico kept moving east: First he sold go-go recordings on the Metro trains; then from a downtown Washington mobile stand; then at a music store on Fourteenth Street across from Club U; then roughly two blocks east of Ben's Chili Bowl. His final stop in the District was in the city's Northeast quadrant on the gentrifying H Street corridor. In the spring of 2007, Nico moved most of his business to Prince George's County, living and working outside the city for the first time since his military service. Nico's go-go store was shuttered just as gentrification marched east across the H Street corridor, with a new trolley line under construction, giving new life to another major black economic hub that had been devastated by the riots of 1968.

Nico's encyclopedic knowledge of his collection of thousands of go-go recordings demonstrates that a history of Washington can be told through go-go music. Thousands of recordings in Nico's collection tell the story of the time. The onstage battles between Fat Rodney and DC Scorpio told the story of the transition from D.C. to Murder Capital. Other recordings spoke of shootings, killings, and personalities that rocked the city. Private collections such as Nico's form a rich archive of the history and culture of black Washington. The trade of recordings also contributes to the continued vitality of go-go as a cultural information channel. Nico and other self-appointed cultural stewards in this colorful underground economy guard the borders of the go-go sphere, and they archive and preserve stories that otherwise would live on only in the memories of participant individuals. In the summer of 2010, Nico still managed Suttle Thoughts and had also started a new venture called gogoradio.com, which recorded at a club not far from Branch Avenue. In August 2010 the web site received six million page views, proving the continued vitality of the go-go community as a black-owned business.

Go-Go Live, 1986–2006

In the "Club U" and "1986" chapters I bring to light two historically and geographically specific moments, occurring twenty years apart. Both performances tell the news of their time. The transcript of the performance of 1986 narrates the zeitgeist of the era of Barry, Reagan, and Bush. In this recording of Rare Essence, bottles of champagne began to pop as the drug economy was poised to boom in the city, preceding and foreshadowing the city's influx of drug money, as well as the attendant violence and mayhem of that era. The recording shows a number of key newsmakers emerge in these years of the underground economy before the mainstream media caught on to what was happening. We hear of Rayful Edmond III and Tony Lewis, partners in what would become one of the city's most successful criminal enterprises. The crowd was also introduced to the rapper Fat Rodney. All three of these individuals went on to headline mainstream news three years later. The 1986 performance took place at the pivotal moment at which go-go reached the height of its popularity, slowly beginning to take a different trajectory from hip-hop, to which I will return shortly.

This recording also illustrates how deeply the official, federal Washington and the go-go public sphere are intertwined and how the content of their debates overlap. Many debates on the Senate floor are mirrored in the go-go industry. In 1986, the Reagan administration's policies encouraged the loosening of control over financial markets and raised public safety concerns about drunk driving and the war on drugs. A parallel debate raged in the underground go-go economy on display at Breeze's Metro Club. Here, street entrepreneurs capitalized on the loosening of controls in the riot-scarred city.

Just as the dynamics of juju musical productions were strongly influenced by the vicissitudes of the Nigerian oil economy, and hip-hop was influenced by the entertainment infrastructure in New York and Los Angeles, the city of Washington's identity as the center of federal power birthed the musical form of go-go and dictated its trajectory. The federal economic base helped make Washington one of the most economically stable black markets, which allowed its residents more control over the stewardship of cultural capital. The federal economy's stability trickled down to the black regional community as well; the federal economy, combined with the influx of money from the crack cocaine trade, financially sustained the go-go industry.

This local economy made it possible for go-go to resist the pull of youth culture's standardization created by the expansion of the public sphere to cable television and radio. In these mainstream media, everything from fashion, to slang, and music became nationalized through the influence of hip-hop. Go-go maintained its unique identity partly as a function of the black community that continues to support it.

Skip forward to another performance twenty years later at the University of Maryland in 2006. In chapter 3 I demonstrated how go-go has preserved basic cultural scripts around dance, fashion, and ritual that are updated and performed in the still vibrant contemporary go-go scene. The heart of the go-go's storytelling continues to be the live show; it constitutes the essence of the go-go experience, maintaining a community and telling the news. The bands look and sound different, but they report similarly.

An Answer to Hip-Hop

Once black and youth cultures possessed regional quirks, textures, and accents that reflected the places of the music's creation. Thanks to the dynamic rise of hip-hop, that is now less frequently the case. Go-go took such a wildly different trajectory to hip-hop that it could be seen as a counterdiscourse to this standardization of youth culture. Both art forms have roots in urban youth culture, and their origins are both a byproduct of the urban centers' sociopolitical outlook following the collapse of the industrial economy in the 1970s, which caused middle-class flight and required the emergence of new urban public spheres. This power vacuum led to the rise of underground economies that snatched their own cultural and economic power. In the mid-1970s Bronx, that was hip-hop. In the mid-1970s Washington, D.C., it came in the form of go-go.

Hip-hop culture's path is better known to most people. It rose above its New York origins, traveled around the world, and became a global youth movement distributed by multinational corporations. With the help of cable networks such as BET and MTV, hip-hop came to standardize black youth culture styles in slang, dress, and popular music throughout the United States and then the world. Three decades after black and Latino youth created it in the Bronx, the face of hip-hop remains dominated by black urban imagery. Yet hip-hop no longer constitutes a uniquely black public sphere; rather, it has become a global commodity whose profits rarely go to the communities the music ostensibly reflects. Hip-hop no longer speaks to the needs or realities of young people in black urban communities who now represent just a fraction of its consumers. While underground hip-hop continues to function as a "Black CNN," the majority of hip-hop consumed worldwide grossly distorts the reality of black life in the United States. Far from its block-by-block origins, mainstream hip-hop is a platform that aggrandizes and exploits black pathology and dysfunction and then offers it up for the consumption of global audiences for corporate profit.

Go-go's divergent path allowed it to maintain its function as a uniquely black public sphere. Its fidelity to time-honored cultural scripts such as live call and response, as well as its locally rooted distribution and economic system, makes a statement about how a public sphere should be structured culturally, aesthetically, and economically. Simply put: go-go never sold out. Go-go, with its live, heavily percussive instrumentation and discursive, nonlinear narrative forms, remains aesthetically faithful to a long history of uniquely black public spheres. It lacks the polish and sheen of the high-tech production of contemporary hip-hop recordings or other kinds of popular music. There is a grit and texture to the music that accurately reflects, represents, and speaks to the communities of its creation, the communities where it is consumed and from which profits are taken. The content of the recordings are aggressively zoned toward individuals and neighborhoods otherwise ignored by mainstream news media. The lyrical content is not devoid of the negative influences that exist in all communities. However, the individuals both calling and responding to the messages reflect on black life in a way that is not distorted by multinational profit motives or the international gaze.

Go-go began as a discursive space in which to speak to the reality of life in Washington, D.C. It has guarded the function of this network by stubbornly refusing to cede its dominance to hip-hop. Go-go has remained the most visible manifestation of black youth culture, with styles in fashion, slang, and dance rooted in D.C. Much like a hypertextual link, each go-go shout-out is also a footnote, referencing the people in the room and the neighborhoods, blocks, and communities where they reside. The sociocultural context of the footnotes presents a flood of unheard stories about the capital city. As a discursive set of communication practices in particular, go-go offers greater validity and specificity than mainstream news reports.

Go-gos are also the place to learn about news that reflects the texture of human life. Here fans find out the latest cultural styles, products, and services available for purchase in the local black economic network. While go-go culture maintains a local news function, it has also evolved into an industry that has capitalized on the links between consumption, identity, and economic power.

Go-go culture as a whole guards an economic and cultural infrastructure that allows the same dollar to circle endlessly through Washington's black community. Fliers advertising concerts are printed in local graphic shops. Clothing worn at go-gos are not bought at shopping malls but designed by local artists, sewn in local factories, and sold in urban storefronts owned by black entrepreneurs. Black proprietors often own the venues where the go-gos take place. The security companies, bartenders, and bands themselves all live, work, and play in the black community. The music itself is pressed and distributed not by national chains or even through iTunes but by the network of local, black-owned mom and pop storefronts. Go-go's survival stands as a testament to the vitality of an autonomous economic network, of the city within a city that was not incinerated by the flames of 1968.

Throughout this book, I have given a tour of black communicative traditions across time, space, and through the lives of individuals. In chapter 4, I reviewed the roots of this storytelling tradition in West Africa, tracing its jagged path across the Atlantic Ocean and back. While its combinations vary and are delivered through evolving technologies, these communicative traditions create a ritual space in which a griot figure moderates a live discussion about the news of the day using time-honored scripts. This call and response is more than just a ritual; it is a deeply transcendent call across the Atlantic Ocean.

American Violence

It has been heartbreaking to hear go-go music tell the story of the holocaust of D.C.'s Murder Capital days, when hundreds of young people — mostly young black men — lost their lives. Violence, and coping with the effects of violence, is a common theme in go-go. From the RIP T-shirts worn by fans, to the live tributes to lost members of the community that form part of some live go-go performances, to the discourse about the future of a high-profile venue, violence is an unmistakable part of the history of go-go. Go-go is an art form that remembers the dead and allows them to live on through surrogates, or through what Joseph Roach called "living effigies."[3] It is the ultimate expression of the twin themes of freedom and death that run through the black vernacular.

Some of the violence can be attributed to the nocturnal, sometimes illicit underground economy in Washington. As we saw in chapter 6 about the life of Grandview Ron, some players in the underground economy are also fans of go-go, and they bring their turf battles with them. These battles are exacerbated by the competition over whose crew or neighborhood will get shouted out on the mike. I have heard others speculate that the violence at go-go shows is just a part of American culture, mirrored in the local punk scene frequented by mostly white young fans. "Kids like to fight," my friend, Joel Dias-Porter (aka DJ Renegade) shrugged. In chapter 2, one police officer concurred, speculating that youth, immaturity, and too much alcohol simply made for a toxic combination. Even Chuck Brown said of his days as a young man, "Fistfight, that was the fun part"; "finish, shake hands again. Then when we got older we shake hands and go get drunk together. Both of us have a bloody nose. Nobody came back with no guns and weapons."

Male fighting is part of working-class culture that should not be racialized. It was also in evidence with the Grits, a white gang in Prince George's County in the 1960s. The escalation to murder seen during D.C.'s Murder Capital days derived from access to handguns and increasing competition over lucrative drug profits. It should not be referred to as "black-on-black violence." This term came about with the rise of Chocolate Cities and is an example of the many pitfalls of segregation. It came into vogue as cities underwent a radical economic transformation: manufacturing jobs, once the staple of the black working class, were being replaced by unemployment and illicit industries such as the volatile crack trade. Instead of attributing the spike in violence to middle-class flight, poverty, hopelessness, or the larger social and economic shifts in cities, the media's "emphasis became looking at a supposedly defective, aberrant black culture," the geographer David Wilson, the author of the book *Inventing Black-on-Black Violence*, told me in an interview in 2010.[4] "It's as though there is something defective about black culture and moderate income, and low-income, working-class kids and families live in different worlds. Supposedly we saw youth that were going astray and that was the problem. The media imposed this narrow [black-on-black] lens that looked at the category of culture. The culture was deemed as problematically different than the mainstream."

Of course, any loss of life is cause to scream from the mountaintops. But language like *black-on-black violence* effectively smacks a racial label on problems that are socioeconomic and thus the collective, moral responsibility of every American. These kinds of racialized explanations continue to be used to slander public school children as incapable of learning or to deem affordable housing a hopeless cause. In gentrifying cities, "black-on-black crime" is used as a weapon to encourage public policies that treat black people as blights on the new urban aesthetic. There is a moral imperative to challenge these assumptions.

These racialized explanations of social ills are an unfortunate side effect of the Chocolate City. Segregated communities effectively quarantine all the hurt, pain, history, and dysfunction—and are then given a "Chocolate" label. Segregation allows things to be labeled racial that are historical, social, and the economic to be cast in terms of black and white. Outside the Chocolate City, the former mayor of D.C., Marion Barry, is seen as the cause of the city's problems; inside the Chocolate City, Barry's human frailties are seen as the ultimate symbol of how bad things were.

Take Dorothy Brizill, a black woman who had for decades operated a good governance watchdog publication, *DCWatch*. She offers the perfect example of the best of the Chocolate City—standing in the trenches holding D.C. politicians and the local media to the fire, working to make a difficult situation viable. When I spoke to her in the summer of 2010 at the polls, weariness tinged her voice when she talked about her new neighbors in gentrifying Columbia Heights: "They don't speak. And if you've been here for longer than ten years, you are part of the problem."

It is infuriating to me to see this slander of the best of Chocolate City. The demonization of black public school teachers. The conscientious city bureaucrats who, under unbelievably challenging circumstances, managed to keep the doors to raggedy buildings open, underfunded and under the volatile watch of Congress. And of course I fume about the criminalization of our modern-day griots, the go-go artists who speak to this reality every single night at shows. It is a tragedy that so many people lost their lives in the Murder Capital. But it is a testament to the resilience of their spirit, of the ability of the countless city bureaucrats, public school teachers, clergy, and the go-go industry that the majority of Chocolate City residents made it out. This community has institutional memory, hard-earned wisdom, and an investment in the city that is being honored less and less. Democracy demands inclusion, in ways that are both symbolic and concrete. A major reason why Adrian Fenty lost his job is that no voter wants to be treated like dead weight. As one voter told the *Washington Post*, "Black people are not going to go out quietly."

The rich trove of go-go recordings I tapped into for this study will not last forever. Cassette tapes have a finite shelf life before they degrade and can no longer be heard. Archivists that Nico and I spoke to noted that even the recordings that have been converted to CD will deteriorate. It is imperative that as many of these live recordings as possible are catalogued and preserved. Viewed as oral time capsules, these recordings offer a rich source of historical data for cultural historians and those interested in urban life in Washington, D.C., in the last three decades of the twentieth century. A searchable archive of older recordings could provide information about specific people, places, styles, and times. Much like Lexis-Nexis, older go-go recordings can be seen as a primary source that can be put into conversation with what is known about the city at that time. More recordings should be transcribed to provide a searchable database of information on places, neighborhoods, names and nicknames, dances, and fashion styles. All would provide a more complete picture of the nation's capital and its residents. Go-go is all about preserving and celebrating each life — before it's too late. It loudly affirms, "I'm here!," from communities that are often ignored. A shout-out during a live show provides a moment of glory, but it is fleeting. The recordings should be preserved so that the lives lost are not forever erased.

Evolution

Personally and professionally I find myself at a crossroads where the future of the city, the future of go-go, and the future of the industries supporting journalism and music intersect. All these spheres are in a state of transition due to market forces spinning beyond their control. For the music and journalism industries, technology has devalued the product from which they previously profited handsomely.

For all of its history, go-go has always faced challenges in finding venues. It's built into the way things work: space is never fixed, the music and promoters are always in search of the next stop. But that old challenge has been exacerbated by gentrification. The city's nightclub scene on U and H Streets has gone upscale, further pushing out the live go-go scene and the attendant network of mom and pop stores. The Ibex, the former go-go club on Georgia Avenue, was transformed into luxury condos. The flagship store for the local urban wear designer We R One on Florida Avenue went out of business in the summer of 2007. A few steps away, the retail distributor Central Communications at the corner of Seventh Street and Florida Avenue painted over the "Go-Go" part of its sign. The mall that held the flagship go-go distributor P. A. Palace was bulldozed months ago to make way for a Walmart. The H Street record store Nico worked at was briefly a children's beauty salon owned by a black couple called "Spoiled Rotten."

Go-go is by nature an itinerant sphere, thus life goes on. Go-go bands continue to play, seven days a week. New bands crop up every day. A storefront that may be booming at one point is not promised to do so tomorrow. Venues such as Club U open for business, make a lot of money, and then close. For months and even years, local teenagers will pay exorbitant prices for a brand of T-shirt, and then it goes out of style. Just as go-go musicians are constantly trying new musical combinations, experimenting with reggae, neo-soul, and hip-hop, go-go's architects embrace economic principles that demand constant evolution and updating. Kevin "Kato" Hammond was an early technology adopter, founding his online magazine *Take Me Out to the Go-Go* in 1996. "Ten years from now I don't know if I'll still be doing this," Andre "Whiteboy" Johnson, the longest-serving member of Rare Essence, told me in October 2011 at Jasper's restaurant in Largo. Then he paused, and shrugged: "But that's what I said ten years ago." In 2011, Go-Go Nico's online Go-Go Radio, based in Prince George's County, was booming, with millions of page views. In the summer of 2011, it had snagged its first sponsor: Industrial Bank, a black-owned bank established on U Street in 1934.

This is the nature of the black public sphere, constant evolution; as Donnell Floyd of Familiar Faces described it, it requires finding the "right formula." Go-go is a social media network. In the age of new and emerging media, the very essence of go-go "liveness" means motion, innovation, and aggressively playing to the needs of local fans. Go-go's future (and the future of journalism and of the music industry) hinges on its ability to continue to be a cultural steward for its constituents. If it manages, go-go will continue to be a history that is remade and forgotten each day, giving a voice to future generations of residents of "the DMV" (D.C., Maryland, and Virginia).

I do take some comfort in that many of the same cultural and social scripts once found in D.C. are still thriving outside its borders in Prince George's County, Maryland. But the Chocolate City drew its subversive authority from its juxtaposition to the seat of power. So even as I appreciate the power of a single black man in shaping Mr. Obama's Washington, and running past the towering monument to Martin Luther King Jr. on the Mall, there remains a need for institutions to provide an alternate view of world power through the collective voices of many. That is the power of art: being different, seeing things differently. That is how we as a country can get the clearest picture of who we are and who we want to be.

On Inauguration Day on U Street in 2009, a red, white, and blue wreath lay at the foot of a monument of black soldiers who gave their lives for the Union. Nearby, a street peddler thrust out an Obama button to passersby, calling out "Yes, you can—buy this button!" A red, white, and blue Obama ice sculpture sat outside Ben's Chili Bowl, where a line stretched around the block. Down on the Mall, Aretha Franklin was not first lady but sang "My Country 'Tis of Thee." Next to a stand peddling "Obama" bottled water, I met a fifteen-year-old high school student named Ray. His school, Thurgood Marshall Academy in Southeast Washington, was entirely black. The teaching staff is largely white. Even more white people moving into Washington could "be better for us or worse," Ray told me. "Since it never happened before, I don't know."[5]

I don't know either, but for my children's sake, I am hoping for forward movement. I have loved the Chocolate City. I have loved its rhythms, its characters, its functioning dysfunction. As someone who never felt I had a place in the world as a black woman, it has been delicious to taste it right outside the gates of the White House. The black family living at the White House is just the beginning of a transformation happening across the globe. It is a change in which power is tilting decidedly east. The death of a Chocolate City is just part of the global movement of voices from the margins to the center.

A region with such a large and powerful black middle class helps mask the ongoing inequities and the racial and socioeconomic fires that continue to burn. They are still there, the child poverty rates worse than that of Mississippi. As I try to make sense of the tragic story of Grandview Ron in chapter 6, that is the best I can come up with. As Mary Patillo-McCoy wrote, the black middle class is the bridge between the white mainstream and the poor disenfranchised masses.[6] We are wedged between the height of privilege and the depths of the peril of the prison industrial complex. The black middle class has no choice but to be connected to the struggle because at any moment any of us can tip to either side. I also hope that Prince George's County embraces its own demographic shift as increasing numbers of Latino immigrants settle there. In some ways, that brings go-go full circle to its musical origins, when Brown and his classmate Joe Manley played with the Los Latinos band.

My neighbor and friend Hope Witherspoon sees the death of the Chocolate City as a sign of white people returning to the "energy source." She also fears the implications for black people's ability to hold their grip on the city as it gets more expensive. Where will we find a spiritual home? "I just feel like we will become like the Israelites, wandering in the darkness," she told me. But, maybe gentrification will result in the kind of integration that the buses could not force. Ultimately, the socioeconomic integration that comes along with gentrification could lead to better life chances for black children in Washington, D.C.

Tony Lee of the Community of Hope agreed. "It probably will be a better city for *your* kids," he said. "It is expedient to push out poor people," he said. "It is effective to push out poor people. But the question we must ask is, 'Is it right?' Because one day we will all face a judgment." I think of Lee's words constantly as my family enjoys the new art galleries, restaurants, shiny new grocery stores and recreation centers, and other luxuries that white privilege has brought to D.C.

Whatever the levels of Chocolate that remain inside the Washington, D.C., limits, the good news is that go-go is still alive and crankin'. Whatever the geography, go-go is the cultural capital. It is at Lee's church, it is at schools and the clubs, on the street corners, in cars driving by. Too much of the region's identity is invested in go-go — financially, politically, spiritually, and otherwise — to abandon it. But even if go-go — the soul of Washington — retreats deeper and deeper into the suburbs, or worse, fades to black, I do not worry about its future. If history is a judge, some other iteration of the black musical tradition will pop up in its place. Someone will make the call. Someone will give a response. This is the essence of the story told by black music. Change. Movement. Rinse. Repeat. Never death — only freedom.

9 ★ Roll Call, 1986

The following transcription of a seminal Rare Essence recording captures a moment in history when Washington, D.C., was about to change in instantaneous and spectacular fashion. But of course no one knew it yet. The performance was recorded sometime in 1986 at Breeze's Metro Club (later Deno's)[1] located at 2335 Bladensburg Road in Northeast Washington. The year 1986 was the height of go-go's popularity.[2] "Go-go is here to stay," Warren Doles, then seventeen years old, told the *Washington Post*. "Go-go was born here. I don't know how long rap is going to be around."[3] This year marked the watershed release of a major motion picture backed by Island Records (*Good to Go*) as a vehicle to commercialize go-go

1 Breeze's was one of the longest serving go-go venues. By 2011, it was headquarters for a corporate catering company.
2 Lornell and Stephenson, *The Beat* (2001).
3 Harris, "D.C. B-Boys Say It's Good to Go-Go, But It's Fresh to Rap."

like its musical cousins reggae and hip-hop. The buzz around the film helped inspire national recording companies to sign deals with several go-go bands, including Rare Essence.

This recording also paints a picture of the year that champagne bottles began to pop as the underground economy took control of Washington, D.C., foreshadowing the city's metamorphosis into "Murder Capital." Several anthropologists, sociologists, and media researchers also established the significance of 1986 in terms of the debate over the so-called war on drugs waged in "the other" Washington.[4] The media and congressional frenzy over drug policy was fueled by the death of Len Bias, the Prince George's County, Maryland, native and University of Maryland basketball star (and go-go enthusiast) who overdosed on cocaine the night in 1986 after he was drafted to the NBA to play for the Boston Celtics.

I analyzed the coverage of the drug scare of 1986 published in the mainstream daily *Washington Post* and the black weekly *Washington Afro American* in a conference paper titled "Black Representation during the Drug Scare of 1986." I found, for example, that aside from a single photo and caption of Chuck Brown, the *Washington Afro American*, a major black newspaper, carried no coverage of go-go that year. This omission had to be intentional given the local popularity of the music and the attention it received outside the city. Thus, much like Howard University, the bourgeois-oriented black press of Washington, D.C., appeared to deliberately distance itself from this segment of the black community.[5]

The following transcription identifies a number of key newsmakers that would emerge in the city's underground economy in coming years. At the time of the show, personalities like Rayful Edmond III and Tony Lewis were in their early twenties and building an empire that would bring in hundreds of millions of dollars.[6] But it would be years before they made mainstream headlines.

In a conversation with me twenty-five years later in October 2011, Rare Essence's longtime lead guitarist Andre "Whiteboy" Johnson recalled the excitement and anticipation among the audience that night because it

---

4 Shoemaker, *Communication Campaigns about Drugs*; Orcutt and Turner, "Shocking Numbers and Graphic Accounts"; Reinarman and Levine, *Crack in America*; Agar, "Literary Journalism as Ethnography."

5 Hopkinson, "Black Representation during Washington's Drug Scare of 1986."

6 Davidson, "How a 24-Year-Old Reigned as a Local Hero until His Arrest."

was being recorded as an album. He remembered getting on the bus the next day to travel to Detroit to appear in Aretha Franklin's "Jimmy Lee" video. This transcript shows all of the cultural scripts described in previous chapters. With references to graffiti artists, neighborhood crews, popular dances and the exuberance of beginning a new school year, the recording captures the joy, whimsy, and cheery optimism of go-go—just before a generation lost its innocence.

Rare Essence: Live at Breeze's Metro Club[7]

"THE ALBUM THAT KEPT THE WHOLE
NEIGHBORHOOD ROCKIN'"[8] 1986 Kolossal Records[9]
Transcription by Al[10]

[*beat: roll call*][11]
JAS. FUNK:[12] All they rolling now y'all,

7 Rare Essence, known as the "wickedest band alive," was founded by a group of St. Thomas More Catholic School kids in Southeast Washington in 1976 (Wartofsky, "The Mother Who Gave Go-Go Its First Big Push"). The band has been a staple of the go-go scene ever since. Despite the rotation of most of the roster, Rare Essence remains one of the best brands in go-go outside of Chuck Brown. They began as a funk-influenced Top 40 band and then adapted to the go-go sound created and popularized by Brown as an alternative to disco.

8 This album is deeply established in the canon of go-go, according to several of my research partners. It also continues to be referenced and traded online.

9 Kolossal Records was a go-go label in the late 1980s based in Suitland, Maryland, that released this now classic record.

10 "Al" (by his request—not his real name) is a research partner whom I hired to do the transcriptions in 2006 and whom I also interviewed about his experiences at the show. At the time of the performance in 1986, Al was an eighteen-year-old high school student. One of his middle school teachers, JB, was one of the band members performing with Rare Essence at this show. Al said he enjoyed transcribing the recording as many memories flooded back to him, and it was remarkably accurate. I edited the transcript only for formatting, punctuation, and typos, and corrected a few minor errors. However, I left the majority of the transcription as he typed it. The transcript is not meant to be read as a 100 percent faithful account of what was said at the show, but as an artifact of how a teenager heard and remembered the show twenty years later.

11 The "Roll Call" beat is a rhythm done when the lead talker surveys who is there. This is one of the cultural traditions that link go-go to the school systems. The other tradition is the music programs in the school system and the city's marching bands, which provide a steady supply of musicians (Lornell and Stephenson, *The Beat* [2001]).

12 Jas Funk, also known as James "Funk" Thomas, is the lead talker for Rare

Special dedication, going out to the whole Washington, D.C., crew.
Yes, indeed, we love all of you.
Big Brother KT and all the rest of the friends.[13]
My main man Duck and all the Dom Perignon crew[14]
Yeah, Houseman and all the friends,
Yeah, roll that tape man[15]
Do it for Big Brother Wayne out of Langdon Park,[16] y'all.

Essence, considered one of the greatest lead talkers of all time. His mother, Annie "Miss Mack" Thomas, served as the longtime manager for the band. Funk's brother, Quentin "Footz" Davidson, was also onstage at this performance, where he did percussion. Jas and Footz were in elementary school when they started rehearsing in the basement of their home on Xenia Street (Wartofsky, "The Mother Who Gave Go-Go Its First Big Push"). In 1986, Funk was in and out of rehab for drug addiction. The artist was later lauded for his outspokenness about his struggle overcoming drug addiction at a time when substance abuse plagued many in the city (Nelson, "Mourning for Rap Singer Is Tapped Out in Tears").

13 Funk uses the appellation "Big Brother" to show affection and respect, emphasizing the family community feeling among R.E. enthusiasts.

14 The Dom Perignon crew was a well-known local crew whose members were major patrons of go-go. The crew took the name of Dom Perignon, the French champagne brand named for a seventeenth-century monk who created the sparkling wine that also symbolized the excess of the 1980s. Dom Perignon was considered the best champagne, and in 1986, it often sold for more than $100 per bottle (Ringle, "Bottoms Up").

   According to DJ Renegade, a prominent deejay in D.C. clubs at the time, D.C. club goers started ordering Dom Perignon champagne in 1986. "We had these drug dealers this was like '86 and this was crack. . . . D.C. was still relatively wide open at that point. Within six months, kids were getting shot in D.C., I would get $50 a mix-tape. [Another major go-go deejay] used to get $100 a mix-tape. It had to be drug dealers. Who else had that kind of money? We went from five [dollars] to seven to ten to get in [to the club]. The comparable go-go club was the Black Hole, Breeze's Metro Club — was like a little joint in terms of square footage. All the clubs were making money" (personal communication, 2005).

15 This was a reminder to the audience that the show was going to be recorded. Often when the show is recorded fans try even harder, by moving to the front of the stage and jumping up throughout the performance, to be acknowledged by the lead talker and have it recorded for posterity. Go-Go Nico describes being immortalized on a go-go recording as being every Washingtonian's "birthright" (personal communication, 2006).

16 Langdon Park is a working-class neighborhood in Northeast Washington located near the Washington Arboretum, with the main arteries being New York Avenue and Bladensburg Road where Breeze's Metro Club was located.

Special dedication going out to Jazzy Jeff and friends

Yes indeed, and all our friends, Big Brother Winston,

I said every time we blend, it gets better again and again,

I said every time we blend y'all, we meet new friends

[*repeat 2x*]

So if we leave anything anybody out,

Just come down front and scream and shout

Cause we wanna make sure that y'all turns it out now

[*repeat 2x*]

JAS FUNK: I said hello?

CROWD: Hello, hello, hello

JAS FUNK: Welcome back to the Metro

[*repeat 4x*]

ROLL CALL: We got Tammy and Devon, y'all

Sheila and Monica,[17] y'all

Tammy and Lisa

TC and Stacy y'all

Tracy and Googie,[18] y'all

Lisa of the World, y'all[19]

Supa Dupa Cooper, we got the whole darn crew in the house tonight

We got Duck and Nuno

We got Cle and Rio

We got Boomie and King Tut[20]

We got all that DP crew[21]

We got all that DP crew

We got Lisa of the World

17 Al recalls that first Tammy and Devon were known as the TM crew. Then Sheila joined, but they were still known as the TM crew, by which Funk refers to them throughout this recording.

18 Googie was a sound engineer for Rare Essence.

19 Lisa of the World was a go-go fan and a graffiti artist. During the 1980s Lisa of the World's tag (in Magic Marker) was ubiquitous throughout neighborhoods, on buses, and on buildings, according to Al. Magic Marker graffiti was a fad in 1986. Lisa of the World would be acknowledged in the *Washington Post* five years after this show in a profile of another famous graffiti writer, Disco Dan (Hendrickson, "Mark of the Urban Phantom").

20 The previous four call names were members of the DP, or Dom Perignon crew.

21 It was always a struggle to get a shout-out, even harder when a show was recorded as an album. Some lead talkers were known to remember names of fans that provided them with other kinds of party favors popular at the time.

We got Tonya and Junior, y'all
We got Lisa and Deenie, y'all
We got the whole darn crew in the house tonight, all do it
We got a lady by the name of Yvette, and she's the prettiest
    I've seen yet.
We got Lisa and Precious Pen
And sweet lady Lucious Lynn
Sweet Lil Lady Sydnee and Sweet Lady Sheila
May main man Pee Wee Herman[22] and Archie and Jeff and Tony
We got Big Brother Wayne, y'all, from out of Langdon Park
We got Sexy Sax, y'all, and Big Brother Ellis too.
007 and the Darnell crew
Hi-C y'all they from that Largo crew[23]
We got Winston and Daria
We got my main man Dynomite Darnell, yeah, he shonuff well
We got her and Samantha, y'all
Big Brother Bob and Nell
We gotta sweet lil' lady name Darnell outta Old Town Virginia,[24]
    all do it
CROWD [*chants*]: Wind me up, Funk
JAS FUNK: Do what now? [*crowd chants*]
Do what, baby? [*crowd chants*]
What u want me to do? [*crowd chants*]
Cause I sure hear you? [*crowd chants*]
What u want me to do? [*crowd chants*]

22 Sometimes if the lead talker did not know your name, he would give you one. "Pee Wee" was the name Funk gave to a fan that used to dance a lot. Rare Essence often played a version of the Pee Wee Herman dance and song, taken from a popular children's show, *Pee Wee's Playhouse*, a spinoff from a film of 1985, which aired on television from 1986 to 1991. This practice of assigning names and bynames rooted in history or culture is also found in John Miller Chernoff's discussion of the Dagbamba of Ghana ("Music and Historical Consciousness among the Dagbamba of Ghana").

23 Largo is a community in Prince George's County, Maryland, which is on the eastern border of Washington, D.C. In 1986, Prince George's was just beginning its transformation from a rural, sleepy area dominated by white residents to the wealthiest majority black jurisdiction in the United States.

24 Old Town is the oldest part of Alexandria, Virginia, established in 1779. It is located across the Potomac River from Washington, D.C., and originally formed part of the District.

We got my main man Keith, y'all, outta Special K Productions[25]
We got Big Brother Flood and Duck and Snacks too
We got Tony and Tom, y'all, Keith and Tina, y'all
We got Sheila and Shirley
We got Wanda and Lisa of the World
We got Monica and Monie
We got Rizzio and Go-Go John
We got Jazzy Jeff, y'all, and Sweet Devon
We got that Sweet Felicia, Sweet Monina, Sweet Nita
We got the whole darn crew in the house tonight, all do it
We got to do it one time for my main man Hollywood Breeze[26]
For lettin' us come over here and rock 'n' roll each and every
    Thursday night.
Ladies and gentlemen, thanks so much Breeze,
And also going out to my main man Big Brother Skip and
    Big Brother Norm
And Big Brother Bug and Pittsburgh Slim on the camera stand[27]
Freakbody on the turntables and,
Big Brother Rerun, put in a lil' fun, say what, y'all
CROWD: Wind me up Funk
JAS FUNK: Do what now? [*crowd chants*]
I don't believe my ears? [*crowd chants*]
What am I hearing? [*crowd chants*]
What did I hear? [*crowd chants*]
I don't believe my ears? [*crowd chants*]
Now did I leave, say what?
Did I leave anybody out?
    [*repeat 4x*]
JAS FUNK: We left out?
    [*repeat 16x*]
    [*Every time Funk says "We left out," a crowd member
    says his or her name*]

25 Special K Productions was a popular promoter.
26 Hollywood Breeze is also known as Daniel Clayton. He told reporters he began hosting music events there in the mid 1970s. In the early 2000s he went on to battle with the city's alcohol control board after some violent incidents at the club (Cherkis and Godfrey, "Last Shot"). The club continued to host go-gos as late as 2009, but by 2011, the building was operating as a corporate caterer.
27 This would be the corner where go-go fans could pay for Polaroid portraits.

Everybody from Uptown,[28] everybody from downtown, cross-town,
   outta town, yes
indeed
We love you too, outta sight.
Big Brother Kevin outta Prophecy Band,[29] too
Say what now,
Do it like this,
Then do it like that
Do it like this,
And then do it like that,
You say do it like this,
And then do it like that,
   [*beat change: "One on One"*[30]]
JAS FUNK: Is that Reggie? My goodness all the old band
All the old crews up in here, y'all
My goodness, we sure feel good up here, y'all
Maverick Room crew[31]
Howard Theatre[32]

28 Uptown is known as the northern part of the city, mostly in the upper North-west east of Sixteenth Street, including the Georgia Avenue, Shepherd Park and Brightwood, and Petworth neighborhoods.

29 Prophecy Band was a go-go act formed by several Oxon Hill High School students.

30 The "One on One" groove is a rhythmic pattern that Al describes as his "all-time favorite groove. They have always hit the One on One, some version of it. All the call and response. Some parts of the One on One, he always asks for participation. One of the original beats with a little socket in it. No other band can play it—that would be like robbery." Other research partners have described the One on One as being kind of a D.C. anthem. In an interview with Little Benny, a former Rare Essence member, Mark Ward asked him to explain. "Actually, I think we probably named it the 'One on One' because of the rolls that Footz did to bring us into the groove. Funk would hold up one finger on each hand, and we knew to play 'One On One'" (Ward, "Picking Stan 'Da Man' Cooper's Brain").

31 The Maverick Room was a go-go located at Fourth and Rhode Island Avenues, Northeast (Gregg, "A Teen-Ager's D.C. Is Filled with Go-Go"). Its name was borrowed by Thomas Sayers Ellis for the title of his book of poems which eventually earned him a prestigious Whiting Prize. In a 2010 interview with me, Chuck Brown pinpointed this location as the place where he developed and fine tuned the go-go sound in collaboration with the Maverick Room audience.

32 The Howard Theatre, located at 620 T Street, first opened in 1910 and served the city's black community for more than seven decades, helping launch the careers of musical greats such as Billy Eckstine, Pearl Bailey, and the Clovers. Its history

The DP crew
The TM crew and the Metro crew
We love you too, say what now
When school was closed, we was good to go.
We didn't wanna leave until we closed the show, shonuff
    [*repeat 2x*]
JAS FUNK: When school was closed [*crowd repeats*]
JAS FUNK: It was good to go [*crowd repeats*]
JAS FUNK: We didn't wanna leave [*crowd repeats*]
JAS FUNK: Until we closed the show [*crowd repeats*]
    [*repeat 2x*]
JAS FUNK: Now the school has reopened [*crowd repeats*]
JAS FUNK: We have returned [*crowd repeats*]
JAS FUNK: Gonna open them books [*crowd repeats*]
JAS FUNK: And really learn [*crowd repeats*]
    [*repeat 2x*]
    [*ad libs*]
I been walking, been talking
    [*crowd says "go head" 4x*]
I am groovin' cause D.C. got y'all moving
    [*crowd says "go head" 4x*]
I been thinking and also peepin'
    [*crowd says "go head" 4x*]
I can't be mumblin' cause I do hear something
    [*crowd says "go head" 4x*]
We want to tell you about the "One on One"
    [*repeat 3x*]
Hang in there Yvette, we see you baby
Big Brother Moe Gentry,[33] yes indeed

---

rings with names like Duke Ellington, Billy Daniels, Sister Rosetta Tharpe, Fats Domino, Marvin Gaye, Laverne Baker, and the Temptations (Trescott, "City Seeks to Buy Howard Theatre: Barry Offer Would Prevent Foreclosure"). The theater had a seating capacity of more than twelve hundred. After the 1968 riots devastated much of the neighborhood, the theater was closed in 1970. Its reopening in the mid-1970s was boosted by the emerging go-go scene including Rare Essence and Chuck Brown (Cultural Tourism DC, "Howard Theatre"). The theater was closed again in the early 1980s. In 2010, the city broke ground on its restoration.

33 Moe Gentry ran the sound for this show.

Thank you so much for coming through man

Some of that old Highland crew,[34] y'all

Some of the crew, grew up with us too

It's like Jack and Jill going up the hill to have a little fun

On the way, he met the Metro crew and he told them about the "One
on One"

It's like Jack and Jill going up the hill to have a little fun

On the way he met the Godfather and he told them about the,[35] he
said _____

    [*crowd singalong*]

If you been thinking about leaving home and going to Hollywood,

It doesn't necessarily mean that you gonna be living good,

You might get hungry, cold, and weak and you may have to sleep
outside,

Then you feel like you been let down, then you crawl inside your
pride.

If you want to deal with the world you gotta love yourself,

And once you learn to love yourself, you can love everybody else

We done been all around and seen the rest

But tonight we getting' down with the very best

And that's you, you, you, and the DP crew

    [*crowd chanting "go head, go head"*]

JAS FUNK: Let me tell you about "One on One," y'all, yes indeed

Talking about Damon and all the rest

Talking about Damon and all the rest of the stars and celebrities

In the house with us this morning

Let me tell you about the "One on One."

Good to see you Outta Sight Mike

Here's a toast to the boogie,

I said here's a toast to the boogie, y'all

    [*fading out*]

    [*beat change: "I Must Be Dreamin'" fading in*]

CROWD: Do the mickey

JAS FUNK: Do what now? [*crowd response*]

JAS FUNK: Do what Darnell? [*crowd response*]

JAS FUNK: Make it well? [*crowd response*]

34 Highland is a part of Southeast Washington off Wheeler Road.

35 Godfather played keyboard.

JAS FUNK: Do what y'all? [*crowd response*]

JAS FUNK: Do what now? [*crowd response*]

JAS FUNK: Do what y'all? [*crowd response*]

[*horn section leading into new groove: "I Must Be Dreamin'"*]

JAS FUNK: Gon do it for that Dom Perignon crew:

Duck, Rio, Nuno, and all the gang, y'all, yes indeed

Big Brother Tony Lewis, is Rayful here too, man?[36]

Yes indeed, Rayful and the fellas, thank you so much for coming
through

Big Brother Ray and Rodney and all the gang[37]

36 Tony Lewis was a business associate of Rayful Edmond III. Police told the *Washington Post* that the combined drug network of Edmond and Lewis employed hundreds of people and brought hundreds of pounds of almost pure cocaine into the District (Lewis and Horowitz, "Area Sweet Nabs Alleged Drug Leaders").

Edmond received his first cocaine brick from his father in 1985 or 1986 (Davidson, "How a 24-Year-Old Reigned as a Local Hero until His Arrest"). At the time of this Rare Essence performance, Edmonds was just beginning his ascent running one of the largest drug organizations in the history of Washington, which, had it been legitimate, would have constituted the city's fifth-largest private enterprise (Davidson, "How a 24-Year-Old Reigned as a Local Hero until His Arrest"). In 1997 Edmond would become the subject of a *Sixty Minutes* television interview, with him behind bars. Until his arrest in 1989 at age twenty-four, he controlled a large part of the D.C. drug trade (Cauvin, "A Drug Kingpin's Hot-Selling Story"). He brought in millions of dollars of Colombian cocaine each week from Los Angeles. The city's streets were awash in the drug, and Edmond was flush with cash. He spent lavishly on cars, clothing, and clubbing. He would drop thousands of dollars in boutiques or nightspots (Cauvin, "A Drug Kingpin's Hot-Selling Story"). In 2005, Edmond was the subject of a biopic film co-produced by Curtis "Curtbone" Chambers, the founder of the urban wear line ALLDAZ.

37 Rodney Tyrone Martin was also known as "Fat Rodney" (Nelson, "Mourning for Rap Singer Is Tapped Out in Tears"). During a series of battles in the mid-1980s, Fat Rodney, one of the best-known drug dealers in the city, squared off against DC Scorpio, a college boy who rapped about the evils of drugs. For several years they battled each other backed by Rare Essence. Fat Rodney was gunned down as he left a go-go at a skating rink in Temple Hills, Maryland, in 1989, just as he was poised to release *Busting Out*, a record and video (Nelson, "Mourning for Rap Singer Is Tapped Out in Tears"). At the first annual WKYS Go-Go Awards on 19 November 2006 I met Fat Rodney's son, whose picture I have included in the book. He is wearing an RIP T-shirt bearing an image of his father, with the phrase "Stuntin' Like My Daddy," an allusion to a radio hit of 2006 by the rap artist Li'l Wayne. Born in 1990, Rodney Jr. was in his mother's

I said when I went into the dance hall to see who I could see,
All I could see getting down was some buddies and some fine
   honeys
So I went on over to the honey, and ask her if I could dance,
They said anything that moves you got to move it to
I said, I must be dreamin'
We said, we must be dreamin'
We said, we must be dreamin'
We never felt this good before
Well the music was getting' stronger
Can't you feel it in your feet,
The crowds getting' down everywhere, y'all, as they groove in
   they seats
And I believe what I'm saying, you ought to come on through
Because anything that moves you got to move your crew too
I said, I must be dreamin'
We said, we must be dreamin'
We said, we must be dreamin'
We never felt this good before
   [*horns*]³⁸
JAS FUNK: Crystal, you should smack my face, girl
You said I'm always forgettin' your name like that
Who you bring with you, Tony?
Did you bring the rest of the fellas with you?
Everything alright, Duck? Alright?
All y'all sure got that new dance up here, my goodness
Almost time for that Go-Go Mickey stuff
Y'all sure got that Cabbage Patch going,³⁹ though, yes you do

---

belly when his father died. At one point at the awards ceremony, the host Big G
of Backyard Band welcomed Rodney Jr. onstage and led the audience in a moment of remembrance for Fat Rodney.

38 Donnell Floyd was Rare Essence's original horn player, from 1983 to 2000
(Wartofsky, "The Mother Who Gave Go-Go Its First Big Push"), who played
that night.

39 The Cabbage Patch was a go-go dance that several years later became a national dance craze. I remember being a teenager in Indianapolis and watching the Black Entertainment Television personality Donnie Simpson on *Video
Soul* joking about learning how to do it. The Miami-based rap group the Gucci
Crew II released a song called "The Cabbage Patch," which also gave directions,

Well let me tell you baby, things never slow you down
Everyone's on the floor, lettin' it all hang out
I just couldn't stand there and watch everybody scream and shout
Because anything that moves you got to move me too,
I said, I must be dreamin'
I said, I must be dreamin'
I said, we must be dreamin'
We never felt this good before
  [*ad libs*]
  [*beat change*]
  [*The medley: Friends don't let friends drive drunk* [40]]
JAS FUNK: Brother Duck, Tony and Rayful
Yeah, don't get drunk back there at the bar
Don't' get drunk back there at the bar Rayful, because
Friends do not let friends drive drunk, no they don't
  [*repeat 4x*]
  [*beat change*]
ELECTRONIC VOICE: R.E. get busy one time
  [*ad libs*]
  [*beat change: "Shake It (But Don't Break It)"*]
JAS FUNK: Shake it (but don't break it)
Testing, Testing 1, 2, 3 in the place to be, hit it
I'm talkin' to you, soul brothers, jitta bugs
Hip cats with them fancy hats
Pretty ladies with them pretty smiles

---

in 1987. The District's version of this and several other dances differed from the national ones.

40 In 1983 the Ad Council and the National Highway Traffic Safety Administration (under the U.S. Department of Transportation) partnered to launch the Drunk Driving Prevention campaign. The campaign, with its tag line "Drinking and Driving Can Kill a Friendship," was originally designed to reach people aged sixteen to twenty-four, who accounted for 42 percent of all fatal alcohol-related car crashes, and to inspire personal responsibility to prevent drinking and driving. The public service advertisement, which emphasized the grave consequences of drinking and driving with a depiction of two glasses crashing into each other, won the classic CLIO award for best overall ad campaign in 1984. There was also a comparable antidrug campaign in 1986 that incorporated the go-go community, which Lornell and Stephenson (*The Beat* [2001], 246) detail. The city's Regional Addiction Program (RAP) requested city funding to record an album and video called the *Go-Go Drug Free Project* in June 1986.

All decked out in the latest styles
Hips shakin', breath takin', devastatin' and fascinatin'
Gatherin' here from far and near
To get on down in this atmosphere
Shonuff [*crowd repeats*]
  [*repeat 4x*]
We want you to shake it to the east, shake it to the west
We want you to shake it to the east, shake it to the west,
Shake it to the one that you love the best
And that's who?
CROWD: R.E.
  [*repeat 4x*]
We want to make you sweat, 'til you get wet
Just to see how funky you can get
Don't want no tears, don't want no lies
And furthermore, I don't want no alibis
Cause y'all moves are hip, that ain't all
This groove's designed for the big and small
Thank you so much for comin' again
Grab you a friend and blend on in, all do it
You know you really come to boogie
CROWD: Yeah, boy
  [*repeat 4x*]
Shake it, but don't' break it, y'all
Gon' and loosen your body
  [*repeat 4x*]
  [*ad libs*]
  [*beat change to "Do the Mickey"*[41]]
  [*beat breakdown*]
JAS FUNK: If you like champagne, just pop the cork
Stir it a while, and give it time to work
If you like it a lot, just make it a double
That's why the Dom Perignon crew is supposed to give a bubble
Hey Shonuff
  [*repeat 4x*]

41 "Do the Mickey" was a go-go cover of an old Smokey Robinson song, which
   became a dance created by Rare Essence's new conga player, Milton "Go-Go
   Mickey" Freeman.

CROWD: Do the Mickey

JAS FUNK: Do what?

CROWD: Do the Mickey

JAS FUNK: Say what y'all?

CROWD: Do the Mickey

JAS FUNK: Say what now?

CROWD: Do the Mickey

JAS FUNK: What did I hear?

CROWD: Do the Mickey

You feel it in your heart. You feel it in your soul

Go-Go Mickey just make you wanna rock and roll, shonuff

JAS FUNK: Repeat after me

You feel it in your heart [*crowd repeats*]

You feel it in your soul [*crowd repeats*]

Go-Go Mickey make us [*crowd repeats*]

Rock and roll [*crowd repeats*]

   [*repeat 2x*]

There's a cat named Mickey from outta town,

Dum, d, dum, d, dum, d, di, I

Aw wait, wait a minute, y'all, break it back down, Footz[42]

This how it go

The ladies say: dum, d, i

The fellas say: dum, d, oh

   [*repeat 4x*]

JAS FUNK: There's a cat name Mickey from outta town

LADIES' REFRAIN: dum, d, i

He spreadin' a new dance all around

FELLAS' REFRAIN: dum, d, oh

In just a matter of few days

His thing became a new dance craze

JAS FUNK: Do the Mickey [*crowd repeats*]

Go-Go Mickey [*crowd repeats*]

   [*repeat 4x*]

   [*crowd chanting "Go-Go Mickey"*]

---

42 Quentin "Footz" Davidson is considered by many to be the greatest go-go drummer of all time. In the fall of 1994, his body was found along a highway in Landover. He had been shot in the back of the head at age thirty-three (Wartofsky, "For Rapper, a 911 Call").

When people see him play, they begin to see [*ladies say their refrain*]
This cat named Mickey, doing the go-go thing
    [*fellas say their refrain*]
And it's really something to see, yeah [*ladies say their refrain*]
This cat named Mickey, doing the go-go thing
    [*fellas say their refrain*]
Do the Mickey [*crowd repeats*]
Go-Go Mickey [*crowd repeats*]
    [*repeat 4x*]
On behalf of that Dom Perignon crew, Nuno, Rio and Duck
And all the gang
Boomie, King Tut, Cle Pop and Rob on there Job, Big Brother Cliff
    and Cornell
And the TM crew, yes indeed we love you too
Big brother Tony, Brother ain't no phony
Supa Dupa Cooper, Lisa of the World
Y'all sure got this dance now.
And the TM crew, y'all
Break it on down
Hang in there, Pee Wee
If we left anything, anybody out,
Shoulda came down front and scream and shout
Cause we didn't wanna leave anybody out, y'all
    [*fades out*]
Please leave carefully, when y'all leave
Y'all got a record that's gonna keep the whole neighborhood rockin'
My goodness![43]

---

43 Go-Go Nico agrees that this recording accomplished as much. Nico says it was
released on Christmas 1986, but the recording date remains unclear. This was
the album that "really grabbed the city by its ears," Nico explained to me at his
H Street store in 2006. Rare Essence had just lost Lil' Benny, who left to start
his own band, Little Benny and the Masters. Nico notes that street vendors
sold T-Shirts inspired by the album with a cartoon character of Mickey Mouse
doing the Go-Go Mickey dance. The T-shirts may have been pressed by a company called Madness Connection, a Georgia Avenue clothing store established
in 1984 and among the first to sell monogrammed hats and T-shirts emblazoned
with a coveted logo.

Notes

1 A Black Body Politic

1 There are two editions of *The Beat*: the first extended scholarly treatment of go-go was published by Billboard Press in 2001; in 2009, an updated edition with a slightly different title (*The Beat: Go-Go Music from Washington, D.C.*) was published by the University Press of Mississippi with photos by Thomas Sayers Ellis.

2 Lornell and Stephenson, *The Beat* (2001), 15.

3 Lornell and Stephenson, *The Beat* (2009), 47.

4 Marc Barnes, perhaps D.C.'s best-known black promoter who owned the popular clubs Republic Gardens, Dream, Love, and Park, which drew upscale black crowds, famously said he would fire any deejay that played go-go. See Godfrey, "Bourgie Nights."

5 Rondeaux and Helderman, "Amid Wave of Killings, Pr. George's Shuts Clubs."

6 Hopkinson, "Go-Go Is the Soul of Washington."

7 Allah, "NYPD Admits to Rap Intelligence Unit."

8 The Fenty administration got off to an inauspicious start when one of the mayor's education aides had a legendary, longtime government watchdog, an older black woman named Dorothy Brizill, arrested and carried out of City Hall in handcuffs in June 2007 when she sought

more information about the schools takeover (Stewart and Labbe, "Activist Charged in Clash with Aide"). The *Washington Post* columnist Courtland Milloy ("Adrian Fenty's Snubs of Black Women Make a Win at the Polls Unlikely") cited snubs of several high-profile black women, including Dorothy I. Height, Maya Angelou, Oracene Price (the mother of Venus and Serena Williams), Susan L. Taylor of *Essence* magazine, and the former D.C. first lady Cora Masters Barry, to explain Fenty's eroding support among black female voters.

9   Aizenman and Keating, "Income Soaring in 'Egghead Capital.'"

10 Pugh, "America's Humming Economy Leaves More and More Behind as Poverty Deepens to Record Levels."

11 Morello and Keating, "D.C. Suburbs Show Disturbing Increases in Child Poverty."

12 Roig-Franzia, "Michelle Fenty's Battle Cry in D.C. Mayoral Campaign That Brought Her to Tears."

13 The longtime D.C. activist Phil Pannell unfavorably compared Adrian Fenty to his predecessor, Anthony A. Williams, the mayor who sparked the city's most aggressive wave of gentrification in 1999–2007. "He makes Tony Williams look like Chaka Zulu," Pannell quipped. See Jones, "Geography Lesson."

14 For a longer discussion of the history of D.C. education reform and congressional meddling, see Witt, "Worn Down by Waves of Change." For a skeptical look at Rhee's education reform policies, see Dingerson, "The Proving Grounds." And for a look at the corporate interests, including the charitable arm of Walmart, that poured millions of dollars into D.C. public schools on the condition that Fenty and Rhee stay in power, see Hopkinson, "Why Michelle Rhee's Education 'Brand' Failed in D.C."

15 A poll in the *Washington Post* in January 2010 showed that among white Democrats, 68 percent said Rhee was a reason to support Fenty. Fifty-four percent of black Democrats cited her as a reason to vote against the mayor. See Turque, "Poll."

16 Turque, "DC Parents Raise Concerns about Middle Schools."

17 *Time*, "How to Fix America's Schools," 8 December 2008.

18 At a speech to CEOs, Rhee said: "Collaboration and consensus-building are quite frankly overrated in my mind. None of you CEOs run your companies by committee, so why should we run a school district by committee?" (CEO Council, "Tough Talk from DC Schools Chief Michelle Rhee").

19 Debonis, "Fast Company."

20 Anderson, "What Cost Peace?"

21 During the election of 2010, competing interpretations of public school reform became a proxy for the historic disconnection between the *Washington Post* newspaper and the city's black community. For a discussion of the tensions between the *Washington Post* and Washington's black community, see *Volunteer Slavery*, a memoir written by the former *Washington Post* writer Jill Nelson in 1994. The book covers Nelson's tenure at the *Post* from 1986 through the coverage of the 1990 drug charges trial of the former D.C. mayor Marion Barry. In

it, Nelson shows how newsroom politics and institutional forces conspired to provide a skewed picture of the black community, which led to a boycott and thirteen weeks of protests by black readers outside the *Post* building. In 2007, D.C.'s public school board was abolished and control was given to the mayor. Before the newly elected Fenty introduced his choice for schools chief to the public, he personally walked Rhee into the *Washington Post* building to introduce her to the editorial board in 2007. The editorial board went on to become rabidly pro-Fenty/Rhee, writing unsigned editorials on their behalf and attacking his opponent. The board was forced to take the unusual step of running a full-column correction of one of the editorials that had falsely accused Gray of meddling in a personnel issue at one school (*Washington Post*, "D.C. Teacher's Ouster Raises Questions about Vincent Gray's Reform Steadfastness").

22 Habermas, *The Structural Transformation of the Public Sphere*, 40.

23 Ibid., 32.

24 Ibid., 203.

25 The Black Public Sphere Collective emerged from two conferences, "Toward an Ethnography of the Institutions of the Black Community," organized by the Africana Studies Program of New York University in the spring of 1993, and "The Black Public Sphere in the Reagan Bush Era," organized by the Chicago Humanities Institute of the University of Chicago in 1994. The published form of the collaboration drew from the fields of anthropology, history, political science, sociology, film, music, and publishing to examine the topic of the black public sphere. It first appeared in the fall of 1994 as a special issue of the journal *Public Culture*, and then, a year later, as a book produced by the University of Chicago Press (Black Public Sphere Collective, *The Black Public Sphere*).

26 Neal, *What the Music Said*, 3.

27 Kelley, *Race Rebels*, 44.

28 Baker, "Critical Memory and the Black Public Sphere."

29 D with Jah, *Fight the Power*, 256.

30 The go-go industry is almost entirely owned and operated by blacks, and it employs hundreds of people in the Washington area. Aside from the top nightclubs that are required to report their substantial tax revenue, most of the industry comprises small, independent companies that do not necessarily report their income to the IRS. As J. T. Foxx ("Show Me da Money") notes, the "off the books" nature of go-go is compounded by the fact that the majority of go-go CDs and tapes are purchased via the "Live P.A. underground" or mom and pop storefronts that sell live go-go recordings (also discussed in chapter 5). Foxx notes that "in other music genres this would be termed bootlegging, but in go-go it is an accepted fact of life that is embraced by both bands and fans alike."

One notable exception to the black-owned and "off the books" rule in the go-go industry is the distribution company Liaison Records. This Maryland-based independent distribution company is the primary "mainstream" channel for go-go recordings, holding a back catalogue of recordings from almost all the major go-go bands (www.liaisonrecords.com/gogo.html). Foxx estimates that Liaison Records distributed more than one hundred thousand units of new go-go recordings by three groups (Chuck Brown, Rare Essence, and 911) in 2001 alone. Other major moneymakers are sound companies, PA (live "public address" recordings) distributors, clothing companies, bouncers, and promoters. All of this adds up to a multimillion-dollar industry (Foxx, "Show Me da Money").

31 Patillo-McCoy, *Black Picket Fences*.

32 Hopkinson, "Tempest in a T-shirt."

33 Stewart and Cohen, "Polls Show D.C. Mayor Fenty Getting More Credit Than Support in Primary Race against Gray."

34 That is exactly what black D.C. voters did in the primary of September 2010, in which Gray was supported four to one by black D.C. voters and Fenty was supported four to one by white voters, resulting in an overwhelming Gray victory. The black population was steadily decreasing in the city, but partly due to the influx in voter registration during the 2008 presidential election, the number of black registered D.C. democratic voters actually increased slightly from the previous election.

Because D.C. remains an overwhelmingly Democratic city, the Democratic primaries are the de facto general elections. (In 2010, the Republican Party did not bother fielding a candidate for mayor.) D.C. has a "closed" primary system in which only registered Democratic voters could elect the party's candidate. Roughly half of states have closed systems similar to that of the District of Columbia (Center for Voting and Democracy, "Congressional Primaries"). Yet, in the aftermath of Fenty's crushing defeat, the *Washington Post's* editorial board called for the D.C. council to "correct its mistake" of having a closed Democratic primary system. See "Unaffiliated Voters Deserve to Have Their Voices Heard in Primaries," *Washington Post*, 18 September 2010. If the city council "corrected the mistake" per the *Washington Post's* recommendation, it would give the white minority of D.C. voters a larger voice.

2 Club U

1 Details from this night were taken from testimony given at the city's Alcoholic Beverage Control Board by police and witnesses. See District of Columbia Alcoholic Beverage Control Board, case no. 28078–05/012C, order no. 2005–76, Levelle, Inc. t/a the Coach & IV Restaurant, 29 June 2005; District of Columbia Alcoholic Beverage Control Board, Hearing Transcripts, 19 February 2005; District of Columbia Alcoholic Beverage Control Board, hearing transcripts, 2 March 2005.

2 *Washington Post*, "Why Club U Matters."

3 Wiltz, "U Turn."

4 Green, *The Secret City*, 37.

5 Ibid., 38.

6 Mintz, "A Historical Ethnography of Black Washington, D.C."

7   Hughes, "Our Wonderful Society."

8   Anderson, *Deep River*, 260.

9   Ellington, *Music Is My Mistress*, 17.

10 Modan, *Turf Wars*, 43.

11 Williams and Smith, *City within a City*.

12 The comments from Snipes and from all other speakers were taken from the Alcoholic Beverage Control Board hearings in 2005 unless noted otherwise (see note 1).

13 Gilbert, *Ten Blocks from the White House*.

14 Ibid., 208.

15 Five years later, Sinclair Skinner's feelings about gentrification changed, since he pursued millions in city contracts to tear down the Sursum Corda public housing project on North Capitol Street and to rebuild it into "mixed-income" public housing. See Debonis, "Adrian Fenty, Some Frat Buddies, and $86 Million in City Spending."

16 Layton and Keating, "Most Blacks, Hispanics in Area Own Homes."

17 Bulletin board, http://www.tmottgogo.com, 29 June 2005.

3   What's Happening

1   Hopkinson, "The Guru of Go-Go."

2   Lornell and Stephenson, *The Beat* (2001), 58.

3   Change, *Can't Stop Won't Stop*, 409.

4   For a larger discussion of the Great Migration, see the work of a native Washington author, Wilkerson, *The Warmth of Other Suns*.

5   Petey Greene was a legendary radio personality and community activist later immortalized in a film of 2007 starring Don Cheadle, *Talk to Me*.

6   Hopkinson, "Roderick Valentine, Sixteen."

7   Hopkinson, "Giving Go-Go a Hotfoot."

8   On the process of adaptation in black music, see also Ramsey, *Race Music*, 36.

9   Hurston, "Characteristics of Negro Expression," 28.

10 Gates, *The Signifying Monkey*.

11 Gilroy, *There Ain't No Black in the Union Jack*, 165.

12 Westmoreland, "Go-Go and the Bad Boys."

13 Nketia, *The Music of Africa*, 180.

14 *Washington Post*, "Following Shooting, Teenagers Weigh Dancing with Danger."

15 Spearchucker, "Beat Your Feet."

16 Hopkinson, "Giving Go-Go a Hotfoot."

17 For a detailed discussion of the central role of dance in black musical culture, see Gaunt, *The Games Black Girls Play*. Gaunt writes: "We are constantly negotiating an artificial split between the mind (supposedly the exclusive realm of the intellect) and the body (the supposed realm of impulse, rhythm, and pleasure, rather than control)" (5).

18 Nketia, *The Music of Africa*, 18.

19 Fahrenthold, "Use of PCP Rebounds with New Generation: Drug's Rising Popularity Brings Violence."

20 Scott, *Domination and the Arts of Resistance.*

4 Call and Response

1 The central role of sexuality and the gendered nature of go-go and well-nigh all black musical cultures is a rich area of inquiry neglected in this book. For an excellent look at the role of gender in black music, see Gaunt, *The Games Black Girls Play.* "While [gender] has always played a role in what, and how, scholars write about music history (often at the expense of her-story), musical performance among African Americans remains a gendered, or intersex phenomenon, from juba-patting and corn shucking, to field hollering and gospel shouting, from griots and giottes, from (male) master drummers to (female) blues queens. All musical practice and discourse exists inside the structures of gender and sexuality that shape our interpretations of African American musical behavior, our language about black music and identity, and our notions of power in and out of musical contexts" (114).

2 My Caribbean identity also helped me connect with several key individuals on the go-go scene. For one with Richard O'Connor, a writer for *Tmottgogo* who wrote under several pen names, including Jamie Tha Foxx and Bubba Ray Spearchucker, who did sound, co-owned Bag of Beats records, and managed a go-go band called Fatal Attraction. After I interviewed a gospel go-go band, Richard slipped me a note explaining his secret online identity and told me he would help me. I later found out his family hailed from Trinidad. Ditto for one of my students at the University of Maryland, a talented young writer named Delece Smith-Barrow. We had bonded over go-go and later realized that we both had parents from Guyana. Delece linked me with some of her childhood friends at the University of Maryland's campus who were members of INI Band, a go-go and reggae fusion band, a majority of whose members had roots in the West Indies.

3 Monson, "Riffs, Repetition, and Theories of Globalization."

4 Agawu, *Representing African Music*, 15.

5 Alexander, "'Can You Be BLACK and Look at This?,'" 15.

6 See also Ramsey, *Race Music*, 41 for a discussion of the tightrope of avoiding the essentializing of black culture while "rescuing from the guillotine the idea of a collective black critique, a collective sensibility, however contested it may be."

7 For a more detailed account of Manley and Brown's relationship see Fisher 2007.

8 Nketia, *The Music of Africa*; Bebey, *African Music.*

9 Echeruo, *Victorian Lagos.*

10 Agawu, *Representing African Music*, 15.

11 Waterman, *Juju.*

12 Lornell and Stephenson, *The Beat* (2009), 47.

13 Nketia, *The Music of Africa*.
14 Smith, "Hip Hop as Performance and Ritual."
15 Hagedorn, *Divine Utterances*.
16 Allen, "Commerce, Politics, and Musical Hybridity."
17 Waterman, *Juju*, 34.
18 Kelley, *Race Rebels*, 190.
19 Rose, *Black Noise*, 11.
20 Waterman, *Juju*.
21 Davis, *Blues Legacies and Black Feminism*, 25.
22 Mushengyezi, "Rethinking Indigenous Media."
23 Letts and Nobakht, *Culture Clash*, 158.
24 Lornell and Stephenson, *The Beat* (2001), 210.
25 Letts with Nobakht, *Culture Clash*, 91.
26 Ibid., 171.
27 Richard Harrington, "Getting Go-Go on Film."
28 Richard Harrington, "Bad Vibes and Good to Go."
29 Lornell and Stephenson, *The Beat* (2009), 212–13.
30 Lee with Jones, *Uplift the Race*.
31 Waterman, *Juju*, 144.
32 Perry, "Chris Blackwell Interview."
33 Letts and Nobakht, *Culture Clash*, 173.
34 Gilroy, *Against the Race*, 194.
35 Roach, *Cities of the Dead*.

5 The Archive

1 Lornell and Stephenson, *The Beat* (2001), 174.
2 Lornell and Stephenson, *The Beat* (2001).
3 Venkatesh, *Off the Books*, 93.
4 Waterman, *Juju*, 116.
5 Price, "White Public Spaces in Black Places."
6 Liebow, *Tally's Corner*.
7 Schwartzman, "Whose H Street Is It Anyway?"

6 The Boondocks

1 The name, city, and some minor details have been changed to protect the identity of Grandview Ron. All the details about his involvement with the legal system have been verified when possible by newspaper accounts or public records.
2 Less than a month after Grandview Ron and I visited the convenience store, a clerk there was killed during an armed robbery. The clerk had moved from an African country eight months before his murder.
3 Chappelle, "America's Wealthiest Black County."
4 Patillo-McCoy, *Black Picket Fences*, 6.

5 Rend Smith, "Crime Stats Show D.C. Leads Nation in Per Capita Marijuana Arrests."

6 See Frazier, "Judge Ends Busing," and Cashin, "Middle-Class Suburbs."

7 For a longer discussion of the practice of tracking white children into gifted and talented education programs, see Barlow and Dunbar, "Race, Class, and Whiteness in Gifted and Talented Identification."

8 The name of this high school is fictional.

9 This arrest was verified with a *Baltimore Sun* article.

10 Len Bias was a Prince George's County native and University of Maryland All-American basketball player who was the second-round draft pick for the Boston Celtics. He died two days after being drafted due to a heart attack induced by a cocaine overdose.

11 Briscoe's novel was marketed as an "African American Peyton Place." See Briscoe, *P.G. County.*

12 According to the Federal Bureau of Investigation, MS-13, also known as Mara Salvatrucha 13, is believed to be a criminal organization with roots in El Salvador and extant in the United States and Canada. See "The MS-13 Threat: A National Assessment," FBI, http://www.fbi.gov.

13 A teardrop tattoo beneath a certain eye can mean you have killed someone or have lost someone to violence.

14 Law enforcement officials in Prince George's and D.C. have noted an increase in membership among the national Crips and Bloods gangs. See Thomas-Lester, "West Coast Gangs Are Making Inroads." She noted: "Some authorities said local gangs might be copying what they perceive to be the behavior of two predominantly African American gangs sometimes glamorized in popular culture.... [Capt. Bill Lynn, commander of the Prince George's police gang unit] said that even if local gang affiliates might be less organized than established sets elsewhere, they are no less dangerous. 'A lot of people like to say someone is a "wannabe," he said. 'Someone who wants to be is more dangerous than someone who is because they are trying to prove something.'"

15 See Aizenman and Birnbaum, "Latinos Anxious over End of School Liaisons in Pr. George's." Here is an excerpt from this article: "African Americans have been losing ground in the school system since 2003, when their numbers peaked at 78 percent of the student population. By contrast, the Hispanic student population is growing rapidly, doubling between 2002 and 2009. Nearly one in five Prince George's public school students are Hispanic; some schools have concentrations as high as 98 percent."

16 Partlow, "Teenager Slashed in Langley Park."

17 See Hopkinson and Williams, "Urban Outfitter."

7 Redemption Song

Parts of this chapter were adapted from Hopkinson, "Roderick Valentine, Sixteen," "Giving Go-Go a Hotfoot," "Go-Go, and Sin No More," "New Genre Sets Gospel to a Go-Go Beat," and "Tempest in a T-shirt."

1 See the Marlow Heights 60s and 70s web site at http://www.marlowheights 60sand70s.com.
2 Kelly, "Living in Marlow Heights Past and Loving Every Minute of It."
3 Stoughton, "The Decline and Fall of a Mall."
4 Karibu Books ended its fifteen-year run in 2008. After a dispute over ownership all six stores in the area comprising Prince George's, Baltimore, and northern Virginia were closed. Another independent black book store, Urban Knowledge, subsequently opened at Iverson Mall.
5 Wiltz, "U Turn."
6 Hazzard-Gordon, *Jookin'*, 116–19.
7 See the church's web site at http://www.ebenezerame.org.

8 Mr. Obama's Washington, D.C.

1 For a longer discussion of the role of black music in creating a "home," see Gaunt, *The Games Black Girls Play*: "Musical blackness is an imagined 'home,' constructed to represent a place of return, a place of social and political comfort. It is a *learned* place of inhabitance; an embodied dwelling that might be viewed as a protection from real and imagined threats. This kind of musical homework is not simply about a return to contemporary Nigeria or ancient Yorubaland imagined or constituted by the descendants of African slaves living in the United States" (49).
2 Florida, *The Rise of the Creative Class*.
3 Roach, *Cities of the Dead*, 36.
4 For a larger discussion of Wilson's work, see Hopkinson, "Go-Go Is the Soul of Washington."
5 For an extended scene of inauguration day on U Street, see Hopkinson, "Mr. Obama's Washington."
6 Patillo-McCoy, *Black Picket Fences*.

Bibliography

Ad Council. N.d. "Drunk Driving Prevention (1983–Present)." Ad Council, http://www.adcouncil.org (accessed 17 August 2011).

Agar, Michael. 1995. "Literary Journalism as Ethnography." *Representations in Ethnography*, ed. John Van Maanen, 112–29. Thousand Oaks, Calif.: Sage Publications.

———. 2003. "The Story of Crack: Towards a Theory of Illicit Drug Trends." *Addiction Research and Theory* 11, no. 1, 3–29.

Agawu, Kofi. 2003. *Representing African Music: Postcolonial Notes, Queries, Positions*. New York: Routledge.

Ahrens, Frank. 2006. "Competitions, Lower Ratings Hurt Radio One Profit." *Washington Post*, 8 August.

Aizenman, N. C., and Michael Birnbaum. 2010. "Latinos Anxious over End of School Liaisons in Pr. George's." *Washington Post*, 7 March.

Aizenman, N. C., and Dan Keating. 2007. "Income Soaring in 'Egghead Capital.'" *Washington Post*, 2 September.

Alaja-Browne, Afolabi. 1989. "A Diachronic Study of Change in Juju Music." *Popular Music* 8, no. 3, 231–42.

Alexander, Elizabeth. 1995. "'Can You Be BLACK and Look at This?' Reading the Rodney King Video(s)." *The Black Public Sphere: A Public Culture Book*, ed. Black Public Sphere Collective, 81–98. Chicago: University of Chicago Press.

Allah, Dasun. 2004. "NYPD Admits to Rap Intelligence Unit: A Look inside the NYPD's Secret 'Hiphop Task Force.'" *Village Voice*, 16 March.

Allen, Lara. 2003. "Commerce, Politics, and Musical Hybridity: Vocalising Urban Black South African Identity during the 1950s." *Ethnomusicology* 47, no. 2, 228–49.

Anderson, Jeffrey. 2009. "What Cost Peace? The D.C. Government Has Given Ronald Moten's Peaceaholics $10 Million to Quash Street Beefs. What Has It Gotten?" *Washington City Paper*, 9 October.

Anderson, Paul Allen. 2001. *Deep River: Music and Memory in Harlem Renaissance Thought*. Durham: Duke University Press.

Arendt, Hannah. 1958. *The Human Condition*. Chicago: University of Chicago Press.

Asante, Molefi Kete. 1987. *The Afrocentric Idea*. Philadelphia: Temple University Press.

Asim, Jabari. 2003. "Tony Morrison Composes a 'Love' Supreme." *Crisis Magazine*, November–December.

Auslander, Philip. 1999. *Liveness: Performance in a Mediatized Culture*. London. Routledge.

Austin, Regina. 1995. "A Nation of Thieves: Consumption, Commerce, and the Black Public Sphere." *The Black Public Sphere: A Public Culture Book*, ed. Black Public Sphere Collective, 229–52. Chicago: University of Chicago Press.

Bacon, Perry, Jr. 2002. "Prince George's Wants to See Some Go-Gos Gone: Despite Security Rules, Clubs May Breed Climate of Violence, Police Say." *Washington Post*, 3 August.

Baker, Houston A., Jr. 1995. "Critical Memory and the Black Public Sphere." *The Black Public Sphere: A Public Culture Book*, ed. Black Public Sphere Collective, 7–37. Chicago: University of Chicago Press.

Barlow, Kathleen, and C. Elaine Dunbar. 2010. "Race, Class, and Whiteness in Gifted and Talented Identification: A Case Study." *Berkeley Review of Education* 1, no. 1, 63–85.

Barlow, William. 1999. *Voice Over: The Making of Black Radio*. Philadelphia: Temple University Press.

Barz, Gregory, and Timothy J. Cooley, eds. 1997. *Shadows in the Field: New Perspectives for Fieldwork in Ethnomusicology*. New York: Oxford University Press.

Baym, Geoffrey. 2005. "The Daily Show: Discursive Integration and the Reinvention of Political Journalism." *Political Communication* 22, no. 3, 259–76.

Bebey, Francis. 1969. *African Music: A People's Art*. Brooklyn, N.Y.: Lawrence Hill.

Benjamin, Walter. 1969. "The Work of Art in the Age of Mechanical Reproduction." *Illuminations: Essays and Reflections*, 217–51. Ed. Hannah Arendt. Trans. Harry Zohn. New York: Schocken Books.

Bennett, Andy, and Keith Kahn-Harris. 2004. *After Subculture: Critical Studies in Contemporary Youth Culture*. New York: Palgrave Macmillan.

Berke, Richard L. 1989. "Capital Offers a Ripe Market to Drug Dealers." *New York Times*, 28 March.

Bhabha, Homi K. 1994. *The Location of Culture*. New York: Routledge.

Bird, S. Elizabeth, and Robert W. Dardenne. 1988. "Myth, Chronicle, and Story: Exploring the Narrative Qualities of News." *Social Meanings of News*, ed. Dan Berkowitz, 333–50. Newbury Park, Calif.: Sage Publications.

Black Public Sphere Collective, ed. 1995. *The Black Public Sphere: A Public Culture Book*. Chicago: University of Chicago Press.

Briscoe. Connie. 2002. *P.G. County*. New York: Doubleday.

Broadway, Bill. 2005. "Patron Killed outside NW Club: Some Seek to Close Bar in City Building." *Washington Post*, 14 February.

Burnim, Mellonee. 1985. "Culture Bearer and Tradition Bearer: An Ethnomusicologist's Research on Gospel Music." *Ethnomusicology* 29, no. 3, 432–47.

Calhoun, Craig, ed. 1992. *Habermas and the Public Sphere*. Cambridge: MIT Press.

Carroll, Kenneth. 1998. "The Meanings of Funk." *Washington Post*, 1 February.

Cashin, Sheryll D. 2000. "Middle-Class Suburbs and the State of Integration: A Post-integrationist Vision for Metropolitan America." *Cornell Law Review* 86, 729–65.

Caughey, John L. 2006. *Negotiating Cultures and Identities: Life History Issues, Methods, and Readings*. Lincoln: University of Nebraska Press.

Cauvin, Henri. 2005. "A Drug Kingpin's Hot-Selling Story: DVD on Rayful Edmond III has Captivated Washington." *Washington Post*, 22 July.

Center for Voting and Democracy. 2011. "Congressional Primaries: Open, Closed, Semi-closed, and 'Top Two.'" Fairvote.org.

CEO Council. 2009. "Tough Talk from DC Schools Chief Michelle Rhee." *Wall Street Journal*, 17 November.

Chang, Jeff. 2005. *Can't Stop Won't Stop: A History of the Hip-Hop Generation*. New York: St. Martin's Press.

Chappelle, Kevin. 2006. "America's Wealthiest Black County." *Ebony*, November.

Cherkis, Jason, and Sarah Godfrey. 2003. "Last Shot: Daniel 'Hollywood Breeze' Clayton Has Cultivated a Go-Go Following by Booking Top Acts and Promoting the Hell out of His Club." *Washington City Paper*. 26 September.

Chernoff, John Miller. 1997. "Music and Historical Consciousness among the Dagbamba of Ghana." *Enchanting Powers: Music in the World's Religions*, ed. Lawrence E. Sullivan, 91–120. Cambridge: Harvard University Press.

Chidester, David, and Edward T. Linenthal, eds. 1995. *American Sacred Space*. Bloomington: Indiana University Press.

Clifford, James. 1988. *The Predicament of Culture: Twentieth-Century Ethnography, Literature, and Art*. Cambridge: Harvard University Press.

Coates, Ta-Nehisi. 2000. "Dropping the Bomb: An Oral History of Go-Go." *Washington City Paper*. 14 January.

Cohen, Sarah. 1994. "Identity, Place, and the 'Liverpool Sound.'" *Ethnicity, Identity, and Music: The Musical Construction of Place*, ed. Martin Stokes, 117–34. Oxford: Berg.

Cole, Ardra L., and J. Gary Knowles, eds. 2001. *Lives in Context: The Art of Life History Research*. Walnut Creek, Calif.: AltaMira Press.

Collins, John. 1992. *West African Pop Roots*. Philadelphia: Temple University Press.

Collins, Patricia Hill. 2000. *Black Feminist Thought: Knowledge, Consciousness, and the Politics of Empowerment.* 2nd ed. New York: Routledge.

Coombe, Rosemary J., and Paul Stoller. 1995. "X Marks the Spot: The Ambiguities of African Trading in the Commerce of the Black Public Sphere." *The Black Public Sphere: A Public Culture Book,* ed. Black Public Sphere Collective, 253–78. Chicago: University of Chicago Press.

Cross, Ian. 2005. "Music and Meaning, Ambiguity and Evolution." *Musical Communication,* ed. Dorothy Miell, Raymond MacDonald, and David J. Hargreaves, 27–43. Oxford: Oxford University Press.

Cultural Tourism DC. 1999–2007. "Howard Theatre." African American Heritage Trail Database, http://www.culturaltourismdc.org/things-do-see/howard-theatre-african-american-heritage-trail (accessed October 2011).

D, Chuck, with Yusuf Jah. 1997. *Fight the Power: Rap, Race, and Reality.* New York: Delacorte.

Davidson, Joe. 1989. "How a 24-Year-Old Reigned as a Local Hero until His Arrest." *Washington Post,* 13 November.

Davis, Angela Y. 1998. *Blues Legacies and Black Feminism: Gertrude "Ma" Rainey, Bessie Smith, and Billie Holiday.* New York: Vintage.

Dawson, Michael C. 1995. "A Black Counterpublic? Economic Earthquakes, Racial Agenda(s), and Black Politics." *The Black Public Sphere: A Public Culture Book,* ed. Black Public Sphere Collective, 199–227. Chicago: University of Chicago Press.

Debonis, Mike. 2009. "Adrian Fenty, Some Frat Buddies, and $86 Million in City Spending." *Washington City Paper,* 30 October.

———. 2010. "Fast Company: Is Speed an Excuse for Fenty's Crony Contracts?" *Washington City Paper,* 9 November.

Denzin, Norman K., and Yvonna S. Lincoln, eds. 2003. *The Landscape of Qualitative Research: Theories and Issues.* Thousand Oaks, Calif.: Sage Publications.

Dimitriadis, Greg. 1996. "Hip-Hop: From Live Performance to Mediated Narrative." *Popular Music* 15, no. 2, 179–94.

———. 2001. *Performing Identity/Performing Culture: Hip Hop as Text, Pedagogy, and Lived Practice.* New York: Peter Lang.

Dingerson, Leigh. 2010. "The Proving Grounds: School 'Rheeform' in Washington, D.C." http://www.commondreams.org, 13 September.

District of Columbia City Council. N.d. "History of Self-Government in the District of Columbia." District of Columbia City Council, http://www.dccouncil.washington.dc.us (accessed 1 May 2007).

Du Bois, W. E. B. 1990. *The Souls of Black Folk.* New York: Vintage Books/Library of America.

Dudley, Shannon. 2004. *Carnival Music in Trinidad: Experiencing Music, Expressing Culture.* New York: Oxford University Press.

Eakin, Paul John, ed. 2004. *The Ethics of Life Writing.* Ithaca: Cornell University Press.

Echeruo, Michael J. C. 1977. *Victorian Lagos: Aspects of Nineteenth Century Lagos Life.* London: Macmillan.

Ellington, Duke. 1973. *Music Is My Mistress*. New York: Da Capo.

Ellis, Thomas Sayers. 2005. *The Maverick Room: Poems*. St. Paul, Minn.: Graywolf.

Emerson, Robert M., Rachel I. Fretz, and Linda L. Shaw, eds. 1995. *Writing Ethnographic Fieldnotes*. Chicago: University of Chicago Press.

Fahrenthold, David A. 2003. "Use of PCP Rebounds with New Generation: Drug's Rising Popularity Brings Violence." *Washington Post*, 5 January.

Fanon, Frantz. 1967. *Black Skin, White Masks*. Trans. Charles Lam Markmann. New York: Grove.

Fine, Michelle, Lois Weiss, Susan Weseen, and Loonmun Wong. 2003. "For Whom? Qualitative Research, Representations, and Social Responsibilities." *The Landscape of Qualitative Research: Theories and Issues*, ed. Norman K. Denzin and Yvonna S. Lincoln, 167–207. Thousand Oaks, Calif.: Sage Publications.

Fisher, Marc. "The Godfather Is Back: Chuck Brown's New Tunes." *Washington Post*, 28 March.

Fiske, John. 1987. *Television Culture*. London: Routledge.

Florida, Richard. 2002. *The Rise of the Creative Class: And How It's Transforming Work, Leisure, Community and Everyday Life*. New York: Basic Books.

Foucault, Michel. 1972. *The Archaeology of Knowledge*. Trans. A. M. Sheridan Smith. London: Tavistock.

Foxx, Jamie Tha. 2002. "Show Me da Money: The Top Ten Loot Makers in Go-Go." http://www.tmottgogo.com, 12 February.

Frank, Gelya. 2000. *Venus on Wheels: Two Decades of Dialogue on Disability, Biography, and Being Female in America*. Berkeley: University of California Press.

Fraser, Nancy. 1992. "Rethinking the Public Sphere: A Contribution to the Critique of Actually Existing Democracy." *Habermas and the Public Sphere*, ed. Craig Calhoun, 109–42. Cambridge: MIT Press.

Frazier, Lisa. 1998. "Judge Ends Busing in Prince George's." *Washington Post*, 2 September.

Gates, Henry Louis, Jr. 1988. *The Signifying Monkey: A Theory of African-American Literary Criticism*. New York: Oxford University Press.

Gaunt, Kyra D. 2006. *The Games Black Girls Play: Learning the Ropes from Double-Dutch to Hip-Hop*. New York: New York University Press.

Geertz, Clifford. 1973. *The Interpretation of Cultures: Selected Essays*. New York: Basic Books.

George, Nelson. 1998. *Hip Hop America*. New York: Viking.

Getler, Michael. 2004. "Readers Tee Off on T-Shirts." *Washington Post*, 22 August.

Gilbert, Ben W. 1968. *Ten Blocks from the White House: An Anatomy of the Washington Riots of 1968*. New York: Praeger.

Gilbert, Daniel T. 1991. "How Mental Systems Believe." *American Psychologist* 46, no. 2, 107–19.

Gilroy, Paul. 1987. *There Ain't No Black in the Union Jack: The Cultural Politics of Race and Nation*. Chicago: University of Chicago Press.

———. 2000. *Against the Race: Imagining Political Culture beyond the Color Line*. Cambridge: Harvard University Press.

Godfrey, Sarah. 2002. "Bourgie Nights: Marc Barnes Defines the Status Quo at D.C.'s Hottest Nightclub." *Washington City Paper*, 26 July.

———. 2005. "Scotched Tapes: Go-Go Acts Are Cutting Back on the Release of Pas, Leaving Fans Starved for New Material." *Washington City Paper*, 4 November.

Go-Go Coalition. 2007. "Letter to Honorable Jack B. Johnson, County Executive." http://www.gogocoalition.org, 3 April.

Green, Constance McLaughlin. 1967. *The Secret City: A History of Race Relations in the Nation's Capital*. Princeton: Princeton University Press.

Gregg, Sandra R. 1982. "A Teen-Ager's D.C. Is Filled with Go-Go." *Washington Post*, 23 August.

Habermas, Jürgen. 1991. *The Structural Transformation of the Public Sphere: An Inquiry into a Category of Bourgeois Society*. Trans. Thomas Burger and Frederick Lawrence. Cambridge: MIT Press.

Habermas, Jürgen, Sarah Lennox, and Frank Lennox. 1974. "The Public Sphere: An Encyclopedia Article (1964)." *New German Critique*, no. 3, 49–55.

Hagedorn, Katherine J. 2001. *Divine Utterances: The Performance of Afro-Cuban Santería*. Washington: Smithsonian Institution Press.

Hall, Stuart. 1980. "Encoding/Decoding." *Culture, Media, Language: Working Papers in Cultural Studies, 1972–79*, ed. Hall et al., 128–38. London: Hutchinson.

Hall, Stuart, and Tony Jefferson, eds. 1993. *Resistance through Rituals: Youth Subcultures in Post-war Britain*. London: Routledge.

Hammond, Kato. 2001. "Backyard Band Hits Michel Wright's Mhz2 Urban." http://www.tmottgogo.com, December 6.

———. 2006. "A Conversation with DJ Flexx on Go-Go: Radio, Covers, and His Point of View." http://www.tmottgogo.com, 12 March.

Hammond, Kato, and Mark Ward. 1998. "Interview with Little Benny." http://www.tmottgogo.com.

Hanchard, Michael. 1995. "Race and the Public Sphere in Brazil. *The Black Public Sphere: A Public Culture Book*, ed. Black Public Sphere Collective, 169–89. Chicago: University of Chicago Press.

Harrington, Richard. 1985. "Getting Go-Go on Film: Past the Hype, Bidding for Breakthrough to Success." *Washington Post*, 20 May.

———. 1986. "Bad Vibes and Good to Go: Controversy Clouds Washington Based Film." *Washington Post*, 1 August.

Harrington, Walt. 2003. "What Journalism Can Offer Ethnography." *Qualitative Inquiry* 9, no. 1, 90–104.

Harris, Lyle V. 1986. "D.C. B-Boys Say It's Good to Go-Go, But It's Fresh to Rap." *Washington Post*, 1 September.

Hazzard-Gordon, K. 1990. *Jookin': The Rise of Social Dance Formations in African-American Culture*. Philadelphia: Temple University Press.

Hebdige, Dick. 1987. *Subculture: The Meaning of Style*. London: Routledge.

Hendrickson, Paul. 1991. "Mark of the Urban Phantom: Cool Disco Dan, the Man behind the Writing on the Wall." *Washington Post*, 9 October.

Hoggart, Keith, Loretta Lees, and Anna Davies. 2002. *Researching Human Geography*. London: Arnold.

Hopkinson, Natalie. 1999. "Nightclub Keeps the Bodies Movin': Classics Draw a Loyal Crowd." *Washington Post*, 1 December.

———. 2001. "I Won't Let D.C. Lose Its Flavor." *Washington Post*, 17 June.

———. 2002. "Giving Go-Go a Hotfoot: Free-Form 'Beat Your Feet' Is the Latest Club Craze." *Washington Post*, 25 May.

———. 2002. "Go-Go, and Sin No More: The Gospel Dance Club That Was the Answer to Their Prayers Has Turned into a Test of Faith." *Washington Post*, 27 August.

———. 2002. "New Genre Sets Gospel to a Go-Go Beat: Band Winning Fans in Church, on Street." *Washington Post*, 14 March.

———. 2003. "Building Blocks: Amid Dealers and Boarded Windows, Brian Brown's Vision Took Root." *Washington Post*, 2 August.

———. 2003. "Culture Club: Republic Gardens' New Owners Are Looking for the Ultimate Mix." *Washington Post*, 9 November.

———. 2003. "The Guru of Go-Go: As He Hits Thirty, Backyard Band's Big G Tries to Reach beyond a Troubled Past." *Washington Post*, 26 April.

———. 2004. "Roderick Valentine, Sixteen." *Washington Post*, 16 May.

———. 2004. "Tempest in a T-shirt: Visionz Clothing Line Sews Discontent and Activism among Rivals." *Washington Post*, 10 August.

———. 2006. "Black Representation during Washington's Drug Scare of 1986: A Case Study in Ethnic and General Circulation Newspaper Coverage." Paper presented at the annual meeting of the Association for Education in Journalism and Mass Communication, San Francisco, August.

———. 2009. "Mr. Obama's Washington: Washingtonians Celebrated as One, But Can a Black President Unite Washington and D.C.?" *The Root*, 20 January.

———. 2010. "Go-Go Is the Soul of Washington: But It's Slipping Away." *Washington Post*, 11 April.

———. 2010. "The Myth of Black-on-Black Violence." *The Root*, 16 June.

———. 2010. "Why Michelle Rhee's Education 'Brand' Failed in D.C." http://www.theatlantic.com, 15 September.

Hopkinson, Natalie, and Natalie Y. Moore. 2006. *Deconstructing Tyrone: A New Look at Black Masculinity in the Hip-Hop Generation*. San Francisco: Cleis Press.

Hopkinson, Natalie, and Krissah Williams. 2003. "Urban Outfitter: Vusi Mchunu's Fashions Are Drawing Notice beyond the Beltway." *Washington Post*, 23 April.

Hughes, Langston. 1927. "Our Wonderful Society: Washington." *Opportunity*, 226–27.

Hurston, Zora Neale. 1996 [1934]. "Characteristics of Negro Expression." *Negro: An Anthology*, ed. Nancy Cunard, 39–61. London: Continuum.

Ives, Edward D. 1980. *The Tape-Recorded Interview: A Manual for Field Workers in Folklore and Oral History*. Knoxville: University of Tennessee Press.

Jackson, Bruce. 1987. *Fieldwork*. Urbana: University of Illinois Press.

Jervey, Gay. 2005. "A Revitalization for Washington's U Street Corridor." *New York Times*, 12 June.

Johnston, Lloyd D. 1989. "America's Drug Problem in the Media: Is It Real or Is It Memorex?" *Communication Campaigns about Drugs: Government, Media, and the Public*, ed. Pamela J. Shoemaker, 97–111. Hillsdale, N.J.: Lawrence Erlbaum.

Jones, James. 2007. "Geography Lesson: Few of Fenty's Nominees Hail from the East Side of the Anacostia." *Washington City Paper*, 16 March.

Kelley, Robin D. G. 1994. *Race Rebels: Culture, Politics, and the Black Working Class*. New York: Free Press.

Kellner, Douglas. 2000. "Habermas, the Public Sphere, and Democracy: A Critical Intervention." *Perspectives on Habermas*, ed. Lewis Edwin Hahn, 259–87. Chicago: Open Court.

Kelly, John. 2009. "Living in Marlow Heights Past and Loving Every Minute of It." *Washington Post*, 11 March.

King, Colbert I. 2006. "A Tale of Two Councils." *Washington Post*, 25 November.

Kisliuk, Michelle. 1997. "(Un)Doing Fieldwork: Sharing Songs, Sharing Lives." *Shadows in the Field: New Perspectives for Fieldwork in Ethnomusicology*, ed. Gregory Barz and Timothy J. Cooley, 23–44. New York: Oxford University Press.

———. 1998. *Seize the Dance! BaAka Musical Life and the Ethnography of Performance*. New York: Oxford University Press.

Klein, Allison. 2010. "Homicide Totals for 2009 Plummet in District, Prince George's." *Washington Post*, 1 January.

Korr, Jeremy Louis. 2001. "Cultural Landscape Analysis Fieldwork Model." Appendix A to "Washington's Main Street: Consensus and Conflict on the Capital Beltway, 1952–2001." PhD diss., University of Maryland.

Lachter, Susan B., and Avraham Forman. 1989. "Drug Abuse in the United States." *Communication Campaigns about Drugs: Government, Media, and the Public*, ed. Pamela J. Shoemaker, 7–22. Hillsdale, N.J.: Lawrence Erlbaum.

Ladson-Bilings, Gloria. 2003. "Racialized Discourses and Ethnic Epistemologies." *The Landscape of Qualitative Research: Theories and Issues*, ed. Norman K. Denzin and Yvonna S. Lincoln, 398–432. Thousand Oaks, Calif.: Sage Publications.

Landow, George P. 1992. *Hypertext: The Convergence of Contemporary Critical Theory and Technology*. Baltimore: Johns Hopkins University Press.

Lane, Belden C. 1988. *Landscapes of the Sacred: Geography and Narrative in American Spirituality*. Baltimore: Johns Hopkins University Press.

Lang, A. 2000. "The Limited Capacity Model of Mediated Message Processing." *Journal of Communication* 50, no. 1, 46–70.

Layton, Lyndsey, and Dan Keating. 2006. "Most Blacks, Hispanics in Area Own Homes." *Washington Post*, 3 October.

Lee, Spike, with Lisa Jones. 1988. *Uplift the Race: The Construction of "School Daze."* New York: Simon and Schuster.

Lehman, Alan Robertson. 1994. "Music as Symbolic Communication: The Grateful Dead and Their Fans." PhD diss., University of Maryland.

Letts, Don, with David Nobakht. 2007. *Culture Clash: Dread Meets Punk Rockers*. London: SAF.

Lewis, Hylan. 1967. Introduction to *Tally's Corner: A Study of Negro Streetcorner Men*, by Elliot Liebow, 3–28. Boston: Little, Brown.

Lewis, Nancy, and Sari Horowitz. 1989. "Area Sweet Nabs Alleged Drug Leaders: Federal, D.C. Forces Conduct Joint Raids." *Washington Post*, 16 April.

Liebow, Elliot. 1967. *Tally's Corner: A Study of Negro Streetcorner Men*. Boston: Little, Brown.

Lindlof, Thomas R., and Brian C. Taylor. 2002. *Qualitative Communication Research Methods*. 2nd ed. Thousand Oaks, Calif.: Sage Publications.

Lornell, Kip, and Charles C. Stephenson Jr. 2001. *The Beat: Go-Go's Fusion of Funk and Hip-Hop*. New York: Billboard Books.

———. 2009. *The Beat: Go-Go Music in Washington, D.C.* Jackson: University Press of Mississippi.

Manuel, Peter. 1993. *Cassette Culture: Popular Music and Technology in North India*. Chicago: University of Chicago Press.

———. 1995. "Music as Symbol, Music as Simulacrum: Postmodern, Premodern, and Modern Aesthetics in Subcultural Popular Music." *Popular Music* 44, no. 2, 227–39.

Martel, Brett. 2006. "Storms Payback from God, Nagin Says." Associated Press. 17 January.

McArdle, Megan. 2010. "Gray Defeats Fenty: What Does That Mean for the City?" http://www.theatlantic.com, 15 September.

McCrery, Johnette Hawkins, and John E. Newhagen. 2004. "Conceptual Elasticity of the Public Sphere: Tracking Media and Psychological Determinants to Access." *Media Access: Social and Psychological Dimensions of New Technology Use*, ed. Erik P. Bucy and Newhagen, 187–206. Mahwah, N.J.: Lawrence Erlbaum.

Merriam, John E. 1989. "National Media Coverage of Drug Issues, 1983–1987." *Communication Campaigns about Drugs: Government, Media, and the Public*, ed. Pamela J. Shoemaker, 21. Hillsdale, N.J.: Lawrence Erlbaum.

Meyer, Eugene L. 2006. "New Day in the City." *Washingtonian Magazine*, April.

Milloy, Courtland. 2010. "Adrian Fenty's Snubs of Black Women Make a Win at the Polls Unlikely." *Washington Post*, 25 August.

Mills, Claudia. 2004. "Friendship, Fiction, and Memoir: Trust and Betrayal in Writing from One's Own Life." *The Ethics of Life Writing*, ed. Paul John Eakin, 101–20. Ithaca: Cornell University Press.

Mintz, Steven. 1989. "A Historical Ethnography of Black Washington, D.C." Records of the Columbia Historical Society, Washington, D.C., no. 52, 235–53.

Modan, Gabriella Gahlia. 2007. *Turf Wars: Discourse, Diversity, and the Politics of Place*. Malden, Mass.: Blackwell Publishing.

Monson, Ingrid. 1999. "Riffs, Repetition, and Theories of Globalization." *Ethnomusicology* 43, no. 1, 31–65.

Morello, Carol, and Dan Keating. 2010. "D.C. Suburbs Show Disturbing Increases in Child Poverty." *Washington Post*, 29 September.

———. 2011. "Number of Black D.C. Residents Plummets as Majority Status Slips Away." *Washington Post*, 24 March.

Muggleton, David, and Rupert Weinzierl, eds. 2003. *The Post-subcultures Reader.* New York: Berg.

Mushengyezi, Aaron. 2003. "Rethinking Indigenous Media: Rituals, 'Talking' Drums, and Orality as Forms of Public Communication in Uganda." *Journal of African Cultural Studies* 16, no. 1, 107–17.

Neal, Mark Anthony. 1999. *What the Music Said: Black Popular Music and Black Public Culture.* New York: Routledge.

Nelson, Jill. 1989. "Mourning for Rap Singer Is Tapped Out in Tears: 'Fat Rodney' Slain Awaiting His Moment." *Washington Post,* 16 June.

———. 1994. *Volunteer Slavery: My Authentic Negro Experience.* New York: Penguin.

Newhagen, John E. 2004. "Interactivity, Dynamic Symbol Processing, and the Emergence of Content in Human Communication." *Information Society* 20, no. 5, 397–402.

Newhagen, John E., and Byron Reeves. 1992. "This Evening's Bad News: Effects of Compelling Negative Television News Images on Memory." *Journal of Communication* 42, no. 2, 25–41.

Nketia, J. H. Kwabena. 1974. *The Music of Africa.* New York: W. W. Norton.

Oakley, Giles. 1976. *The Devil's Music: A History of the Blues.* Ed. Madalena Fagandini. London: British Broadcasting Corporation.

O'Hara, Terence. 2006. "FBR Reports Loss Related to Subprime Lending Venture: Radio One Profit Falls." *Washington Post,* 3 November.

Orcutt, James D., and J. Blake Turner. 1993. "Shocking Numbers and Graphic Accounts: Quantified Images of Drug Problems in the Print Media." *Social Problems* 40, no. 2, 190–206.

Partlow, Joshua. 2005. "Teenager Slashed in Langley Park: Police Uncertain If Gangs Were Involved." *Washington Post,* 14 August.

Patillo-McCoy. 1999. *Black Picket Fences: Privilege and Peril among the Black Middle Class.* Chicago: University of Chicago Press.

Perry, Andrew. 2009. "Chris Blackwell Interview: Island Records; British Pop's Greatest Surviving Mogul Is in London to Celebrate the Fiftieth Anniversary of His Brainchild, Island Records." *London Telegraph,* 20 May.

Price, Tanya Y. 1999. "White Public Spaces in Black Places: The Social Reconstruction of Whiteness in Washington, D.C." *Sage Urban Studies Abstracts* 27, no. 3, 301–44.

Pugh, Tony. 2007. "America's Humming Economy Leaves More and More Behind as Poverty Deepens to Record Levels." *Miami Herald,* 25 February.

Ramsey, Guthrie P., Jr. 2003. *Race Music: Black Cultures from Bebop to Hip-Hop.* Berkeley: University of California Press.

Reagon, Bernice. 1974. "World War II Reflected in Black Music: Uncle Sam Called Me." *Southern Exposure* 1, nos. 3–4, 169–84.

Reese, Stephen D., and Lucig H. Danielian. 1989. "Intermedia Influence and the Drug Issue: Converging on Cocaine." *Communication Campaigns about Drugs: Government, Media, and the Public,* ed. Pamela J. Shoemaker, 29–47. Hillsdale, N.J.: Lawrence Erlbaum.

Reinarman, Craig, and Harry G. Levine, eds. 1997. *Crack in America: Demon Drugs and Social Justice.* Berkeley: University of California Press.

Ringle, Ken. 1986. "Bottoms Up: All Things Bright and Bubbly; A Spirited Toast to Champagne." *Washington Post,* 31 December.

Roach, Joseph. 1996. *Cities of the Dead: Circum-Atlantic Performance.* New York: Columbia University Press.

Rogers, Everett M., ed. 1995. *Diffusion of Innovations.* 4th ed. New York: Free Press.

Roig-Franzia, Manuel. 2010. "Michelle Fenty's Battle Cry in D.C. Mayoral Campaign That Brought Her to Tears." *Washington Post,* 11 September.

Rondeaux, Candace, and Rosalind S. Helderman. 2007. "Amid Wave of Killings, Pr. George's Shuts Clubs." *Washington Post,* 30 March.

———. 2007. "Pr. George's Judge Temporarily Bars County from Closing Five Clubs." *Washington Post,* 31 March.

Rose, Tricia. 1994. *Black Noise: Rap Music and Black Culture in Contemporary America.* Middletown, Conn.: Wesleyan University Press.

Sawyer, R. Keith. 2005. "Music and Conversation." *Musical Communication,* ed. Dorothy Miell, Raymond A. R. MacDonald, and David J. Hargreaves, 45–60. Oxford: Oxford University Press.

Schwartzman, Paul. 2006. "Whose H Street Is It Anyway? A Dispute over Restaurant Zoning Creates a Chasm between Northeast Washington's Old and New Residents." *Washington Post,* 4 April.

Schwartzman, Paul, and Chris L. Jenkins. 2010. "How Fenty Lost the Black Vote." *Washington Post.* 18 September.

Scott, James C. 1990. *Domination and the Arts of Resistance: Hidden Transcripts.* New Haven: Yale University Press.

Shannon, Claude E., and Warren Weaver. 1949. *The Mathematical Theory of Communication.* Urbana: University of Illinois Press.

Shelemay, Kay Kaufman. 1991. *A Song of Longing: An Ethiopian Journey.* Urbana: University of Illinois Press.

Shoemaker, Pamela J., ed. 1989. *Communication Campaigns about Drugs: Government, Media, and the Public.* Hillsdale, N.J.: Lawrence Erlbaum.

Shudson, Michael. 2001. "The Emergence of the Objectivity Norm in American Journalism." *Social Norms,* ed. Michael Hechter and Karl-Dieter Opp, 149–70. New York: Russell Sage Foundation.

Shurmer-Smith, Pamela, ed. 2002. *Doing Cultural Geography.* London: Sage Publications.

Smith, Rend. 2010. "Crime Stats Show D.C. Leads Nation in Per Capita Marijuana Arrests: The Vast Majority of People Arrested on Pot Charges Are Black. Why?" *Washington City Paper,* 13 August.

Smith, William E. 2003. "Hip Hop as Performance and Ritual: A Biographical and Ethnomusicological Construction of a Washington, D.C., Hip Hop Artist Named Priest da Nomad." PhD diss., University of Maryland.

Smith-Barrow, Delece. 2006. "Awards Celebrate Go-Go's Funk." *Washington Post,* 30 November.

Smitherman, Geneva. 1994. *Black Talk: Words and Phrases from the Amen Corner*. New York: Houghton Mifflin.

————. 1997. "The Chain Remain the Same: Communicative Practices in the Hip-Hop Nation." *Journal of Black Studies* 28, no. 1, 3–25.

Spearchucker, Bubba Ray. 2002. "Beat Your Feet: The New Dance Craze." http://www.tmottgogo.com, 13 January.

Squires, Catherine R. 2000. "Black Talk Radio: Defining Community Needs and Identity." *Harvard International Journal of Press/Politics* 5, no. 2, 73–95.

Startt, James D., and William David Sloan. 2003. *Historical Methods in Mass Communication*, rev. ed. Northport, Ala.: Vision Press.

Stephens, Mitchell. 2005. "We're All Postmodern Now: Even Journalists Have Realized That Facts Don't Always Add Up to the Truth." *Columbia Journalism Review*, July–August, 60–64.

Stewart, Nikita, and Jon Cohen. 2010. "Polls Show D.C. Mayor Fenty Getting More Credit Than Support in Primary Race against Gray." *Washington Post*, 28 August.

Stewart, Nikita, and Theola Labbe. 2007. "Activist Charged in Clash with Aide." *Washington Post*, 13 June.

Stewart, Nikita, and Paul Schwartzman. 2010. "How Adrian Fenty Lost His Reelection Bid for D.C. Mayor." 16 September.

Stock, Jonathan P. J. 2001. "Toward an Ethnomusicology of the Individual; or, Biographical Writing in Ethnomusicology." *World of Music* 43, no. 1, 5–19.

Stokes, Martin, ed. 1994. *Ethnicity, Identity, and Music: The Musical Construction of Place*. Oxford: Berg.

Stoughton, Stephanie. 1999. "The Decline and Fall of a Mall: Landover Seen as a Drag on Retail Efforts." *Washington Post*, 4 August.

Swope, Christopher. 2004. "Reinventing the District: A Pro-planning Mayor and His Planning Director Set a New Course for a Troubled City." *Planning* 70, no. 2, 4.

Tavernise, Sabrina. 2011. "A Population Changes, Uneasily." *New York Times*, 17 July.

Thomas-Lester, Avis. 2007. "Protestors Offer to Be Part of Solution: Go-Go Community Criticizes Closing of Night Spots But Suggests Ways to Stop Violence." *Washington Post*, 4 April.

————. 2008. "West Coast Gangs Are Making Inroads: Bloods, Crips Tied to Area Crimes." *Washington Post*, 29 August.

Thornton, Sarah. 1996. *Club Cultures: Music, Media, and Subcultural Capital*. Hanover, N.H.: University Press of New England.

Time. 2008. "How to Fix America's Schools," 8 December, cover.

Titon, Jeff Todd. 1992. "Representation and Authority in Ethnographic Film/Video: Production." *Ethnomusicology* 36, no. 1, 89–94.

————. 1997. "Knowing Fieldwork." *Shadows in the Field: New Perspectives for Fieldwork in Ethnomusicology*, ed. Gregory Barz and Timothy J. Cooley, 87–100. New York: Oxford University Press.

Trescott, Jacqueline. 1985. "City Seeks to Buy Howard Theatre: Barry Offer Would Prevent Foreclosure." *Washington Post*, 7 December.

Tuchman, Gaye. 1973. "Making News by Doing Work: Routinizing the Unexpected." *American Journal of Sociology* 79, no. 1, 110–31.

Turque, Bill. 2010. "Poll: Polarizing D.C. Schools Chief Rhee Helps, Hurts Fenty." *Washington Post*, 1 September.

———. 2011. "DC Parents Raise Concerns about Middle Schools." *Washington Post*, 25 September.

Vargas, Jose Antonio. 2005. "The Changing Complexion of U Street: On Historic Black Broadway, a Tanning Salon Sets up Shop." *Washington Post*, 16 April.

Venkatesh, Sudhir Alladi. 2006. *Off the Books: The Underground Economy of the Urban Poor*. Cambridge: Harvard University Press.

Vidich, Arthur J., and Stanford M. Lyman. 2003. "Qualitative Methods: Their History in Sociology and Anthropology." *The Landscape of Qualitative Research: Theories and Issues*, ed. Norman K. Denzin and Yvonna S. Lincoln, 55–129. Thousand Oaks, Calif.: Sage Publications.

Ward, Mark (Teago). 1994. "Picking Stan 'Da Man' Cooper's Brain." http://www.tmottgogo.com, 17 September.

Wartofsky, Alona. 2001. "For Rapper, a 911 Call: Frontman Starts New Band, But Rare Essence Goes On." *Washington Post*, 2 January.

———. 2003. "The Mother Who Gave Go-Go Its First Big Push." *Washington Post*, February 1.

Wartofsky, Alona, and Philip P. Pan. 1997. "Go-Go Singer Wounded in Prince George's Club: Alleged Gunman Apprehended by Guards." *Washington Post*, 15 October.

Washington Post. 2005. "Why Club U Matters." Editorial. 20 February.

———. 2007. "Following Shooting, Teenagers Weigh Dancing with Danger." 22 February.

———. 2010. "D.C. Teacher's Ouster Raises Questions about Vincent Gray's Reform Steadfastness." Editorial. 27 July.

Waterman, Christopher Alan. 1990. *Juju: A Social History and Ethnography of an African Popular Music*. Chicago: University of Chicago Press.

Westmoreland, Bobbie. 2001. "Go-Go and the Bad Boys." http://www.tmottgogo.com, 6 November.

Wilkerson, Isabel. 2010. *The Warmth of Other Suns: The Epic Story of America's Great Migration*. New York: Random House.

Williams, Paul K., and Kathryn S. Smith. 2001. *City within a City: Greater U Street Heritage Trail*. Washington: Historical Society of Washington, D.C., and Cultural Tourism D.C.

Williamson, Elizabeth, and V. Dion Haynes. 2005. "Md. Teen Dies after Nightclub Shooting." *Washington Post*, 7 November.

Wilson II, Clint C. 1991. *Black Journalists in Paradox: Historical Perspectives and Current Dilemmas*. New York: Greenwood Press.

Wilson II, Clint C., and Félix Gutiérrez. 1995. *Race, Multiculturalism, and the Media: From Mass to Class Communication*. Thousand Oaks, Calif.: Sage Publications.

Wilson, David. 2005. *Inventing Black-on-Black Violence: Discourse, Space, and Representation*. Syracuse, N.Y.: Syracuse University Press.

Wiltz, Teresa. 2006. "U Turn: The Fabled Street That Played Host to Duke Ellington and Pearl Baily Reinvents Itself Once More." *Washington Post*, 5 March.

Winston, Brian. 1995. *Claiming the Real: The Griersonian Documentary and Its Legiti-
   mations*. London: British Film Institute.

Witt, April. 2007. "Worn Down by Waves of Change: Bureaucracy, Politics Beat
   Back Succession of Superintendents and Plans." *Washington Post*, 6 July.

Index

Italicized page numbers indicate an illustration on the page or its caption.

Natalie Hopkinson is a contributing editor of *The Root* magazine, teaches journalism at Georgetown University, and directs the Future of the Arts and Society project as a fellow of the Interactivity Foundation. She is the author, with Natalie Y. Moore, of *Deconstructing Tyrone: A New Look at Black Masculinity in the Hip-Hop Generation* (2006).

Library of Congress Cataloging-in-Publication Data

Hopkinson, Natalie.
Go-go live : the musical life and death of a chocolate city /
Natalie Hopkinson.
p. cm.
Includes bibliographical references and index.
ISBN 978-0-8223-5200-6 (cloth : alk. paper)
ISBN 978-0-8223-5211-2 (pbk. : alk. paper)
1. Go-go (Music)—Washington (D.C.)
  —History and criticism.
2. Go-go (Music)—Social aspects—Washington (D.C.)
3. African Americans—Washington (D.C.)
  —Music—20th century.
4. African Americans—Washington (D.C.)
  —Social life and customs—20th century.
I. Title.
ML3527.84.H67 2012
306.4′84240975309045—dc23   2011041902